POLLINATORS
OF NATIVE PLANTS

Attract, Observe and Identify
Pollinators and Beneficial Insects with Native Plants

Pollinators of Native Plants
Attract, Observe and Identify Pollinators and Beneficial Insects with Native Plants
www.PollinatorsNativePlants.com

Published by Pollination Press LLC
Minnetonka, MN 55345
www.pollinationpress.com

First edition, fifteenth printing.

Printed in the United States.

ISBN 978-0-9913563-0-0

Keywords: pollination, pollinators, insects, bees, beneficial insects, biodiversity, ecology, ecosystem services, ecosystem management, landscape, landscape ecology, native plants, plant communities, climate change

POLLINATORS
OF NATIVE PLANTS

Attract, Observe and Identify
Pollinators and Beneficial Insects
with Native Plants

Heather Holm

Pollination Press LLC
Minnesota

ACKNOWLEDGEMENTS

This book would not be possible without the assistance and support of many people. Their contributions were diverse and from many perspectives. I am very grateful for the entomological information, technical assistance, review, and suggestions from Elaine Evans, Joel Gardner, Dr. Marla Spivak and Dr. Karl Foord from the University of Minnesota and Crystal Boyd for her entomological information and thorough review of the manuscript. Among those I am very grateful for assistance, for sharing their insights and suggestions, and agreeing to review a draft manuscript are Michelle Kalantari and Ruth Peterson. Ruth has shared her enthusiasm for this project and has thoughtfully listened to me talk about the book, even when it was just an idea. Michelle Kalantari continues to share her passion for pollinators and insects and her love of photography with me and graciously made available photographs for this book. I also have relied on wildflower enthusiasts for their photography and support of this project including Michael Lynch, Katy Chayka and Peter Dzuik. Shirley Mah Kooyman has also been very supportive of this project and has helped me find speaking engagements to promote the book. I would like to thank Larry Wade for his enthusiasm for pollinators and for inviting me to take photographs of the pollinators in the prairie he maintains. I would also like to thank Anita Poplin, Kim Phillips and Alex Surcica for agreeing to let me use their wonderful pollinator images in the book. Kim and Alex generously responded to last minute requests.

With all my endeavors, my spouse, Brent, has been a constant supporter and, for this project, a willing editor. He delayed many vacations the last few years so I could photograph pollinators and do research for this project. My mother, Gail, has also been invaluable reading and editing many drafts and versions of this book, helping me refine the writing and supporting me and this project. I am very grateful because without Gail and Brent this project would not have happened.

PREFACE

As a landscape designer and horticulturist, I have been using native plants in designs for over fifteen years. All this time, I was also ardently photographing native plants and plant communities. In order to capture the plants and landscape, I was forced to slow down and observe these plant communities. It was this focused observation that led me to notice the diversity and quantity of insects that were visiting native plants; the same species would return year after year to the same plants.

Photographing these insect visitors took me on a fascinating journey: What is this insect? Why does it visit this particular native plant? How does it interact with other insects and the food web? The story of their life cycles and interactions opened up a new and intriguing world of discovery. It reinforced that all wildlife depends on native plants and that native plants support and feed the entire food web. When pollinators are scarce, seed set and the reproduction of plants is at risk. Without pollinators, native plant communities are in jeopardy.

After moving to Minnesota ten years ago and restoring our entire suburban yard with native plants, I began to document and research the interactions of pollinators and native plants in earnest. Douglas Tallamy's book *Bringing Nature Home* reinforced what I was already observing: Native plants and insects are the foundation of a diverse, sustainable ecosystem.

I searched for more information about native pollinators, especially bees. So much attention and research have been directed toward honey bees that our native bees have been largely ignored for their contribution to the pollination of plants. My final springboard was the release of the Xerces Society's book *Attracting Native Pollinators*, the first of its kind to highlight the importance of native pollinators and the book that helped me learn more about the bees I have been documenting.

This book combines my research of native pollinators with my knowledge of native plants and interest in photography. It is a result of over ten years of observations and research starting in my own native landscape and expanding into restored and remnant plant communities. The book illustrates common, specific interactions of native plants with their pollinators. With its publication, my goal is to inspire readers to plant for, observe, attract and foster pollinators in their landscape, ultimately helping to sustain pollinator populations.

All pollinators are in trouble, not just bees. Major factors impacting pollinator populations include the loss of forage plants and nesting habitat, the spread of pathogens, competition from introduced species, and the use of pesticides. Native plants play a critical role in supporting pollinator and beneficial insect populations. Pollinators have evolved with native plants over thousands of years developing unique and interdependent relationships. Incorporating more native plants into the home garden, agricultural or large natural landscape can have an extremely positive impact on pollinators and all wildlife. Every individual can make a difference by planting native plants.

INTRODUCTION

Insect Pollination

This book focuses on pollination by insects (**entomophily**), highlighting the interactions between native plants and native pollinators as well as beneficial insects and other floral visitors. Readers learn about these interactions, how the plants are pollinated and how they can use native plants to attract, observe and identify pollinators and ultimately sustain pollinator populations.

This book covers common native bee species. See the **Common Bee Genera** section (p. 257) for other bee genera not included in the book. The plant and insect ranges do not overlap entirely: some insects in the book may not occur in the geographic ranges that the plants cover. Flowering times reflect the upper Midwest, Great Lakes region, Northeast and southern Canada. For areas outside of this range, flowering times may be earlier or later.

Pollination By Honey Bees

This book includes limited information on **honey bees, *Apis mellifera***. A honey bee symbol is located at the top of the **Plant-Insect Interactions** page if the plant is visited by honey bees. Honey bees were introduced to North America by European settlers in the early 1600s to provide them with a source of honey and wax for candles. Their managed contribution to the pollination of crops is well documented and beyond the scope of this book.

Pollination By Hummingbirds

Information about how hummingbirds pollinate plants is not included. Besides the difficulty in photographing hummingbirds, they do not play a large role in pollinating plants in the northern temperate regions of North America, unlike their active role in tropical regions. It is still important to provide forage plants, insects and habitat for these amazing birds. If a plant is visited by hummingbirds, a hummingbird symbol is located at the top of the right page in the **Plant-Insect Interactions** chapters.

WRITING ABOUT A POLLINATOR IN 1900

White Turtlehead ~ *Chelone Glabra*

"It requires something of a struggle for even so strong and vigorous an insect as the bumblebee to gain admission to this inhospitable-looking flower before maturity; and even he abandons the attempt over and over again in its earliest stage before the little heart-shaped anthers are prepared to dust him over. As they mature, it opens slightly, but his weight alone is insufficient to bend down the stiff, yet elastic, lower lip. Energetic prying admits first his head, then he squeezes his body through, brushing past the stamens as he finally disappears inside.

At the moment when he is forcing his way in, causing the lower lip to spring up and down, the eyeless turtle seems to chew and chew until the most sedate beholder must smile at the paradoxical show. Of course it is the bee that is feeding, though the flower would seem to be masticating the bee with the keenest relish! The counterfeit tortoise soon disgorges its lively mouthful, however, and away flies the bee, carrying pollen on his velvety back to rub on the stigma of an older flower."

Neltje Blanchan, *Nature's Garden*, 1900

TABLE OF CONTENTS

TABLE OF CONTENTS

TABLE OF CONTENTS

COMMON BEE GENERA (Cont'd)

CHAPTER ONE
POLLINATION

POLLINATION

Importance of Pollination

Pollination is *the* crucial event in a plant's life because it is essential for production of seed and future generations of a species. While some plants depend on the whims of wind or water for pollen transport, the vast majority of terrestrial flowering plants are pollinated by animals, usually insects. The reasons for these amazing interrelationships are simple - insects provide the mobility and targeted delivery of pollen that the plants require and the insects obtain food and resources for their role in plant reproduction.

Pollination By Insects

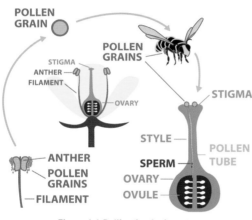

Figure 1.1 Pollination by Insects
(Modified from Willmer, 2011.)

The analogy of a straight forward exchange quickly breaks down, however, when one considers the amazing diversity of insects and their myriad roles in the food web. Some pollinate plants effectively; others consume resources but do not effectively transfer pollen. Some hunt prey; others become parasitized. Pollinators and beneficial insects detailed in this book are integral to a healthy, functioning ecosystem. Their role in the transfer of pollen facilitates the production of viable seed/fruit

in plants sustaining plant communities. All animals depend on plants or the animals that feed on plants. Without pollinators, a plant community relies on the minority of plants that are self-compatible (*see* p. 3). Long term reliance on self-compatible plants results in a decrease in genetic diversity and opportunities for adaptation in plants, and the overall loss of biodiversity.

Pollination Process

The pollination process begins when a pollinator transfers a pollen grain from one flower's anthers to another flower's stigmatic surface. The pollen grain germinates on the stigmatic surface and a pollen tube grows down the style to the ovary, penetrating through the ovary, delivering two male sperm. One of the male sperm enters the female egg cell producing a seed. The other male sperm unites with two polar nuclei to develop into the nutrient-providing tissue surrounding the seed (**endosperm**).

Ensuring Pollination

Plants lure pollinators to visit their flowers by offering rewards including pollen, nectar, resin and oil. Plants have also devised a number of ways to attract pollinators with visual and olfactory cues including nectar guides, flower color and flower fragrance. *More information about resources and rewards, p. 4.*

SELF-POLLINATION

A minority of plants has the ability to be self-pollinating (self-compatible). Seeds develop if pollen comes into contact with the stigmatic surface on the same plant. Some plants self-pollinate when pollinators are not available.

Bloodroot, *Sanguinaria canadensis*

Bloodroot, *Sanguinaria canadensis* (p. 164), flowers in early spring during periods of fluctuating spring temperatures, potentially unseasonable weather and therefore low pollinator activity. Bloodroot flowers can self-pollinate; their stamens (**filaments** and **anthers**) bend toward the stigma around the third day of flowering after insects have had ample opportunities to visit the flowers. The bending stamens transfer pollen to the stigmatic surface and self-pollinate the plant.

Plants have devised several strategies to avoid self-pollination. The most common strategy is the devel-

opment of anthers and stigmas at different times (**dichogamy**), for example wild geranium, *Geranium maculatum* (below & p. 150). The majority of plants have anthers that dehisce before the stigma becomes receptive (**protandry**). The opposite, less common strategy is **protogyny** where stigmas develop before the anthers shed pollen as in American pasqueflower, *Anenome patens*, p. 54.

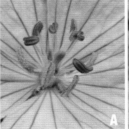

Wild Geranium, *Geranium maculatum*
A: Flower in the male phase with anthers dehiscing
B: Flower in the female phase with stigma receptive

The arrangement of anthers and stigmas combined with flower morphology also helps prevent self-pollination. If the anthers and stigmas have spatial separation (**herkogamy**), the visiting insect may be guided by the flower shape and form to one but not both of the reproductive parts or rewards.

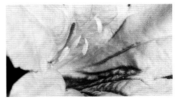

Wild Petunia, *Ruellia humilis*
Spatial separation between anthers (below) and stigma (above)

The other technique plants employ to prevent self-pollination is to have male and female flowers on separate (**dioecious**) plants. Many of these plants are wind- or water-pollinated when anthers dehisce and pollen is transferred by these mechanisms from the male plant to the female plant.

CROSS-POLLINATION & FLOWER DEVELOPMENT

Cross-Pollination

The most successful pollination is cross-pollination, especially with pollen from plants that are geographically distant. Cross-pollinated plants generate robust and genetically diverse seed, helping to suppress undesirable mutations and keeping unfavorable recessive traits ineffective. Plant offspring from cross-pollination have more variability of traits and therefore increase overall differences in the plant population. Plants prevent self-pollination through self-sterility or incompatibility. Self-incompatible plants inhibit the germination of the pollen grain on the stigmatic surface or the growth of the pollen tube when pollen from the same plant is deposited on the plant's stigma.

Flower Development

Flowers typically develop in a sequence, with their male and female reproductive parts maturing at different stages during the flower development. Nectar production may begin when flowers first open or initiate during a certain part of the flower development such as when the stigma becomes receptive in the female phase. The floral development sequence can influence the timing and types of floral visits by pollinators. If the flowers are protandrous (anthers dehisce before the stigma becomes receptive), initial visits by pollinators are to collect and feed on pollen, and, if nectar is offered, feed on nectar. Pollinators have shown preferences for visiting flowers in a particular floral phase, avoiding the female phase flowers for example. *See foraging behavior of bees on wild bergamot, p. 97.* Plants have devised many different strategies of presenting floral rewards so that the probability of pollinator contact and transfer of pollen is maximized.

FLORAL RESOURCES & REWARDS

Pollen

Many insects, including bees, flies and beetles visit flowers to feed on or collect pollen. Pollen is an important source of protein containing between 2.5 and 61 percent protein along with fats, starches, vitamins and minerals. Female bees collect pollen and combine it with nectar to form bee bread. Eggs are laid on the bee bread which larvae consume as they develop. *More information on larval development pp. 16 & 17.*

Yellow-Faced Bee, *Hylaeus* sp.

Some bees such as yellow-faced bees, *Hylaeus* spp. (above), do not have pollen collecting hairs on their legs or abdomen; instead, they feed on pollen, store it in their crop and regurgitate it when they return to their nest. *For more information see pollen collection by bees p. 20 & 21.*

FLORAL RESOURCES & REWARDS

Nectar

Most flower-visiting insects seek out nectar if offered by the plant. Nectar is a source of sugar (carbohydrates) as well as water and helps fuel an insect's activities including foraging and nest construction. Plants such as great St. John's wort, *Hypericum pyramidatum* (p. 204), do not offer nectar as a reward. Instead, the plants entice visitors by offering a large quantity of pollen. Insects often investigate nectarless flowers for nectar. Nectar, if offered, is secreted from a flower's nectaries typically located near the base by the ovary.

Green sweat bee, *Agapostemon* sp. feeds on nectar from a New England aster flower.

Accessing nectar requires insects to insert their mouthparts, head or abdomen into the flower. This action can force the pollinator to come into contact with the anthers or stigma. Some plants offer nectar away from the flower in extra-floral nectaries to discourage stealing of floral rewards; ants are often seen foraging on extra-floral nectaries. The timing of nectar production by a plant can vary; some plants replenish nectar overnight, catering to nocturnal pollinators such as moths. Nectar production early in the morning provides the most rewards to the first foraging insects of the day. A plant that has peak nectar production in the morning may be pollinated by a bee that can forage during cooler temperatures such as a bumble bee. Plants may increase nectar production during a particular part of their floral development. In wild white indigo, *Baptisia lactea* (p. 62), nectar production increases when the flower is in the female phase and the stigma is receptive to pollen.

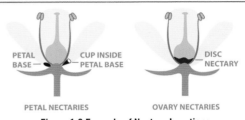

PETAL BASE — CUP INSIDE PETAL BASE — DISC NECTARY

PETAL NECTARIES   OVARY NECTARIES

Figure 1.2 Example of Nectary Locations
See the visual glossary, p. 255 for more examples.
(*Modified from Willmer, 2011*)

Resin & Oil

Several bees including small resin bees, *Heriades* spp., collect resin secreted by plants to line and waterproof their brood cells. Other bees feed on or collect oil to mix with pollen or to line brood cells. Plants secrete oils from glands or hairs (**trichomes**) at the base of flowers and occasionally from leaves. In some plants, the stigma exudes an oil to trap pollen grains and keep the stigmatic surface moistened to help with pollen grain germination. Resins and oils may have anti-microbial properties and when combined with provisions or used to line the brood cell can help deter pathogens from infecting developing larvae.

FLORAL ATTRACTANTS ~ SIGNALS

Nectar Guides

Nectar guides are stripes, spots or color contrasts on flowers that guide the insect visitors past anthers to a nectar reward. Since bees can see in the ultraviolet spectrum, beyond the range of human eyesight, many guides on flowers are not visible to people. Flower parts may either reflect or absorb ultraviolet light to reveal contrasting colors to pollinators. In black-eyed Susan, *Rudbeckia hirta* (p. 117), the outer portion of the rays reflects and the inner portion absorbs ultraviolet light revealing to pollinators a two-toned, contrasting pattern.

Flower Color Change

The flower color on plants may change during the flowering period. These color changes can coincide with the floral development phase (male or female), the depletion of the floral rewards or the completion of pollination.

Flower color change from light pink to violet in **Canada tick trefoil**, *Desmodium canadense*, after flowers are pollinated.

Changes in flower color help redirect pollinators to other flowers that are still offering a reward and require pollination. Two examples of flower color changes in this book include wild lupine, *Lupinus perennis* (p. 92), and Canada tick trefoil, *Desmodium canadense* (above & p. 192).

Shape & Color Contrast

Flower shapes can influence the types of floral visitors they attract. Bees prefer symmetrical flowers with simple outlines and a landing pad such as the bottom lip of bilabiate flowers. Color contrast between more than one color on the corolla or between the color of the anthers and petals also serves as a visual attractant to flower visitors.

Fragrance & Olfactory Guides

Flowers produce volatile organic compounds that release floral fragrances; however, only a few of the compounds released are attractive to floral visitors. Bees typically prefer fruity, flowery, sweet-smelling compounds emitted from flowers. Flies are often attracted to unpleasant smelling flowers with odors resembling carrion or dung. Moths and butterflies prefer flowers emitting sweet scents. Insects detect flower odors with their antennae and mouthparts where olfactory sensilla are located. The sensilla are small pore plates attached to olfactory neurons that send signals to the brain. As with coloration, flower scent may change as the flower ages, signalling to a floral visitor that rewards have been depleted. Male bees use their olfactory sensilla to detect pheromones emitted by females.

FLOWER MORPHOLOGY & RESOURCE ACCESS

Flowers come in numerous shapes, colors and forms, both symmetrical and asymmetrical.

Flower features can dictate what types of pollinating insects visit the flower:

- size, shape and habit of the flower
- corolla width and depth
- location of the nectaries
- presentation of pollen

Composite Flowers

An open, composite flower (below) typically has short disc florets clustered in the center with nectar and pollen accessible to most or all floral visitors including flies, wasps and butterflies. Butterflies prefer composite flowers because they provide a large platform for resting while they nectar.

Umbelliferous Flowers

Like composite flower heads, umbelliferous flower heads have numerous small, shallow flowers and a flat landing platform. These flowers are frequently visited by flies and short-tongued bees such as syrphid flies and sweat bees. See golden alexanders, *Zizia aurea* (p. 132).

Tubular & Bilabiate Flowers

Long, narrow, tubular corollas such as prairie phlox, *Phlox pilosa* flowers, p. 108, have nectaries that are not accessible to shorter-tongued insects. Larger, bilabiate tubular flowers including smooth beardtongue, *Penstemon digitalis,* p. 104, and great blue lobelia, *Lobelia siphilitica*, p. 208, have a flat lower lip that serves as a landing platform for bees and a larger corolla opening for accessing resources.

Nodding Flowers

Flowers that nod or hang downward and can limit visits to hovering insects if no suitable landing area or flower part is available to grasp. Small bees often crawl into nodding flowers as they forage, clinging to floral structures such as the style. Harebell, *Campanula rotundifolia*, below & p. 66, floral resources are accessed in this manner. Many nodding flowers require buzz pollination. *Read more about buzz pollination on p. 21.*

Harebell	Wild Columbine
Campanula rotundifolia	*Aquilegia canadensis*

Complex Flowers

Complex flowers including wild columbine, *Aquilegia canadensis* (above & p. 142), and Dutchman's breeches, *Dicentra cucullaria* (p. 146), have concealed nectar in spurs that can only be reached by visitors with long tongues, mainly bumble bees.

MUTUALISM BETWEEN PLANT & POLLINATOR

Pollination can be a mutualistic relationship between plant and pollinator but often is not. Most visits are by ineffective pollinators; only a minority of visitors are effective pollinators. Ineffective pollinators make visits to feed on or collect floral resources without picking up or transferring pollen grains and pollinating the next plant.

Both plants and insects carefully balance their costs and benefits in the presentation and procurement of floral resources. The quality of the rewards (food) determines whether an insect wants to expend energy or not visiting the flower. The plant's reward is pollination by the visitor; however, the visitor is often feeding or collecting resources at the expense of the plant's energy.

The effectiveness of insect visitors as pollinators is determined by several factors:

- their ability or inability to carry pollen
- their grooming habits
  (how well they handle pollen)
- their foraging behavior including
  the timing of visits
- their body size and shape (tongue length)
  in relation to the flower shape
- their movement between flowers
- their fidelity to a certain plant species

Observing Pollinators

When observing insects visiting a flower, look for how the flower presents rewards and in what ways the insect interacts with the flower that would influence whether they are effective or ineffective pollinators.

TYPES OF FLORAL VISITORS

Plant Specialists

An insect that visits many plants can be a specialist of one of the visited plants (no other pollinators pollinate the plant).

For example, Dutchman's breeches, *Dicentra cucullaria* (above), is only effectively pollinated by queen bumble bees that have the size, strength and tongue length to manipulate the flower, reach the nectar and effectively transfer pollen. Most plants receive visits from many types of insect pollinators, both generalists and specialists.

Generalists

The majority of flower-visiting insects are generalists; they visit many species of plants for the floral rewards offered (nectar, pollen, resin or oil).

TYPES OF FLORAL VISITORS

Pollen Specialists

Most female bee species collect pollen from a wide range of plants within flight distance of their nesting sites. These bees are **polylectic**, collecting pollen from many genera or families of plants. A minority of bee species are pollen specialists (**oligolectic**), collecting pollen from a single plant genus to a few plant genera. Oligolectic bees rely on olfactory cues to find their host plants. They detect the volatile compounds emitted from the oily coating on pollen grains. These olfactory cues are especially important for newly emerged adults lacking foraging experience and the ability to interpret visual cues.

Advantages

There are advantages to being an oligolectic bee: foraging and nest-provisioning are efficient when a sufficient amount of host plants are present nearby. Also, less energy is required to process the nutrition from one set of plant chemistries.

Disadvantages

There are disadvantages as well: habitat fragmentation can decrease the number of forage plants and nesting sites. With climate change, plants may flower earlier or later resulting in a mismatched emergence of an oligolectic bee and the flowering phenology of its host plants.

Thieves

Depending on its tongue length, overall shape and size, a visiting insect may either easily reach nectar in the flower or not reach it at all. Many small insects, for example, sweat bees visiting wild columbine, *Aquilegia canadensis* (p. 142), can reach nectar by climbing into the flower but limit their contact with anthers and therefore perform no pollination service.

When their tongues are not long enough to reach the nectar, several flower-visiting insects such as mason wasps and bumble bees chew holes in the petals to access nectar. These visits are considered a form of theft - stealing floral rewards without pollinating the plant.

A **sweat bee, *Lasioglossum* sp.,** feeds on nectar through a hole (perforation) at the bottom of the long, tubular corolla of wild bergamot, *Monarda fistulosa*.

In wild bergamot, *Monarda fistulosa* flowers, the long, tubular corollas allow nectar access only to pollinators with the longest tongues including bumble bees, butterflies and moths. Many small, short-tongued pollinators such as sweat bees (above) and leafcutter bees gain access to nectar through the holes (**perforations**) chewed by mason wasps. *See p. 95.*

TYPES OF FLORAL VISITORS

Predators

Flower-visiting predators are adult insects or spiders that hunt other insects to feed upon. They may also use the prey to cache in their nests for their larvae to consume. Several insects and spiders such as ambush bugs and crab spiders wait on flowers or foliage to ambush, kill and feed on insects. Many of these predators also feed on floral resources when not hunting prey.

Solitary and social wasps are predators of large insects and actively hunt prey including katydids, crickets, grasshoppers, moth and butterfly larvae and bugs. Many of their prey are foliage-eating insects; the predation by these wasps helps keep populations of potentially destructive insects in balance.

A **jagged ambush bug**, *Phymata* **sp.**, catches an unsuspecting bumble bee while the bee attempts to visit the flowers of **wild bergamot**, *Monarda fistulosa*. Jagged ambush bugs use toxins in their saliva to paralyze prey, then feed on their prey with long, straw-like mouthparts.

A **great golden digger wasp**, *Sphex ichneumoneus*, carries a katydid back to its nest, caching the katydid for the wasp larva to feed upon.

A **crab spider** feeds on a syrphid fly that was ambushed on the flowers of **wild quinine**, *Parthenium integrifolium*. Many crab spiders in the family Thomisidae have the ability to change the color of their head and abdomen to match the color of the flower for camouflage. They inject digestive fluids into prey then suck out the dissolved contents.

A **grass-carrying wasp**, *Isodontia* **sp.**, is a predator of crickets and katydids. Nests are constructed in cavities, often in hollow stems. Females collect pieces of grass used for dividing brood cells and closing nests.

Pollinators of Native Plants

TYPES OF FLORAL VISITORS

Parasitoids

Insect parasitoids differ from predators because they do not attack their prey directly; instead, they lay their eggs on or in a host, or in a host's nest. The parasitoid larvae hatch and feed on the host eventually killing it. Many parasitoids can be found stealthily lurking on plants awaiting prey. It is not uncommon to see parasitoids on flowers that are predominantly visited by their prey. For example, wedge-shaped beetles, *Macrosiagon* spp. (p. 99), lay eggs on flowers such as rattlesnake master, *Eryngium yuccifolium* or Virginia mountain mint, *Pycnanthemum virginianum,* that are frequented by wasps. Beetle larvae climb onto wasps or bees visiting flowers and are transported to the nest where they find, feed on and eventually kill the host larvae.

A **wedge-shaped beetle, *Macrosiagon* sp.,** lurks on the flower heads of rattlesnake master, *Eryngium yuccifolium,* waiting for prey (wasps and bees). A beetle wasp, *Cerceris* sp., forages on the same flower head and risks transporting the parasitic beetle larvae back to its nest.

Parasitoids also visit flowers because their prey may be feeding within the flower head; many moth caterpillars are stem and flower head borers.

After landing on and investigating several flower heads of **false sunflower, *Heliopsis helianthoides***, a female **braconid wasp** inserts her long ovipositor into the flower head to lay eggs in a caterpillar feeding inside.

Some parasitoids even lay their eggs directly on the host in flight. *See thick-headed flies and tachinid flies (pp. 233 & 125) for examples.*

Hyperparasitoids

Hyperparasitoids lay their eggs on or in the larvae of parasitoids. Hyperparasitoids feed on the parasitoid larvae eventually killing it. The sinuous bee fly, *Hemipenthes* sp. (p. 85), parasitizes the parasites inside caterpillars.

Cleptoparasites

Cleptoparasitic insects lay their eggs in the nests of other insects or on flowers that their insect prey visit. The larvae hatch and typically kill the host larvae and any sibling larvae, then feed on provisions provided by the host. Similar to wedge-shaped beetles (photo bottom left), blister beetles, *Nemognatha* spp. (p. 118), lay their eggs on plants that their prey visit. The beetle larvae climb onto the host and are transported back to the nest where they kill the host larvae and feed on the provisions. Cleptoparasitic bees typically lay their eggs directly in the nest of their hosts (other bees).

CHAPTER TWO
POLLINATORS

BEES ~ LEVELS OF SOCIALITY

Worldwide there are close to twenty thousand bee species and North America is home to around four thousand species. Approximately 90% of bees are solitary and the remainder are social. Nesting sociality can change in a species from solitary to social based on a bee's geographic range, for example, social in warm climates and solitary in cold climates. There are several levels of nesting sociality between solitary and social:

Solitary Bees

One solitary, female bee builds and provisions her own nest. Nests are typically constructed in hollow stems, cavities in wood or rocks, or burrows in the ground. Each cell constructed in one of these nesting sites is provisioned with food, an egg is laid and the brood cell is sealed. The female then begins constructing and provisioning another brood cell.

A female **Cellophane Bee, *Colletes* sp.,** excavates a solitary nest in the ground. Cellophane bees often construct nests in aggregations.

In ground-nesting species in particular, solitary nests can be built in **aggregations** with many nests in close proximity, but each female bee is constructing and provisioning her own nest.

Communal Bees

Multiple female bees can also share a nest but they do not take care of each other's brood. These shared nests are **communal**. In solitary and communal nests there is a single generation at any given time with no overlapping generations. The adults are short-lived, surviving for a few weeks and often dying before their offspring pupate.

Quasi-Social & Semi-Social Bees

These bees have nests where multiple female bees cooperate and share nest construction and provisioning duties. Either several or all females (usually sisters) in a quasi-social nest have mated and can lay eggs. Only a few females in a semi-social nest can lay eggs; the remaining females are workers. Semi-social nests can occur when a queen dies and a few of her offspring mate to carry on egg-laying duties.

Subsocial Bees

In subsocial nests, overlapping generations occur with one adult female and several of her offspring residing in the nest. The head female bee protects and feeds her larval offspring then leaves the nest to die before her offspring pupate. There is no cooperative brood care or division of labor in subsocial nests.

Eusocial Bees (Colony)

Eusocial bee nests consist of two generations of bees, a mother and her daughters living in a nest together. Bumble bees are the most common eusocial bees in North America. The mother and daughters work together caring for the brood, protecting the nest and foraging for nest provisions. *Read more about bumble bees on p. 16.*

SOCIALITY, FORAGING EFFICIENCY & POLLINATION

Only one female forages for nest provisions including pollen and lays eggs in solitary, communal and subsocial nest types. Without a division of labor, more energy is expended by the individual female that is required to do all nest and brood rearing tasks. To offset the energy expenditure, solitary bees may have targeted flowers to forage on that offer higher rewards, resulting in the reliance on a narrower set of flower types.

Division of Labor
In a eusocial bumble bee nest, the specialization or division of labor within the nest can lead to higher productivity and a lower energy expenditure per bee. The workers that forage for floral resources collect food in order to amass resources in the nest for the rest of the colony to feed upon. With nectar pots available for storage, nectar can be selectively collected on days when weather conditions are favorable rather than relying on collection every day.

Generalist Foraging Patterns
With many individuals from a eusocial nest out foraging for resources, the higher or easier to access rewards become depleted forcing bees to move on to flowers offering smaller rewards.

Bumble bees have demonstrated they can choose to forage on plants not occupied by their nest mates including plants that they are unfamiliar with or that have unknown floral rewards. The result is a generalist pattern of flower visitation, with bees visiting more types of flowers within their flight range than would a solitary bee. More types of plants are typically pollinated by these generalist eusocial bees.

Foraging Ranges
Eusocial bees typically have larger foraging ranges than solitary bees. Bumble bees, for example, can travel approximately one mile from their nest, the longer distance allowing them to forage on more plants.

Length of Foraging
Eusocial nests also have a longer season of activity with overlapping generations and individuals from the colony relying upon flowering plants from early summer until late fall. They can exploit a variety of resources or flower types at any given time and find new resources when they become available.

Foraging Efficiency
Eusocial bees can influence each other's foraging behavior when an experienced forager demonstrates or directs inexperienced foragers to flowers offering a higher reward. This activity is especially advantageous where there are small patches of flowers or many flower types distributed over a large landscape. Foraging between the same plants offering a higher reward often results in effective cross-pollination of the plant.

Bumble Bees

Bumble bees nest in colonies that are initiated by a single female (queen). Their nests are eusocial where a division of labor occurs among the female offspring along with cooperative brood care.

Bumble bee queens overwinter in the ground. To prevent freezing, the queens circulate an anti-freeze fluid through their bodies. When the queens emerge in the spring, they are reliant on early flowers for food. Nest construction initiates when the queen finds a dry cavity such as an abandoned rodent hole, pile of grass clippings or leaves. The choice of nest location can vary with different bumble bee species.

The queen performs all nest construction, foraging and provisioning until the emergence of female offspring. Like honey bees, bumble bees produce wax used to construct nectar pots and cover eggs. The queen stores nectar in her crop after visiting flowers and once she returns to the nest regurgitates the nectar into the nectar pots. Some nectar is also combined with pollen to form a pollen ball. She lays a batch of eggs (between 8 and 14) on top of the pollen ball and covers the eggs in wax. The eggs hatch and the larvae begin feeding on the pollen ball.

Most eggs laid early in the season are fertilized and produce female offspring that, after pupating into adults, forage for provisions in place of the queen. The queen remains in the nest to continue nectar pot construction and egg-laying. Male offspring are produced near the end of the season to mate with new females that become queens the following season. If female offspring are to become queens, they are typically provided with more food so they develop into large adults. Queens can be

as much as three times the size of worker bumble bees. The entire bumble bee colony dies in the fall except for newly mated females (queens). These queens seek out a place to overwinter in the ground then start a new bumble bee colony in the spring.

Sweat Bees

Other eusocial, quasi-social or sub-social bees include sweat bees, many from the *Lasioglossum* and *Halictus* genera.

Sweat Bee, *Lasioglossum zephyrum*

Lasioglossum zephyrum (male pictured above) is a ground-nesting, quasi-social bee that rears its brood in a colony. Each colony contains an average of fourteen females, including workers and multiple females laying eggs.

BEES ~ SOLITARY NEST PROVISIONING & LIFE CYCLE

Solitary or Communal Bees

An adult female solitary or communal bee's entire life span (usually two to six weeks) is dedicated to creating and providing for the next generation of offspring. She focuses most of her effort foraging on flowers for pollen and nectar. Pollen is transported on pollen-collecting structures on her abdomen or leg. Nectar is held in the crop until it is regurgitated and combined with pollen to form a mixture known as bee bread.

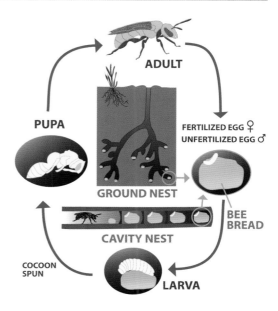

Figure 2.1 Life Cycle of a Solitary or Communal Bee

A **Yellow-faced bee,** *Hylaeus* **sp.** collects pollen and nectar, stores it in her crop and regurgitates both provisions when she returns to the nest.

An exception to this collection method is the yellow-faced bee, *Hylaeus* sp., that lacks external pollen-collecting structures and stores both pollen and nectar in the crop. Depending on the species, adult female bees may augment the bee bread with secretions from their own body or resin or oil collected from plants.

Once enough provisions have been collected, an egg is laid on each bee bread. A fertilized egg produces a female offspring and an unfertilized egg produces a male offspring. An egg usually hatches within one to five days and the tiny larva begins feeding on the bee bread. As it grows, it molts four or five times, defecates, then spins a cocoon to pupate within. After pupation, the bee emerges from the nest as an adult.

Males typically have a shorter egg-to-adult development period. Male eggs are laid near the entrance of cavity and tunnel nests so the males develop and emerge first (**protandry**), followed by the females that are at the back of the cavity or tunnel. Adult males primarily search for suitable mates and obtain their energy from nectar. Females mate, forage for nectar and pollen, construct and provision the nest, then lay eggs.

Pollinators of Native Plants

BEES ~ SOLITARY & SOCIAL NESTING SITES

Bees choose nesting sites that provide protection from predators, parasitoids and the elements. The types of nesting materials vary depending on the bee species: leafcutter bees often use pieces of leaves to create and divide brood cells; other bees divide cells with mud, pith and saliva or line their cells with resin or a cellophane-like gland secretion.

Cavities - 30%

Approximately thirty percent of bees nest in cavities, usually preexisting cavities. Small carpenter bees, *Ceratina* spp., chew the pith from the center of plant stems to excavate nesting cavities. Mason bees, *Osmia* spp., rely on preexisting woodpecker or beetle larvae holes in wood, often in standing dead trees.

CAVITY-NESTING BEES

Hollow Stems

Small Carpenter Bees   Mason Bees
Large Carpenter Bees   Carder Bees
Small Resin Bees   Leafcutter Bees
Yellow-Faced Bees

Holes in Wood

Leafcutter Bees   Mason Bees
Small Carpenter Bees   Digger Bees
Large Carpenter Bees   Small Resin Bees

Figure 2.2 Cavity Nest

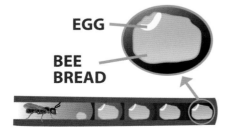

EGG

BEE BREAD

Ground - 70%

Approximately seventy percent of bees nest in the ground, typically excavating nests in bare soil or sparsely vegetated places under plants. All ground nests are excavated by females, preferring sandy, loose, well-drained soils. Nest tunnels can be perpendicular to the soil surface, angled, or built horizontally into slopes or banks.

GROUND-NESTING BEES

Mining Bees	Digger Bees
Cellophane Bees	Alkali Bees
Squash Bees	Sweat Bees
Green Sweat Bees	Sunflower Bees
Long-Horned Bees	Bumble Bees
Leafcutter Bees	

Figure 2.3
Ground Nest

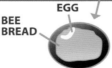

EGG

BEE BREAD

To encourage ground-nesting bees, leave existing nesting sites, areas of bare soil and rodent holes in the landscape. Heavy layers of mulch or landscape fabric can restrict access to new nesting sites. *More information about nesting sites, p. 34.*

BEES ~ MOUTHPARTS

Tongue

Bees can have tongue lengths ranging between two and fourteen millimeters. The arrangement of the mouthparts can also vary with each bee species. *See a chart of tongue lengths on p. 247.* Bees typically visit flowers that have corolla depths that match their tongue lengths. Short-tongued bees such as yellow-faced bees, *Hylaeus* spp. (bottom right), prefer to visit open, composite flowers with easily accessible rewards over complex or tubular flowers. Long-tongued bees visit most flower types but get the most rewards where fewer bees are competing for nectar. For example, long-tongued bumble bees are the only bees that can access nectar in the flowers of bottle gentian, *Gentiana andrewsii* (p. 202).

A bee's tongue (glossa) has a spoon-shaped tip that allows the bee to lap up tiny quantities of nectar onto hairs on the tongue. The nectar naturally clings to and even climbs the hairs, like watercolors saturating a paint brush. Once a sufficient amount of nectar is present on the hairs, the entire mouthpart structure (galea) closes around the tongue to create an airtight chamber. Next, muscles in the bee's head expand the pharynx to create a mild vacuum that draws the nectar upward. At this point, the bee may swallow or store the nectar in its crop.

Mandibles

Bees also have mandibles (chewing mouthparts) used to feed on pollen, collect nesting materials or excavate nests. Female leafcutter bees, *Megachile* spp., have large mandibles for cutting pieces of leaves used in nest construction (p. 86). Male bees use their mandibles to grasp females during mating or to fight with other males over territory or mates.

Bumble Bee, *Bombus* sp.
Tongue Lengths Between 5 and 16 mm

Long-Horned Bee, *Melissodes* sp.

Yellow-Faced Bee, *Hylaeus* sp.
Average Tongue Length Between 1 and 2 mm

BEES ~ VISION & POLLEN COLLECTION

VISION

Bees have a pair of compound eyes and three simple eyes (**ocelli**) with receptors that discern different wavelengths from the human eye. They can see intensity, color and polarization of light and have a high sensitivity to ultraviolet light but are red-blind to longer wavelengths. Because their perception of flower color is offset from humans, many visual cues such as nectar guides and color contrasts in flowers are visible only to bees. On the flowers of marsh marigold, *Caltha palustris*, the outer part of the sepals reflects ultraviolet light and the inner part closest to the center of the flower absorbs ultraviolet light. The result is a two-toned contrast between the outer and inner parts of the flower, despite appearing as a monochromatic yellow to humans. Pollinators are visually guided by the contrasting colors to the center of the flower where the floral resources are located (p. 188). Bees prefer flowers that are pink, purple or blue; their secondary preference is white or yellow flowers (as the colors appear to humans). The amount of light as well as flower reflectance can influence their visibility. Flower shapes are more easily discerned when a contrasting color surrounds the shape, like green foliage or brown soil.

COLOR SPECTRUM

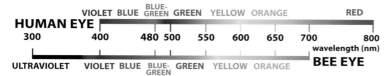

Figure 2.4
Color Spectrum,
Human Eye &
Bee Eye
(*Redrawn from Michener, 1974.*)

POLLEN COLLECTION

Only female bees have pollen-collecting hairs (**scopae**) or pollen baskets (**corbiculae**). Pollen-collecting hairs are located on the lower (sweat bees) or upper (mining and cellophane bees) hind leg or under the abdomen (leafcutter and mason bees).

Abdomen

Only bees in the Megachilidae family collect pollen on their abdomen. The abdominal scopae is comprised of many fine, curved, unbranched hairs. Pollen is collected by rubbing their abdomen on anthers. Alternatively, some bees use comb-like structures on their legs to rake the pollen then comb it to their abdomen. Megachilid bees often forage with their abdomen curved upward when their scopae is full.

Leafcutter Bee, *Megachile* sp.,
has pollen-collecting hairs (scopae)
on the underside of the abdomen.

BEES ~ POLLEN COLLECTION

Leg

Bees release pollen from anthers for collection by raking the grains with their mouthparts, comb-like structures on their legs or foreleg tarsal claws. Some bees have modified hairs on their mouthparts for removing pollen from tubular flowers.

Female **Bumble Bee,** *Bombus impatiens*
Pollen is collected, combined with nectar and pressed
into a pollen basket (corbicula) on the hind leg tibia.

Females package pollen by grooming pollen grains from their head, thorax and abdomen to their pollen-collecting hairs or pollen baskets (**corbiculae**) on the hind legs. Combining nectar with pollen, female bumble bees create a sticky mixture that they press in the pollen basket for transport.

Female **Green Sweat Bee,** *Agapostemon virescens*
Pollen is collected on the lower part of the hind leg.

Buzz Pollination (Sonication)

Buzz pollination is a technique used to release pollen from a flower's anthers through small pores or longitudinal slits, where pollen is difficult to access. Bumble bees, *Bombus* spp., along with some other bee species such as mining bees, *Andrena* spp., perform buzz pollination on flowers. They cling to the anthers with their forelegs or mouthparts and vibrate their flight muscles, releasing pollen.

Female **Bumble Bee,** *Bombus* sp.
Bumble bees buzz-pollinate a number
of flowers including prairie smoke (above) to
release pollen from anthers.

Crop

Yellow-faced bees collect and carry pollen (and nectar) in their crop because they have no pollen-collecting structures on their legs or abdomen. Cleptoparasitic (**cuckoo**) bees do not have any pollen-collecting structures either because they lay their eggs in the nests of other bees.

SOCIAL WASPS

Social wasps nest in colonies, most are constructed with a paper-like material. Wasps create this material by chewing and regurgitating wood fibers. Paper nests are sited on horizontal surfaces such as tree limbs or house soffits, as well as in shrubs and below ground. Similar to eusocial bees such as bumble bees, a mated female wasp (queen) overwinters and begins nest construction in the spring. Flower-visiting social wasps include paper and yellowjacket wasps, and bald-faced hornets.

Yellowjacket Wasp, *Vespula* sp. *left*
Wood fiber collection for paper nest construction
Bald-Faced Hornet, *Dolichovespula maculata* *right*
Visits flowers for nectar in early spring

Wasps visit flowers for nectar, especially flowers with shallow corollas. Their paper nests provide protection from the cold, allowing workers to forage for nectar late into the fall.

Social wasps can aggressively protect their nests by stinging intruders. When visiting flowers for nectar however, they are docile. Social wasps are predators of other insects including caterpillars which they chew and regurgitate to feed their larvae.

Paper Wasp, *Polistes* sp.

SOLITARY WASPS

Solitary wasps build nests in a variety of locations including burrows in the ground, cavities in plant stems and wood, and cavities formed with mud. One adult female performs nest construction and provisioning tasks. Prey may include caterpillars, grasshoppers, sawfly larvae, crickets, katydids, cicadas, and beetles.

Sand Wasp, *Bicyrtes quadrifasciatus*
A female excavates a nest in the ground.

These prey are paralyzed by the female's sting then transported back to the nest. There they remain, entombed but alive, to provide an unspoiled meal for the developing larvae to feed upon.

Most solitary wasps are short-tongued, visiting flowers with shallow corollas or accessible nectar. Solitary wasps do not aggressively defend their nests like social wasps. Once a female has completed nest excavation, provisioning and egg-laying, the nest is closed. The female typically does not revisit the nest or actively defend it.

BEETLES

The most common flower-visiting beetles include soldier beetles, Cantharidae family, long-horned beetles, Cerambycidae family, leaf beetles, Chrysomelidae family, and snout beetles, Curculionidae family. Beetles visit flowers to feed on pollen and nectar.

Soldier beetles (**Cantharidae family**) are common flower visitors in late summer.

Mouthparts

Some beetles have hairs on their tongue tip that scrape and release pollen but they typically use their mandibles for chewing pollen grains. Blister beetles, *Nemognatha* spp., have long, specialized maxillae for feeding on nectar (below).

Blister beetles, *Nemognatha* spp., use specialized mouthparts to feed on nectar.

While feeding on floral resources, beetles can be destructive by chewing the reproductive parts of the flower and/or the petals and foliage. Many beetle larvae are wood boring, feeding on wood fibers or fungi that inhabit decaying wood. Others are parasitoids of other insects; the larvae feed on another insect's larvae as they develop, ultimately killing the host.

Wedge-Shaped Beetles, *Macrosiagon* spp.
These beetles lay eggs on flowers. Beetle larvae climb onto a visiting adult bee or wasp and are transported to the nest where they feed on and eventually kill the host larvae.

With hairy bodies that trap pollen grains, many flower-visiting beetles effectively pollinate plants. Their hard wings (**elytra**) provide some protection from predators while they visit flowers. Other defense mechanisms include chemical defense (blister beetles) and mimicry (soldier beetles' coloring mimics wasps). Not easily scared off by other insects that visit flowers, beetles often spend several minutes on a flower, feeding on pollen or nectar. Because they often remain on one plant for a long period of time or forage between different plant species (lack floral constancy), their effectiveness as pollinators is diminished in many instances.

Floral Preferences

Beetles have a keen sense of smell and prefer open, white, cream or green-colored flowers with a spicy, fruity or fermented fragrance.

BUTTERFLIES & MOTHS

Butterflies and moths have a long proboscis to suck up nectar. The proboscis (**galeae**) has two maxilla, held together by hooks and teeth. In between the maxillae is a central tube. Flexing of the galeae muscle changes the diameter of the maxilla, then a muscular region in their head acts as a suction pump or bellows that draws nectar up the tube.

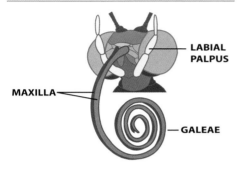

Figure 2.5 Butterfly & Moth Mouthparts
(Redrawn from Barth, 1991.)

A **great spangled fritillary butterfly,**
Speyeria cybele, nectars on pale purple
coneflower, *Echinacea pallida*.

Tiny spines cover the tip of the proboscis and are used to scratch and release sap from the base of flowers, even on plants that lack nectar. To coil back to its resting position, the proboscis does not require muscles. It passively coils because of the elasticity in the outer walls of the maxillae.

Foraging By Moths

Some moths such as hummingbird moths (right) have the ability to hover, allowing them access to a wider variety of flower types. Many moths are nocturnal, foraging at night when some flowers replenish nectar. Flowers pollinated by nocturnal moths are usually white or cream colored and have a strong scent, natural adaptations that help attract pollinators in low light conditions.

A **hummingbird moth,** *Hemaris* **sp.,**
hovers while nectaring on
wild bergamot, *Monarda fistulosa*.

Pollinators of Native Plants

BUTTERFLIES & MOTHS

Larval Host Plants

Female butterflies lay eggs on or near host plants, typically on the underside of the host plant's leaves. Butterfly and moth larvae (caterpillars) feed on the host plant foliage. Monarch caterpillars (below) are specialists, feeding on plants belonging to one genus (milkweeds, *Asclepias* spp.). Most caterpillars are generalists, feeding on host plants from many plant families. Butterflies and moths may have one to many generations per year.

Pollination By Butterflies & Moths

Several native plants are primarily pollinated by butterflies and moths. *See prairie phlox, Phlox pilosa, p. 108.* Large butterflies such as swallowtail butterflies brush their broad wings against anthers while visiting flowers, transferring pollen grains remaining on their wings to other plants. Although pollen grains typically do not persist on moths or butterflies, some grains may remain on their heads or be held in the proboscis when it recoils.

Eastern Tiger Swallowtail Butterfly, *Papilio glaucus*

Floral Preferences

When nectaring, butterflies prefer to land on flat flowers or to cling to some part of the flower structure. They nectar on both deep and shallow corollas but are common on composite flowers with shallow corollas and many disc florets offering nectar.

Orange Sulphur Butterfly,
Colias eurytheme

Dilute nectar is preferred; if it is too concentrated and thick, butterflies and moths cannot draw the fluid upward into their mouthparts. Nectar in flower corollas can become concentrated on hot summer days when flowers do not produce or actively replenish nectar.

Virginia Creeper Clearwing Moth,
Albuna fraxini

FLIES

Many types of flies visit flowers to feed on nectar and/or pollen and are considered effective pollinators of several flower species.

Mouthparts

Most flower-visiting flies have short mouthparts consisting of a labial tube (**labium**) with two suction pads (**labellum**) on the end. Channels (**pseudotracheae**) located on the bottom of the labellum lead to the mouth opening. Small teeth around the mouth opening scrape pollen from anthers or break down larger food particles. Some flies utilize saliva to dissolve food making it easier to ingest.

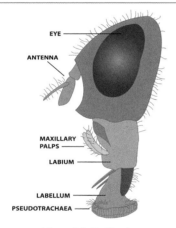

Figure 2.6 Fly Mouthparts
(Redrawn from Barth, 1991.)

Floral Preferences

Flies have demonstrated a preference for flat or bowl shaped flowers with shallow corollas and nectar rewards such as common boneset, *Eupatorium perfoliatum* (p. 194). Umbelliferous flowers that have volatile oils are also attractive to flies. Flies prefer many shallow flowers in a flower head such as plants in the carrot family (Apiaciae) as well as flowers that are white or cream colored and have a musty smell.

A **syrphid fly**, *Eristalis* sp., on common boneset, *Eupatorium perfoliatum,* a white flower frequented by flies.

Bee Flies
(Family Bombyliidae)

The labial tube in some flies, including bee flies, is long enough to access nectar in flowers with lengthy corollas. Many bee flies (Bombyliids) also have the ability to hover and visit many flowers in a short time frame. Bee flies' hairy bodies can carry substantial amounts of pollen. The hair also provides protection from cool temperatures in early spring when they are active looking for hosts (bees). *Read about the life cycle of bee flies on p. 95.*

A **bee fly**, *Bombylius* sp., probes for nectar with its long, modified mouthparts on bloodroot, *Sanguinaria canadensis*.

FLIES

Syrphid Flies (Family Syrphidae)

Syrphid or flower flies are the most common and diverse flower-visiting flies. Many are mimics of bees and wasps with black, yellow or white coloring.

A **syrphid fly,** *Lejops* **sp.,** feeds on pollen of marsh marigold flowers, *Caltha palustris.*

Syrphid flies feed on both pollen and nectar and rely on these food sources for most of their adult lives. To provide protein for egg production, females typically feed on pollen more often than males. Syrphid flies hold anthers with their forelegs (below) as they sponge up pollen with their mouthparts.

A **syrphid fly,** *Toxomerus* **sp.,** feeds on pollen from a long-styled sweet cicely, *Osmorhiza longistylis,* flower.

Many syrphid fly larvae are predators, preying on aphids or other small, soft-bodied insects. Larvae actively feed in the evening, looking for prey on plant foliage, in galls or roots below ground. Some syrphid fly larvae also feed on pollen.

Tachinid Flies (Family Tachinidae)

Tachinid flies typically visit flowers for nectar. They parasitize other insects, usually butterfly and moth larvae, and are common mid- to late summer. They have stout bodies and long bristles on the end of the abdomens. *See profile p. 125.*

A **tachinid fly,** *Archytas* **sp.,** feeds on nectar of yarrow flowers, *Achillea millefolium.*

Thick-Headed Flies (Family Conopidae)

Thick-headed flies visit flowers to feed on nectar. They parasitize many types of insects including wasps, bees, ants, crickets, cockroaches and some types of flies. Several types of thick-headed flies lay their eggs on the host while it is in flight.

Thick-headed fly, *Myopa* **sp.** *left*
Thick-headed fly, *Physocephala* **sp.** *right*

CHAPTER THREE
POLLINATOR CONSERVATION

URBAN/SUBURBAN LANDSCAPES

Foster pollinator populations by planting a diversity of flowering plants native to the region and protecting existing pollinator nesting and foraging habitat. A continuous succession of plants flowering from early spring until late fall provides forage resources for all types of pollinators and floral visitors throughout the growing season.

Right Plant - Right Place

The information in the Plant-Insect Interaction chapters of this book is compiled to match native plants with the most appropriate site conditions. Plants that are native to a region have coevolved with native pollinators; the plants are adapted to local climatic conditions, soils and rainfall. The benefit to the gardener is that properly situated plants require no additional water or fertilizer, and rarely need to be replaced.

Selecting Native Plants

To properly site native plants, determine the types of plant communities occurring locally before selecting or purchasing native plants. **The right plant for the right place can be determined by studying the following:**
- soil type and moisture
- drainage patterns
- rainfall amounts
- solar exposure
- historic and future plant communities

Native plants that are propagated from locally sourced seeds or plants, within a fifty mile radius, contain the genotype and phenotype best suited to local conditions. Plants installed in clumps or masses (at least five of the same plant together) provide a concentrated visual attractant for pollinators and help improve pollinator floral constancy.

Straight Native Species

Straight native species are typically better for pollinators than cultivars or hybrids bred or selected for double blooms, an alteration in the flower form or flower color change. Double blooms can restrict pollinator access and plant breeding may change the amount of nectar or pollen offered. For example, the double-flowered bloodroot plant, *Sanguinaria canadensis* 'Multiplex', has been vegetatively propagated from a plant found in Ohio in the early 1900s. The stamens in this plant are modified into petals resulting in numerous petals or double blooms. This plant lacks reproductive parts and therefore offers no reward to pollinators. Even if the plant did offer floral rewards, it would restrict pollinator access because of the number of petals crowded on the flower.

URBAN/SUBURBAN LANDSCAPES

Water

Many pollinators need an additional source of water beyond what they acquire from nectar. Clean water can be provided (if not naturally occurring) by installing a shallow dish with a sloped edge for easy exiting or by creating a mud puddle that is kept wet. To limit mosquito breeding sites, refresh water every five to seven days.

Butterflies in particular drink water from moist soils or shallow pools, a behavior known as puddling (above). In these puddles, they forage for salts and minerals held in the soil. Plants themselves can have water reservoirs. Cup plant, *Silphium perfoliatum* (below), has clasping leaves that hold water and many types of pollinators visit the plant to drink water in the leaves.

Pesticides

Pesticides harmful to pollinators include many insecticides, some fungicides and herbicides. Pollinator deaths increase when pesticides are used on forage plants, especially when forage plants are flowering. Pollinators can be poisoned from pesticides through floral resources (food) and through coming into contact with the chemical residue on foliage or in the soil. Even naturally-derived insecticides such as pyrethrin formulations are harmful to pollinators.

Systemic insecticides, including neonicotinoid-based insecticides, are incorporated into the plant's vascular system and the floral resources (nectar and pollen). These insecticides can be persistent with their effectiveness lasting from several months to a few years. When applied, even at very low doses, systemic insecticides are harmful to pollinators. Bees in particular are affected because they are foraging, collecting and consuming the most floral resources. Fungicides are also harmful; they can impact bees by reducing or eliminating the beneficial fungi in bee bread.

Non-chemical methods reduce or eliminate the likelihood of pollinator poisoning. Many problem pests cause only cosmetic damage to ornamental plants and they often can be controlled with a healthy population of beneficial insects. *Read more information about pesticides on p. 39, 41 & 43.*

INVASIVE PLANTS

Invasive Plants: Non-native plants that have been introduced by humans and are serious environmental pests. Invasive plants change the structure and diversity of native plant communities. Eradicating invasive plants before enhancing existing or installing new pollinator plantings eliminates this competition for light, nutrients and water. Herbaceous invasive plants without a taproot can be smothered using paper and a thick layer of mulch in the fall. Before covering the soil, it is a good idea to check for ground-nesting bee nests. This smothering material can be left in place for planting through in the spring.

Non-native **honeysuckle shrubs, *Lonicera* sp.,** invade forests and replace native shrubs and herbaceous plants.

Invasive woody plants can be cut to the ground (basal pruned) and stump spot-treated with a concentrated glyphosate-based herbicide. This technique reduces soil disturbance caused from removing the entire woody plant root system and minimizes the amount of herbicide used. Repeated basal pruning (several times per year for two to five years) instead of herbicide treatment can be effective at eliminating some invasive plants. Prescribed fires are another tool used in the control of invasive plants but can cause harm to existing pollinator populations and nesting sites if performed over large areas or when pollinators are active. *See p. 36 for more information.*

Many invasive ornamental plants, (both herbaceous and woody) continue to be sold by the nursery trade. For example, Japanese barberry, *Berberis thunbergii,* is a shrub available for sale throughout the United States and Canada. This shrub invades woodlands and savannas and outcompetes native plant species.

For more information, invasive plant lists are provided by the Department or Ministry of Natural Resources for a particular state or province. Other good resources for invasive plant information include:

- **Center for Invasive Species and Ecosystem Health** www.invasive.org

- **Invasive Plant Atlas** www.invasiveplantatlas.org

- **Midwest Invasive Plant Network** www.mipn.org

European buckthorn, *Rhamnus cathartica,* invades forest understories outcompeting native plants for water and sunlight.

NATIVE PLANTS

Native Plants: plants that exist in a geographic area without direct or indirect human introduction.

Leadplant, *Amorpha canescens,*
in a prairie remnant.

The network of interactions between insects and native plants is the foundation of a complex ecosystem. Fostering these interactions with a diversity of native plants in the urban, natural, restored and agricultural landscape supports healthy, robust ecosystems and pollinator populations.

Pollination ensures the successful reproduction of plants and the long-term survival and diversity of plant communities. Without pollinators performing cross-pollination, fewer viable and genetically-diverse seeds are produced.

With the degradation and fragmentation of most native plant communities, there has been a significant decline in pollinator populations. Even small urban landscapes play an important role in supporting native pollinators when a sufficient amount and diversity of forage plants are provided. Recent research (Frankie et al, 2005; Wojcik et al, 2008) has demonstrated that native flowering plants were four times as likely to attract pollinators than exotic plants. The studies also found that eight or more species of native plants in a landscape increases both the abundance and diversity of native bees.

A diverse native planting not only supports more pollinators but also attracts beneficial insects. These insects suppress problem pests and provide ecosystem services to all types of landscapes. Gardeners and landowners who manage and enhance their landscape with both pollinator forage plants and nesting sites can support almost as many types of pollinators as natural areas.

Pollinators of Native Plants

PROVIDING NESTING SITES

Native bees nest in a variety of habitats, so it is possible to provide additional nesting habitat with a few simple techniques:

Hollow or Pithy Plant Stem Stubble

Native perennials have hollow or pith-filled plant stems. Cavity-nesting insects which include most cavity-nesting bees and some solitary wasps use the hollow stems or a preexisting cavity.

Perennial plant stem stubble from the previous season's growth provides nesting sites for cavity-nesting bees. The stems naturally break down in one to two years limiting reuse.

A few bee species, including small carpenter bees, *Ceratina* spp., and mason bees, *Hoplitis* spp., construct their nests in pith-filled plant stems, chewing the pithy material from the center of the stem to create their nesting cavity. The pith shavings are used as brood cell divisions within the nesting cavity.

After some of the first woodland wildflowers bloom in the garden, cut perennial plant stems down in late spring, leaving 15" of stubble as potential nesting sites. Provide both hollow and pithy stems of varying diameters. Look for pith shavings coming out the tops of some of the small stems in the following weeks.

The top end of a cut stem where the pith is being excavated to create a nesting cavity by a small carpenter bee, *Ceratina* sp.

A small carpenter bee, *Ceratina* sp., enters a nest in a plant stem.

PROVIDING NESTING SITES

Cavities in Wood

Standing dead trees (snags) provide excellent nesting habitat for native pollinators. If a dead tree is a property hazard that needs to be removed, consider leaving a portion of the trunk standing. A native vine such as virgin's bower, *Clematis virginiana,* planted at the base of the tree provides forage resources for pollinators and helps camouflage the tree snag. Banded long-horn beetles, *Typocerus* sp. (p. 96), have wood-boring larva that create nesting holes that bees utilize. Logs lying on the ground are also used for nesting sites.

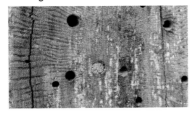

Cavities in Rocks

Porous rocks such as limestone-based rocks often have holes or cavities used by cavity-nesting pollinators. Incorporate rocks with cavities if locally available to provide additional nesting sites.

A **leafcutter bee,** *Megachile* **sp.,** uses a hole in a rock for a nesting site.

Ground Nests

Most ground-nesting bees prefer to construct their nests in sandy, loamy or loose soil. Some ground-nesting bees prefer to nest in slopes or exposed banks. Nests often look like ant hills with a raised entrance where the excavated soil is deposited. Provide areas of bare soil and protect existing nests from disturbances such as tilling, plant removal or compaction.

A newly excavated **cellophane bee,** *Colletes inaequalis,* nest. Many ground nests look similar to ant hills with soil deposited around the entrance.

Rodent Holes & Leaf Piles

For nesting, bumble bees use abandoned rodent holes or mouse nests, leaf or grass clipping piles. Queens overwinter in the ground, often in abandoned rodent holes.

Leaves and downed logs provide important overwintering sites for beetle, butterfly or moth larvae or pupae, and cavity-nesting sites for bees, wasps, and beetles.

NATURAL LANDSCAPES

Native pollinators, already abundant in natural areas, provide important pollination of rare plant species and contribute to the overall health and diversity of a native plant community.

The following conditions can affect pollinator populations in natural landscapes:

- the spread of invasive plants
- fire/prescribed burns
- soil compaction or tilling
- human and livestock disturbance within or around plant communities

Prescribed Burns (Fires)

Prescribed burns are a management tool to maintain or establish prairie plant communities as well as pastures, woodlands and brushlands. These controlled fires help eliminate woody or invasive plant encroachment, improve wildlife habitat, fertilize the soil with ashes, stimulate seed germination and new plant growth and increase plant diversity.

Timing of Burns ~ Late Fall

To minimize pollinator mortality, prescribed burns are typically performed in late fall or early winter when insects are not actively foraging. If insects are beneath the soil surface when a fire is performed, they generally are not harmed. These insects would include ground-nesting bees and wasps whose burrows are deep enough to protect larvae from the heat of the fire.

Timing of Burns ~ Summer

Summer fires performed after many overwintering insects have pupated and are mobile (able to fly) can also reduce pollinator mortality. Mobile species not harmed by the fire of mid-summer burns have demonstrated that they can recolonize burned areas quite quickly - within two years. Insect species with multiple generations per year versus one generation per year are more resilient and recover faster from summer burns.

Since timing for summer burns is site specific, first determine the dominant insect orders in a given habitat to prevent pollinator mortality. Target burns when the majority of insects are in the adult stage of their life cycle or when a remnant-dependent species is mobile.

Size of Burn

Another consideration is to minimize the number of forage plants burned, especially when forage resources are low. A program of a multi-year rotational schedule that burns small portions, less than one quarter of a site yearly, can help minimize the impact of burns on pollinator populations. Patchy burns (fires that meander through a habitat in a mosaic) can stimulate new plant growth, create complex plant compositions and increase the number of forage plants in flower. Timing of patchy burns is site specific in order to achieve the best results for forage plant regeneration and to minimize pollinator mortality.

Positive Impacts of Burns
Ground-nesting bees can benefit from prescribed burns through the creation of more open, bare ground and access to new nesting sites. If burns increase the number of forage plants, the net results to pollinators can be positive.

Negative Impacts of Burns
When prescribed burns are performed in late fall, winter or early spring, insects such as cavity-nesting bees, butterfly or moth larvae in the duff or leaf litter are severely affected. Burns also eliminate valuable cavity-nesting sites for bees, wasps and beetles.

Species that are remnant-dependent, habitat specialists or those with small, fragmented habitats are very vulnerable to prescribed burns. Only burn small isolated, high-quality remnants that host rare plant or pollinator populations in limited portions on a rotational basis. Leave plenty of refugia and forage plants for rare pollinators.

Edge Disturbance
Disturbances such as grazing, compaction, tilling, ground clearing and pesticide use around the edges of intact plant communities can negatively affect pollinator populations and habitat. Disturbed edges are portals for the introduction of invasive plant species, changes in plant structure and decline in habitat.

These degraded edges reduce the overall size of the plant community. The distance between plant communities makes pollinator movement more difficult and, therefore, restricts long distance outcrossing of pollen. Decreasing forage resources within the plant community can result in unsustainable populations of pollinators.

Soil Compaction
Soil compaction has a negative effect on plant community structure and pollinator habitat. Mycorrhizal fungi that colonize roots and aid in the delivery of nutrients to plants can be severely impacted by soil compaction. Plant growth is also impeded when soils are compacted: plant roots are unable to penetrate new spaces and there is a decrease in the amount of oxygen and water available in the soil. Both stem-nesting and ground-nesting pollinators can have nests destroyed from compaction by vehicles or foot traffic.

AGRICULTURAL LANDSCAPES

By introducing native plants to the edges of fields, agricultural crops can receive secondary pollination from native pollinators plus crop pest management from beneficial insects. In many cases, native pollinators have been found to pollinate crops more effectively than honey bees (Garibaldi et al, 2013). Native pollinators are, however, limited by flight distance (200 yards - 1 mile) and cannot access all plants in large fields unless nesting habitat and forage plants are strategically located.

Wild bergamot, *Monarda fistulosa,* is a long-flowering native plant visited by **bumble bees,** *Bombus* **spp.,** and is also an excellent forage plant for bumble bee-pollinated crops.

If habitat (forage and nesting sites) exists near crop fields, native bees can provide a substantial amount of pollination to crops or, on organic farms with valuable habitat nearby, full pollination service. To maintain this service, the existing pollinator habitat must be protected from degradation and restored or enhanced.

Pollination of Crops

The types or numbers of native bees that pollinate a particular crop can vary. For a crop such as cranberries typically pollinated by honey bees, bumble bees supply valuable secondary pollination or can be the primary pollinator when the bog is surrounded with woods. The charts (p. 244) and sample pollinator plans (p. 268) are provided as scalable templates to attract appropriate bee species for the pollination of a particular crop.

Benefits of Native Plantings

Native plantings also attract beneficial insects that help suppress pest populations in crops. The most effective plantings provide a diversity of native plants suited to the site conditions and a continuous sequence of flowering from early spring through late fall. Crop pollination can significantly improve with supplementary native plantings.

Besides crop pollination, other benefits of native plantings in agricultural landscapes include:

- weed suppression when native plants provide good soil coverage
- reduction in soil erosion
- improvement in water quality
- improved aesthetics

Planting Sites & Pollinator Habitat

Forage and nesting sites for native pollinators develop from the protection or enhancement of existing natural habitats. Marginal, open, sunny areas such as grassed waterways, ditches around fields or riparian edges are good sites to create pollinator habitat by adding forage plants. If fragments of potential habitat exist, join the fragments together to create a corridor. If only one fragment exists, expand its size or replicate the plant community in new, strategically spaced locations near the field.

AGRICULTURAL LANDSCAPES

The natural layout of an agricultural site can also determine where the best pollinator habitat can be incorporated. Given the limited flight distance of native pollinators, fields or tracts of land under ten acres work best for pollinators to access and pollinate crops.

Within these tracts, long narrow corridors can be planted with pollinator-specific native plants. Incorporate nesting materials such as plant debris, rock piles, standing dead trees, downed logs and leaves. Combined with areas of bare ground, these materials provide valuable nesting sites in the corridors.

Grazing

If intensive, grazing can have a number of negative impacts on pollinator habitat. The plant community may experience significant changes in its diversity, composition and structure. If grazing is intensive in early spring when caterpillars are foraging, it can limit the number of larval host plants available for butterflies and moths or cause larval mortality. Intensively grazed pastures alter plant composition and pollinator diversity and cause trampling of vegetation and soil compaction. These actions negatively affect the number of ground-nesting sites for bees and wasps. Established ground nests and adult bees can be trampled by livestock.

Less intensive rotational grazing can limit damage to floral resources if it is carefully planned and executed. Rotational grazing allows plants to recover and flower, ensuring a succession of flowering plants for pollinators.

Pesticide Use & Drift

Insect communities are most successful when forage plants and nesting sites are protected from the direct impact of pesticide use or drift. A windrow or hedge row of tall shrubs or evergreen trees can limit pesticide drift from contaminating forage and nesting sites in field margins and reduce soil erosion from wind and water.

A sound integrated pest management (IPM) program with crop monitoring for pests reduces the number of pesticide applications required. When a threshold has been reached and no other non-chemical alternatives are available, pesticides may be used as a last resort. To minimize poisoning, select the least toxic pesticides and avoid applications when crops are in flower or when pollinators are active.

Pollinators of Native Plants

Many predators and parasitoids that are beneficial, natural pest enemies rely on floral rewards for food. Beneficial insects maintain the checks and balances of the insect world and help prevent pest populations from getting out of control and causing damage to crops and garden plants. There are numerous types of beneficial insects including flies, wasps, beetles and true bugs.

The abundance and diversity of beneficial insects in a particular landscape depends on the:

- quality and abundance of forage plants
- availability of prey
- number of nesting sites
- overall health of the plant community
- maintenance of the landscape including pesticide use

Selecting Native Plants

Native plants play an important role in attracting beneficial insects. Beneficial insects visit flowers for nectar and pollen or seek shelter in the foliage when not hunting or parasitizing prey. Similar to selecting plants for pollinators (p. 30), match the site conditions to the plants' requirements. Plant stress is reduced and susceptibility to pest problems minimized.

In a study by Michigan State University (Fiedler et al., 2007), forty-six native plants were selected to provide an overlapping succession of flowers throughout the growing season and were rated on their efficacy in attracting beneficial insects while in flower. Some of the top native plants in the study that attract the most beneficial insects include *Zizia aurea* (p. 132), *Anemone canadensis* (p. 180), *Ratibida pinnata* (p. 112), *Monarda punctata* (p. 98), *Silphium perfoliatum* (p. 216), *Lobelia siphilitica* (p. 208) and *Symphyotrichum novae-angliae* (p. 220).

Predators

Predators feed on insects as adults and/or as larvae. For many predators, prey is cached in the nest for larvae to consume. Predators help control caterpillars, sawfly larvae, katydids, crickets, and grasshoppers - all insects that feed on foliage. Others help control aphid, whitefly and mealybug populations. Soldier beetles, lady bird beetles, syrphid flies, solitary wasps and minute pirate bugs are important predatory beneficial insects.

A syrphid fly larva, *Eupeodes* sp., feeds on aphids.

Adult syrphid flies visit flowers to feed on pollen and nectar. They are often mistaken for bees - their coloring and behavior mimic bees (and wasps). Larvae look like small caterpillars and feed on aphids or other small soft-bodied insects (above). Their larvae can be found on the underside of leaves where a large aphid population occurs. They are voracious predators that can catch and feed on aphids much larger than themselves.

BENEFICIAL INSECTS ~ ECOSYSTEM SERVICES

Brown Lacewing Larva Preying on Aphids

Also known as "aphid lions" lacewing larvae are effective predators of aphids (above), grabbing and chewing prey with their long, curved mandibles. Adult females typically lay their eggs on the underside of leaves; some species suspend the eggs on long, thin stalks from the underside of leaves. Lacewings are insects in the Chrysopidae and Hemerobiidae families.

Ladybird Beetle Larva Feeding on Aphids
Both the adults and larvae of ladybird beetles feed on aphids and other soft-bodied insects.

Wasps are also predators, feeding on or provisioning their nests with a variety of insects including crickets, katydids, caterpillars, sawfly larvae and true bugs. Many wasps are flower visitors feeding on nectar, especially in late summer.

Parasitoids

Parasitoids use insect hosts for their larvae to feed on (or within) and develop. Many wasps are parasitoids such as braconid wasps (p. 87), laying eggs inside the host. Thynnid wasps, *Myzinum* spp. (p. 198), lay their eggs in scarab beetle larvae in the soil. Like all parasitoids, the wasp larvae eventually kill the host by consuming its essential organs. With the host food source depleted, the larvae then pupate.

A tachinid fly feeds on nectar from swamp milkweed, *Asclepias incarnata*.

Tachinid flies lay their eggs directly on their prey. When the egg hatches, the larva burrows into the host to feed. Prey include butterfly, moth and sawfly larvae, grasshoppers, true bugs and immature beetles. These flies are common flower visitors feeding on nectar in July and August.

Pesticides

When an insecticide is used to control an insect population that is causing damage to a plant, it not only kills the problem pest but also harms beneficial insects and pollinators. Studies have found that pest populations recover more quickly from an insecticide treatment than beneficial populations do. Therefore, using insecticides can perpetuate an imbalance of pest and beneficial insect populations and result in more pests.

THREATS TO POLLINATORS

Many factors are contributing to the decline of native pollinators. These include the degradation and fragmentation of natural habitats, the decline of flower-rich plant communities, the spread of pathogens, climate change and pesticide use.

Habitat Degradation & Fragmentation

Habitat degradation from the conversion of natural habitats into agricultural cropland or residential/commercial development is one of the main causes contributing to the decline in pollinator diversity. This degradation and fragmentation directly impacts nesting habitat, floral resources (food sources) and host plants for butterflies and moths. As the natural landscape becomes degraded or fragmented into smaller parcels, native pollinators, challenged to travel long flight distances between habitat fragments, are unable to service the plant community. Some self-compatible plants may survive over time but overall genetic diversity decreases. Plants that are not self-compatible do not survive as long.

The loss of habitat is very disruptive to pollinator populations and it can create an imbalance between effective pollinators and ineffective pollinators, with more of the latter. In a smaller, fragmented landscape, there is a risk of pollinator inbreeding due to small pollinator populations. Reduced pollinator populations result in lower pollinator visitation rates to the remaining plants, decreasing seed set.

Solution

Connecting or enlarging fragmented landscapes by reintroducing native plants can increase the survivability of pollinators and reduce the pressures associated with invasive species and competition. Long, narrow habitat corridors oriented north-south play an important role in the movement of species northward as the climate warms and plant communities' structure changes.

Invasive Plants

Invasive plants displace or decrease native plant populations in natural habitats. They can also spread, covering over valuable ground nesting sites. These introduced plants often steal pollinator visits from native plants, decreasing pollination effectiveness to native plants. In the short term, invasive species can help support pollinator populations if they offer attractive floral rewards.

Purple Loosestrife, *Lythrum salicaria*
Pollination of native *Lythrum* sp. is reduced by floral visits to invasive purple loosestrife.

Long term, as an invasive plant continues to degrade and reduce diversity in a native plant community, pollinators are no longer benefiting. A reduction in plant diversity can lead to a seasonal gap in flowering plants and fewer forage plants for pollinators.

Solution

The best way to restore the diversity of native plant communities and rebalance effective and ineffective pollinator populations is to remove invasive plants and replace them with native flowering plants. *See p. 32 for strategies on removing invasive plants from the landscape.*

THREATS TO POLLINATORS

Pesticides

Herbicides have an indirect impact on native pollinators. They eliminate forage plants for pollinators, host plants for butterflies and moths and decrease overall plant diversity.

Insecticides have a direct impact, some are applied in microcapsule form mimicking pollen. These capsules can be collected by foraging bees where they are incorporated into nest provisions. Applied when pollinators are actively foraging on plants, insecticides can be very harmful.

Systemic insecticides such as neonicotinoid-based insecticides are absorbed into a plant's vascular system and make the entire plant harmful, including the floral resources: nectar and pollen. When these systemic insecticides are applied, plants can remain toxic to bees for several months to years. Systemic insecticides can also have sub-lethal effects on bees when repeated exposure of small doses occurs, decreasing their neurological function and resulting in disorientation.

Fungicides are often combined with agricultural pesticides and can reduce or eliminate important beneficial fungi. These fungi facilitate fermentation of pollen in bee bread which creates a more digestible food for developing larvae. The reduction in beneficial fungi diminishes the quality of bee bread resulting in malnutrition and increased larval susceptibility to disease and pathogens.

Climate Change

Plant-insect interactions may become uncoupled as flowering phenology and pollinator emergences shift with warming temperatures. A recent study (Rafferty, 2011) has shown that when plants flower earlier, they receive more visits from pollinators than plants flowering at historical dates. As many plants flower earlier and earlier, the pollinators may not be able to keep up with the shift, resulting in a reduction or gap in the overlap of flowering species in plant communities. With the predicted increase in extreme weather events and drought, plant growth and flowering periods are likely to shorten, resulting in a decrease in flowering overlap and quality of floral resources offered to pollinators.

Plant community diversity is projected to decrease with climate change. Plants that can adapt to the changing temperatures and weather patterns may survive, but fragile plants may perish. Pollinators have the ability to change their range through corridors or connected fragments where plant communities are stable and offer adequate forage and nesting habitat. These corridors are especially important for pollinators with short flight distances. Riverways and other natural corridors oriented in a north-south direction are projected to be very important pathways in the movement and relocation of both plant and animal species. In the future, specialist plants could lose their pollinators as plants shift to other ranges. Oligolectic (pollen-collecting specialist) bees may be displaced outside the range of their host plants.

POLLINATOR CONSERVATION CHECKLIST

BENEFICIAL ACTIONS

NESTING HABITAT
- [ ] Prevent soil disturbance
- [ ] Prevent soil compaction
- [ ] Leave areas of bare soil, especially where existing ground nests occur
- [ ] Preserve and enhance existing ground-nesting sites
- [ ] Leave standing dead trees
- [ ] Leave or add downed logs
- [ ] Leave leaf litter, use leaf litter as a garden mulch instead of shredded wood mulch
- [ ] Leave perennial stems standing for the winter, then cut the following spring leaving 15" of stem stubble to provide nesting opportunities for bees that season
- [ ] Leave cut perennial plant debris on the ground as a natural mulch
- [ ] Add or leave rocks with holes for nesting cavities
- [ ] Perform rotational prescribed burns in sections of a site with a multi-year time line

FORAGING RESOURCES
- [ ] Provide a continuous succession of flowering plants from spring through fall
- [ ] Plant a diversity of native plants with different flower forms and floral resources
- [ ] Plant butterfly and moth larval host plants
- [ ] Provide a shallow source of water and refresh every 5-7 days (to kill mosquito larvae and prevent disease)

PLANT SELECTION & PLACEMENT
- [ ] Remove invasive plant species while minimizing soil disturbance
- [ ] Use local native plant communities as cues for plant selection
- [ ] Select plants native to the area/region
- [ ] Purchase locally grown native plants
- [ ] Replace a portion of lawn with forage plants
- [ ] Incorporate forage plants in the lawn
- [ ] Plant forage plants in masses to create better visual attractants
- [ ] Build upon/expand/restore/connect existing native plant community fragments
- [ ] Build upon/create corridors for habitat connectivity

PESTICIDE POISONING PREVENTION
- [ ] Purchase plants from retailers that do not use systemic insecticides during nursery production
- [ ] Use non-chemical methods to control pests and look for beneficial insects
- [ ] Restrict or eliminate pesticide use, especially when forage plants are flowering

POLLINATOR CONSERVATION CHECKLIST

DESTRUCTIVE ACTIONS - PRACTICES TO AVOID

NESTING HABITAT
- [ ] Tilling soil
- [ ] Compacting soil by driving vehicles/equipment on landscape
- [ ] Creating large soil disturbances by scraping soil/uprooting large woody plants
- [ ] Cutting down dead trees
- [ ] Removing all leaves from the landscape
- [ ] Removing branches/downed logs
- [ ] Fragmenting existing habitat
- [ ] Increasing the size of the lawn
- [ ] Cutting down and removing plant material/stems in the fall
- [ ] Covering bare soil with mulch especially where nesting sites occur
- [ ] Covering the soil with plastic and/or landscape rock
- [ ] Performing a prescribed burn over the entire site in one season
- [ ] Not replacing liners/stems or cleaning man-made cavity nests every two years
- [ ] Destroying rodent holes

FORAGING RESOURCES
- [ ] Planting hybrids/cultivars bred for color change or double blooms that restrict pollinator access or offer fewer or no floral rewards
- [ ] Planting only annuals and/or herbs
- [ ] Mowing/spraying forage plants and larval host plants

PLANT SELECTION & PLACEMENT
- [ ] Planting/not removing invasive species
- [ ] Removing native forage plants
- [ ] Planting plants not locally grown or unsuitable to climate/region
- [ ] Removing larval host plants of butterflies and moths

PESTICIDE POISONING
- [ ] Planting plants treated with systemic insecticides during nursery production
- [ ] Using insecticides, especially systemic ones
- [ ] Applying fungicides/herbicides to lawn where nesting sites or forage plants occur
- [ ] Using herbicides or insecticides on forage plants or larval host plants
- [ ] Using rodent poison in burrows

HOW TO USE THIS BOOK ~ LEFT SPREAD

Flowering period and **habitat** (exposure, soil type, soil moisture) are provided in scale illustrations for each native plant species. Develop an understanding of the regional native landscape, then match existing site conditions to native plant requirements. An individual native plant may occur in geographically disjunct habitats. For example, harebell, *Campanula rotundifolia* (p. 66), occurs on rocky Lake Superior shorelines and above the treeline in the Rocky Mountains. Insect visitors for a particular plant can be as diverse as the plant's range.

Range maps have been drawn from the USDA Plants Database, **www.plants. usda.gov;** and the Biota of North America Program (BONAP), **www.bonap.org** websites. Refer to these websites for county-level occurrences.

Unshaded: Not native to state, province or territory

Shaded: Native to state, province or territory

Flower, **leaf**, **fruit** and **root** information is provided for identification purposes. *See the **Visual Glossary of Plant Parts** p. 254, for diagrams of leaf, flower and fruit types.*

Plant notes provide horticultural information and cultivation tips for the native plant featured.

COLOR-CODED SECTIONS

The native plants in this book are categorized in one of three main sections: **prairie**, **woodland edge** and **wetland edge**. With any native plant species, there is overlap of these sections and designations are not always distinct. For example, some plants in the wetland edge section also occur in moist prairies. Plants are listed in alphabetical order by genus in each section. See the table of contents for common names.

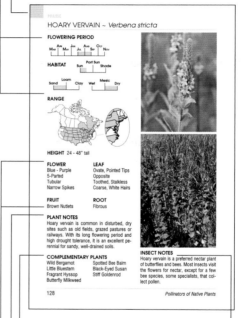

Complementary plants are plants that flower around the same time as the featured plant and typically occur in the same conditions and habitat. Use the lists as a guide for companion plantings.

Insect notes describe the types of floral visitors and plant characteristics that influence pollination.

HOW TO USE THIS BOOK ~ RIGHT SPREAD

POLLINATOR PROFILE OR PLANT CHARACTERISTICS INFLUENCING POLLINATION

A specific pollinator, predator, parasitoid or beneficial insect that interacts with the featured native plant. It also describes information about flower morphology and development that influence the types of pollinators that visit the plant.

LARVAL HOST PLANT

List of butterfly or moth species that feed on the featured native plant as larvae (caterpillars). Butterfly and moth ranges may not occur throughout the entire range of the native plant. Refer to a butterfly or moth field guide to determine if the butterfly or moth occurs in the region.

SPECIALIST BEE(S)

List of bee species that are pollen specialists of this native plant (oligolectic bees) collecting pollen from a narrow range of plants, often from a single plant family or genus.

INSECT INTERACTIONS

Photos of common insect species that visit the featured native plant and their interactions with the plant, whether they are effective or ineffective pollinators, collect and/or feed on pollen, feed on nectar or predate/parasitize other floral visitors.

 LARVAL HOST PLANT OF BUTTERFLY OR MOTH SPECIES

 POLLEN-COLLECTING SPECIALIST BEE(S)

 PLANT VISITED BY HUMMINGBIRDS

 HONEY BEES PLANT VISITED BY HONEY BEES

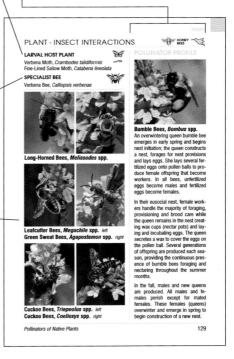

This book covers common native bee species of the upper Midwest, Great Lakes area, Northeast and southern Canada. See the Common Bee Genera section (p. 257) for other bee species not included in the book. The plant and insect ranges do not overlap entirely: some insects in the book may not occur in the geographic ranges that the plants cover. Flowering times reflect the upper Midwest, Great Lakes area, Northeast and southern Canada. For areas outside of this range, flowering times may be earlier or later.

CHAPTER FOUR

Native Plant - Insect Interactions

PRAIRIE

FRAGRANT (Anise) HYSSOP ~ *Agastache foeniculum*

FLOWERING PERIOD

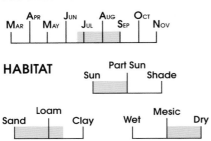

HABITAT

RANGE

HEIGHT 30 - 60" tall

FLOWER	**LEAF**
Blue - Violet	Lanceolate
5-Parted	Opposite
Tubular	Hairy Underneath
Dense Spike, Whorls	Anise Fragrance

FRUIT	**ROOT**
Oval Nutlet	Fibrous

PLANT NOTES

Fragrant hyssop is a very drought toler-ant plant, performing well in sand prairies and landscapes with well-drained soils. Site fragrant hyssop next to soft-textured prai-rie grasses to complement its dark green foliage and upright stature. The leaves give off a pleasant anise scent when crushed or chewed.

COMPLEMENTARY PLANTS

Black-Eyed Susan   Stiff Goldenrod
Little Bluestem

INSECT NOTES

Bees and butterflies are the main visi-tors to fragrant hyssop. As bees probe the flower, pollen from the anthers held in the upper lip is deposited on their head or thorax. A disc at the base of the flower secretes nectar. Look for several types of butterflies and moths nectaring on the flowers.

50

PLANT - INSECT INTERACTIONS

HONEY BEES

As medium- and large-sized bees probe the flower, pollen from the anthers located in the upper lip is deposited onto their head. When visiting subsequent female phase flowers, pollen is transferred to receptive stigmas, also located in the upper lip.

Long-Horned Bee, *Melissodes* **spp.** *left*
Bumble Bees, *Bombus* **spp.** *right*

Small Resin Bees   **Leafcutter Bees**
Heriades **spp.** *left*   *Megachile* **spp.** *right*
Small resin bees, *Heriades* spp., cling to the style to access the flower's nectar. Large leafcutter bees, *Megachile* spp., visit fragrant hyssop for nectar and are effective pollinators. Pollen collects on their abdominal scopae and is transferred onto receptive stigmas on the next plant visited.

Bee Flies, *Bombylius* **spp.** *left*
Bee flies hover in front of the flowers. They reach nectar with their long mouthparts and minimize their contact with pollen.
Soldier Beetles, *Chauliognathus* **spp.** *right*

Butterflies probe each tubular flower on the flower spike for nectar.

Silver Spotted Skipper Butterfly, *Epargyreus clarus*

Peck's Skipper Butterfly
Polites peckius

Great Spangled Fritillary Butterfly, *Speyeria cybele*

NODDING ONION ~ *Allium cernuum*

FLOWERING PERIOD

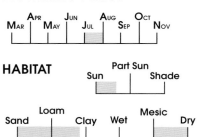

HABITAT

RANGE

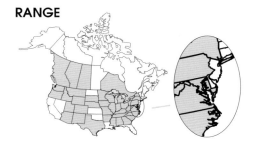

HEIGHT 12 - 24" tall

FLOWER
Pale - Dark Pink
6-Parted
Nodding Umbel

LEAF
Linear
Basal-Like
Clasping
Onion Scent

FRUIT
3-Lobed Capsule
No Bulblets

ROOT
Bulb

PLANT NOTES
Nodding onion is extremely adaptable and thrives in both dry and medium soils. When massed in borders or at the edges of prairie plantings, its unique nodding flower heads and grass-like leaves contrast well with neighboring plants.

COMPLEMENTARY PLANTS
Butterfly Milkweed   Wild Petunia
Purple Prairie Clover   Blue Grama
Hoary Vervain

INSECT NOTES
The nectar is accessed by all floral visitors including beetles and short-tongued bees. Bees visit the flowers primarily for nectar. When visiting the flowers, medium to large bees contact pollen from long stamens that extend past the petals. The flowers are protandrous (the anthers mature before the stigmas). Nectar collects at the base of the three fused filaments. The other three filaments are attached to the petals.

PLANT - INSECT INTERACTIONS

 HONEY BEES

Leafcutter Bees, *Megachile* spp. *left*
Small Resin Bees, *Heriades* spp. *right*
Leafcutter and resin bees have a concave (downward-curving) abdomen and abdominal scopae. When they visit nodding onion to collect pollen and feed on nectar, their scopae contacts the anthers.

Sweat Bees, *Lasioglossum* spp. *left*
Bumble Bees, *Bombus* spp. *right*

Soldier Beetles, *Chauliognathus* spp. *left*
Soldier beetles feed on nectar. *See profile p. 96.*
Tumbling Flower Beetles, *Mordella* spp
When disturbed, these beetles take cover under the flower or foliage or drop off the plant and tumble downward. They feed on the flower's nectar.

Syrphid Flies, *Allograpta* spp.
Syrphid flies visit the flowers for both pollen and nectar. Pictured (left) feeding on pollen.

Cellophane (Polyester) Bees
Colletes spp.
Cellophane bees are one of the principal visitors of nodding onion. As their common name suggests, these bees produce a cellophane-like substance in their Dufour's gland. Once secreted, this substance is spread over brood cells with their bi-lobed tongue to provide waterproofing and protection from pathogens. They often build their ground nests in moist soils, along riparian areas where the waterproof lining can help mitigate flooding.

Cellophane bees are medium-sized, have pale stripes on their abdomen and a heart-shaped face. Their head and thorax are moderately hairy. Pollen is collected on combs on the upper part of their hind legs and the side of their thorax, a characteristic that causes easy confusion with mining bees, *Andrena* spp. When females return to the nest, they mix pollen with nectar to make a liquid bee bread. Instead of laying their egg on top of the provisions like most other bees, they lay their egg on the upper wall of the brood cell.

AMERICAN PASQUEFLOWER ~ *Anemone patens*

FLOWERING PERIOD

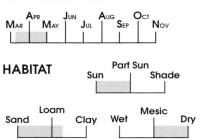

HABITAT

RANGE

HEIGHT 4 - 16" tall

FLOWER	**LEAF**
5- to 7-Parted	Palmately Divided
Blue - White	Thin Segments
Single Flower	Hairy

FRUIT	**ROOT**
Seed	Woody Taproot
Long Fluffy Hairs	

PLANT NOTES

A wonderful alternative to non-native tulips or daffodils, American pasqueflower blooms in early spring and is tolerant of poor, dry soils. The leaves are held tight to the stem when the flowers open then relax and unfurl after flowering. Do not plant in rich soils as the woody root system may rot.

COMPLEMENTARY PLANTS

Field Pussytoes	Wild Lupine
Prairie Smoke	Wild Columbine

INSECT NOTES

American pasqueflower primarily offers pollen to visiting insects and is an important early spring resource for female bees that are provisioning nests. The plant produces small amounts of nectar from the base of the stamens (staminal nectaries). *See the visual glossary for illustrations of nectary locations, p. 255.*

PLANT - INSECT INTERACTIONS

 HONEY BEES

American pasqueflower blooms in early spring during fluctuating temperatures so visits by pollinators can be sporadic. If the sepals are closed on a cool day, bees force their way into the flower to collect pollen.

Sweat Bees
Lasioglossum spp.

Sweat bees collect the white pollen by circling around the stamens on each flower and are frequent visitors.

Syrphid Flies, *Brachypalpus* spp.
These large syrphid flies are excellent mimics of mining bees and bumble bees. They visit American pasqueflower to feed on pollen.

Bee Flies, *Bombylius* spp.
Bee flies are common in dry prairies in early spring where American pasqueflower occurs. Flying low to the ground, bee flies search for nests of ground-nesting bee species where they lay their eggs at the entrance. During their first instar, bee fly larvae have leg-like appendages that allow them to crawl down the nest and find their host larvae. They then feed on the host internally.

SOLAR TRACKING (HELIOTROPISM)

Flower stalk rotation occurs in many plant families. This rotation points the flowers (and foliage) toward the sun throughout the day, an adaptation known as heliotropism.

Heliotropism often occurs in plants that flower in early spring when pollinators are scarce. By creating a warm place for pollinators to forage and raise their body temperatures, heliotropism enhances pollinator visitation rates and movement between flowers. The result in an improvement in the chances of cross-pollination. Plants can benefit from heliotropism as well: warmer temperatures increase the number of pollen grains germinating and can stimulate pollen tube growth.

Large Mining Bees
***Andrena* spp.**
Large mining bees are common in early spring and can be mistaken for bumble bees. They have shiny, black abdomens, unlike bumble bees that have hairy abdomens. Mining bees nest in the ground in sand or loose, loam soils.

PALE INDIAN PLANTAIN ~ *Arnoglossum atriplicifolium*

FLOWERING PERIOD

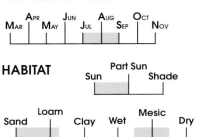

| MAR | APR MAY | JUN JUL | AUG SEP | OCT NOV |

HABITAT

Sun | Part Sun | Shade

Sand | Loam | Clay | Wet | Mesic | Dry

RANGE

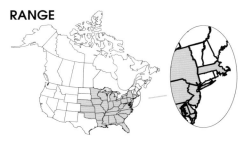

HEIGHT 5 - 10' tall

FLOWER	LEAF
White - Cream	Triangular
5 Bracts	Palmately-Veined
5 Disc Florets	Basal
Tubular	Pale Beneath
Flat-Topped Umbel	Stem: Alternate

FRUIT	ROOT
Achene, White Hairs	Fibrous

PLANT NOTES

Pale Indian plantain is a tall, upright perennial. With basal rosettes forming in the first
year, it typically flowers in the second year.
The single, narrow flower stalk branches into
a large broad umbel at the top. Flower stems
are hollow and utilized by cavity-nesting bees
and wasps.

COMPLEMENTARY PLANTS

Wild Bergamot   Rough Blazingstar
Gray-Headed Coneflower

INSECT NOTES

Pale Indian plantain is primarily visited by
wasps. The white to cream flower color,
shallow corollas and accessible nectar
are flower features preferred by wasps.
The flowers are incompatible and require
cross-pollination by pollinators.

PLANT - INSECT INTERACTIONS

A WASP FAVORITE

Many solitary wasp species visit pale Indian plantain flowers for nectar, a great source of energy for late summer prey-gathering. Nectar is secreted at the base of the style and rises up the corolla allowing access to short-tongued wasps. During hot summer days, wasps have shown a preference for dilute nectar sources. Pale Indian plantain's white flowers, with nectar replenished from the base of the corolla, may help keep nectar cool and more dilute. A significant amount of pollen is transferred onto the head and thorax of wasps when they visit pale Indian plantain flowers because the anthers extend past the corolla.

Four-banded Sand Wasp
Bicyrtes quadrifasciatus
See profile p. 196.

Great Black Wasp
Sphex pensylvanicus
See profile p. 184.

**Great Golden
Digger Wasp**
Sphex ichneumoneus

Thread-waisted Wasps
Ammophila spp.
See profile p. 232.

Potter Wasp
Eumenes fraternus

Grass-Carrying Wasp
Isodontia mexicana
See profile p. 197.

Sweat Bees, *Halictus* spp. *left*
Sweat bees collect pollen and feed on nectar. Their heads get covered with pollen grains from the anthers extending past the corolla as they visit for nectar.

Clematis Clearwing Moth *left*
Alcathoe caudata
These moths visit pale Indian plantain for nectar, especially when their host plant virgin's bower, *Clematis virginiana* grows nearby.

Bumble Bee, *Bombus* sp.
Bumble bees occasionally visit pale Indian plantain. Crawling across the top of the flower head to feed on nectar, their legs, abdomen and head get covered with white pollen.

BUTTERFLY MILKWEED ~ *Asclepias tuberosa*

FLOWERING PERIOD

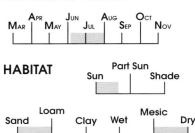

	Apr	Jun	Aug	Oct	
Mar	May	Jul	Sep		Nov

HABITAT

	Part Sun	
Sun		Shade

	Loam			Mesic	
Sand		Clay	Wet		Dry

RANGE

HEIGHT 12 - 36" tall

FLOWER	**LEAF**
Orange - Yellow	Lanceolate
5-Parted with	Narrow
Horn, Hoods Above	Fine Hairs
Petals Below	

FRUIT	**ROOT**
Upright Pod	Taproot
Many Seeds	
Silky Hairs Attached	

PLANT NOTES
Because of its large taproot, butterfly milkweed does not transplant well and requires loose soils (sand to loam). Find a suitable location in full sun and let it grow. Plant in masses to create an unrivaled display of bright orange flowers and a larger visual attractant for monarch butterflies and other pollinators.

COMPLEMENTARY PLANTS
Prairie Phlox   Ohio Spiderwort

INSECT NOTES
Many bee, wasp, butterfly and beetle species visit butterfly milkweed for nectar. Monarch butterfly caterpillars and milkweed leaf beetles feed on the flowers and foliage. Look for pollinia (sacs of pollen) attached to the legs of large visiting insects. *See p. 60 for more information.*

PLANT - INSECT INTERACTIONS

LARVAL HOST PLANT

Monarch Butterfly, *Danaus plexippus*
Queen Butterfly, *Danaus gilippus*
Milkweed Tussock Moth, *Euchaetes egle*

Monarch Butterfly, *Danaus plexippus*

Male and female monarch butterflies visit butterfly milkweed for nectar. Look for females laying eggs on the underside of leaves; monarch butterflies are specialists of milkweeds. Monarch caterpillars consume both the foliage and flowers of milkweed plants undergoing several instars of growth before constructing a chrysalis and pupating.

Sulphur Butterflies, *Colias* spp. *left*

Clouded, *C. philodice,* and orange sulphur butterflies, *C. eurytheme,* are common throughout most of North America and often hybridize. They visit many types of native plants for nectar, especially near open sunny areas in fields, prairies and suburban yards. Look for female clouded sulphur butterflies laying eggs on native legumes such as Canada milkvetch, *Astragalus canadensis* and wild white indigo, *Baptisia lactea* (p. 62), in spring.

Crescent Butterflies, *Phyciodes* spp. *right*

Crescent butterflies are active in late spring and visit a variety of nectar-producing plants.

Great Spangled Fritillary Butterfly, *Speyeria cybele*

The great spangled fritillary has been observed with milkweed pollinia attached to its legs. Look for this butterfly in mid-June through July in prairies and open sunny areas. Butterfly milkweed is one of the first plants in the season that emerging adults visit for nectar.

Females do not typically lay eggs directly on host plants (violets, *Viola* spp.); instead, they lay eggs on grasses and other prairie plants in late summer. The caterpillars hatch two to three weeks later in the fall. They drink water but do not feed.

Caterpillars then seek out a place to overwinter but very few survive hibernation. Many eggs are laid however, so enough survive to maintain a stable population. As temperatures warm in the spring, caterpillars crawl to their host plant to start feeding and ultimately pupate. Caterpillars are ground-dwelling, elusive and feed at night to avoid predation.

Pollinators of Native Plants

BUTTERFLY MILKWEED ~ *Asclepias tuberosa*

POLLEN PACKAGING

Bees, wasps, flies, butterflies and beetles visit butterfly milkweed flowers for nectar. They grasp or prop themselves on one of the five flower hoods, sliding their tongues down the side of the hood to access nectar. Pollen grains are packaged on milkweed flowers into sacs called pollinia. Two sacs are joined together by a filament.

When visiting for nectar, pollinators must be careful not to slip one of their legs into the flower. When pulling their leg out, they risk snagging it on the filament that holds the sticky pollinia sacs together. If snagging occurs, insects carry the pollinia sacs to other milkweed flowers. If their leg slips into the flower again, the sacs can be transferred into the stigmatic slit and cross-pollination occurs.

Large bees such as bumble bees snag and carry the most pollinia sacs. Small bees can become trapped in the flowers and perish because they are unable to pull their leg out. Butterflies and small bees lacking the strength and compatible foraging behavior are rarely seen carrying pollinia sacs.

PLANT - INSECT INTERACTIONS

Leafcutter Bees, *Megachile* spp.
Leafcutter bees are frequent visitors that feed on nectar. They rarely snag their legs on pollinia sacs so are not considered effective pollinators of butterfly milkweed flowers.

These small bees (below) prop themselves on the top of the flower hood and slide their tongue down the side to reach the nectar.

Green Sweat Bee, *Augochlora pura* *left*
Small Carpenter Bees, *Ceratina* spp. *right*

Small Resin Bees, *Heriades* spp. *left*
Sweat Bees, *Lasioglossum* spp. *right*

PLANT - INSECT INTERACTIONS

 HONEY BEES

Milkweed Leaf Beetle
Labidomera clivicollis

The milkweed leaf beetle is one of several beetle species that consume the foliage of milkweed (*Asclepias*) plants. Overwintering adults emerge in the landscape in early spring. Females typically lay their eggs on the underside of milkweed leaves in bright red to orange egg clusters.

 Larvae hatch and undergo several instars during the summer months, feeding on the flowers and foliage as they develop. Adult beetles are active in the fall preparing to overwinter.

Paper Wasp, *Polistes fuscatus* *left*
Butterfly milkweed blooms when paper wasps are constructing and provisioning their nests. They visit for nectar, a source of energy for these early summer activities.

Thread-Waisted Wasps, *Prionyx* spp. *right*
Thread-waisted wasps build nest burrows in the ground. They hunt for their prey, grasshoppers, prior to excavating their nest.

CLEPTOPARASITE PROFILE

Cuckoo Bees, *Coelioxys* spp.
Cuckoo bees lay their eggs in the nests of other bees. When cuckoo bee eggs hatch, the larvae kill the host larvae then develop on the provisions (pollen and nectar) provided by the female host bees.

This particular cuckoo bee is a cleptoparasite of leafcutter bees, *Megachile* spp. *Coelioxys* females have a tapered abdomen ending in a sharp point to break through leafcutter brood cells to lay eggs. Males (above) have a spined abdomen. Cuckoo bees often forage on the same plants as their hosts; butterfly milkweed is frequently visited by leafcutter bees. Look for this cuckoo bee feeding on nectar later in the summer on wild bergamot, prairie coreopsis, joe pye weed and hoary vervain.

Ants, Family Formicidae *left*
Common visitors, ants feed on nectar when milkweed flowers open.
Soldier Beetles
Chauliognathus spp. *right*

WILD WHITE INDIGO ~ *Baptisia lactea* (*B. alba*)

FLOWERING PERIOD

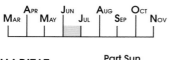

HABITAT

RANGE

HEIGHT 36 - 72" tall

FLOWER	LEAF
5-Parted	Palmately Divided
White	3 - 5 Leaflets
Spike-Like Raceme	2 Large Stipules

FRUIT	ROOT
Erect Cylindrical Pod	Taproot

PLANT NOTES
The narrow racemes of wild white indigo project above prairie forbs and grasses in early spring. This tall, broad plant is statuesque in form, with blue-gray foliage held horizontally on light gray, sturdy stems. Small seedlings take a few years to establish before flowering.

COMPLEMENTARY PLANTS
Smooth Beard Tongue   Butterfly Milkweed
Golden Alexanders   Prairie Phlox
Ohio Spiderwort

INSECT NOTES
Queen and worker bumble bees are the primary pollinators of wild white indigo flowers. Their size and strength allows them to pry open the flowers to access nectar inside. Blister beetles feed on the foliage and weevils feed on the seeds. Butterflies observed visiting the flowers for nectar include cloudless sulphurs and silver spotted skippers.

PLANT - INSECT INTERACTIONS

LARVAL HOST PLANT

Clouded Sulphur Butterfly, *Colias philodice*
Moths: Genista Broom, *Uresiphita reversalis;*
Black-Spotted Prominent, *Dasylophus anguina*

Clouded Sulphur Butterfly *left*
Colias philodice

Female clouded sulphur butterflies lay pale-colored eggs near the center of leaflets on wild white indigo (above left). As eggs age, they turn red after a few days, then gray prior to caterpillars hatching. Other host plants include clovers, *Trifolium* spp. and milk vetches, *Astragalus* spp.

Genista Broom Moth *right*
Uresiphita reversalis

These moth caterpillars hatch in early August and feed on foliage of *Baptisia* sp. during the day. Their long hairs help protect them from predation. Other host plants include *Acacia*, *Genista* and *Sophora* species.

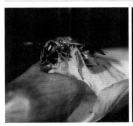

Small Sweat Bees, *Lasioglossum* spp.

Small sweat bees occasionally visit wild white indigo flowers. They access nectar through perforations created at the base of the flower by other nectar thieves. They also crawl into the end of flowers to feed on pollen.

Blister Beetle, *Lytta sayi*

Many species of blister beetles can be destructive feeders of the foliage, flowers and seed pods of *Baptisia* plants. Adults form large aggregations and devour all the plants in a given area. Mating occurs during these feeding aggregations. Females lay eggs in batches in the soil near the entrance of their host's nest (bees) or directly in the nest. Eggs hatch and the first instar larvae crawl into the burrow to seek out the host larvae to parasitize.

The larvae of this blister beetle have been found in the nests of green sweat bees, *Agapostemon* spp.

WILD WHITE INDIGO ~ *Baptisia lactea* (*B. alba*)

FLOWER DEVELOPMENT

The flowers of wild white indigo are protandrous (the anthers dehisce before the stigmas become receptive). Flowers open and mature from the bottom upward on the raceme.

Individual flowers typically last three to four days. During the first two days, the flowers offer pollen to visitors and by the end of the second day the anthers have dehisced. On the third day, the stigma becomes receptive.

The flowers are self-compatible. With so many flowers on a raceme in different phases of development, pollen from one flower is often transferred to receptive stigmas of another flower on the same raceme. Nectar production peaks during the pistillate (female) phase on the third or fourth day offering a large nectar reward to visiting bumble bees. Successfully pollinated ovaries develop into seeds housed in an inflated seed pod that turns from light green to dark gray when the seeds are mature.

PLANT - INSECT INTERACTIONS

Bumble Bees, *Bombus* spp.

Queen and worker bumble bees are the primary pollinators of wild white indigo. Queen bumble bees visit the flowers earlier in the season. Near the end of the flowering period, worker bumble bees collect pollen from the flowers by pressing the keel downward and rubbing their mid and hind legs on the exposed anthers.

Bumble bees fly toward the upright flower raceme to land on one of the lower flowers in the pistillate (female) phase. Pistillate flowers typically produce more nectar than staminate flowers at the top of the raceme. After bumble bees seek out the higher nectar rewards on the pistillate flowers, they work their way up the flower raceme to the staminate flowers. Pollen is therefore transferred onto bees from the staminate flowers during the last stage of their visit. The bumble bees move on to a new flower raceme thus transporting pollen to the next pistillate flower on a new plant's raceme.

PLANT - INSECT INTERACTIONS

Weevil, *Trichapion rostrum (Apion rostrum)*

Small black weevils overwinter as adults and are active in late spring just as pods are starting to develop on *Baptisia* sp. Females drill small holes in the base of the developing pods in June, laying their eggs on the outside then pushing them with their snout into the seed pod. Many eggs are deposited in each pod.

Larvae hatch and consume the developing seeds inside the pod. With an average of thirty-five seeds in each pod and one weevil consuming five or more seeds, it is not uncommon to have all seeds consumed in a pod. The weevils pupate in July. Any remaining seeds ripen and harden, maturing to a dark gray color. The adult weevils either chew an exit hole out of the pod or wait until the pods open, often the following spring.

To save energy, wild white indigo and other *Baptisia* sp. often abort pods during ripening especially those with weevil populations or low numbers of seeds. These pods decay and the developing weevils inside die. A white wild indigo plant typically has one or two flower racemes but has been observed with as many as fourteen. Seed losses from weevil feeding in individual pods of white wild indigo have been documented as high as ninety-six percent (Haddock & Chaplin, 1982).

HAREBELL ~ *Campanula rotundifolia*

FLOWERING PERIOD

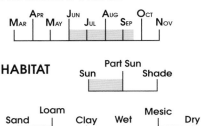

HABITAT

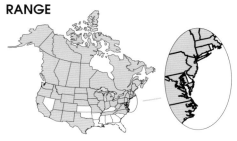

RANGE

HEIGHT 4 - 20" tall

FLOWER
5-Parted
Light Blue - Violet
Nodding, Bell-Shaped

LEAF
Lower: Ovate
Upper: Linear

FRUIT
Narrow Capsule
Opening Near Base
Wind Dispersed

ROOT
Fibrous

PLANT NOTES
Harebell excels in dry, sunny sites and can be found growing in shallow soils in rock crevices, rocky, high alpine terrain and sand prairies. Plant in rock walls, landscape borders and sidewalk edges.

COMPLEMENTARY PLANTS
Prairie Phlox   Hairy Beard Tongue
Cut-Leaved Toothwort   Ohio Spiderwort
Pale Purple Coneflower

INSECT NOTES
Small- to medium-sized bees visit harebell flowers. Small bees climb into the base of the flowers to access nectar; others collect and feed on pollen presented on the style.

PLANT - INSECT INTERACTIONS

Leafcutter Bees, *Megachile* spp. *left*
Feeding on nectar, leafcutter bees are regular visitors of harebell flowers. The pollen-collecting hairs (scopae) on their abdomens contact pollen grains held on the style when visiting the flowers.

Digger Bees, *Anthophora* spp. *right*
Long tongues allow digger bees to reach nectar at the base of the style, minimizing their contact with pollen held on the style.

Green Sweat Bees, *Agapostemon* spp. *left*
Green Sweat Bee, *Augochlora pura* *right*
Green sweat bees climb into the base of harebell flowers for nectar. In these photos, the stigma is receptive to pollen transferred by visiting insects.

Small Carpenter Bees, *Ceratina* spp.
Small carpenter bees feed on pollen stuck to the hairs on the style as well as from the anthers.

Orange Mint Moth
Pyrausta orphisalis
When harebell reblooms in late summer, this moth visits for nectar.

POLLEN PRESENTATION

Filament bases surround the nectar-producing disc at the bottom of the style. Anthers dehisce first and pollen grains accumulate in the cylinder formed by the filaments. As the style elongates, pollen-collecting hairs on the style pick up pollen, exposing it to pollinators.

Small Sweat Bee, *Lasioglossum* sp.

Pollen-collecting hairs on the style are stimulated by visiting insects, more so with pollen feeding and less with nectar feeding. More stimulation of the hairs results in a shorter duration of the male phase. Hairs retract causing the remaining pollen to fall out of the nodding flower. The female phase then begins with the unfurling of the stigma. This pollen presentation technique, accelerated by pollinators, ensures cross-pollination of the flowers.

Mason Bees, *Osmia* spp. *left*
Long-Horned Bees *right*
***Melissodes* spp.**

PRAIRIE COREOPSIS ~ *Coreopsis palmata*

FLOWERING PERIOD

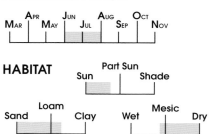

HABITAT

RANGE

HEIGHT 20 - 36" tall

FLOWER
Yellow - Orange
8 - 12 Ray Florets
Many Disc Florets
Short Stalks

LEAF
Dark Green
Linear
Divided: 3 Lobes
Stalkless

FRUIT
Achene
Narrow Wings

ROOT
Rhizome

PLANT NOTES
This native perennial is rhizomatous and spreads forming a loose cluster. The contrast between the dark green linear foliage and bright yellow flowers provides a good visual attractant to pollinators.

COMPLEMENTARY PLANTS
Wild Lupine
Little Bluestem
Side Oats Grama

Butterfly Milkweed
Prairie Phlox

INSECT NOTES
The open flower heads and short disc florets provide access to floral rewards for all bees, especially short-tongued bees. Other regular visitors include butterflies, moths, beetles, wasps, syrphid flies and ants. Ants are also attracted to the developing flower buds which may have extra-floral nectaries along the edges of the petals.

Pollinators of Native Plants

PLANT - INSECT INTERACTIONS

Sulphur Butterflies
Colias spp.

Small Carpenter Bees, *Ceratina* spp.

Long-Horned Bees
Melissodes spp.

Only male long-horned bees (above) have long antennae. As regular visitors of prairie coreopsis, they feed on nectar offered from each tubular, disc floret. Long-horned bees are common pollinators of composite flowers in the Asteraceae family.

Females (below) have long pollen-collecting hairs (scopae) on their hind legs that resemble loaded saddlebags when coated with pollen. Long-horned bees are ground-nesting; females excavate nests on slopes or banks in mid- to late summer. Their larvae are parasitized by cuckoo bees, *Triepeolus* spp.

Leafcutter Bees, *Megachile* spp. *left*
Small Resin Bees, *Heriades* spp. *right*
Leafcutter bees visit prairie coreopsis for nectar and pollen; females collect pollen on their abdominal scopae as they move across the top of the disc florets. *See profile p. 86.*

Cuckoo Bees
Coelioxys spp.
These cuckoo bees visit native plants in the summer months where their hosts (leafcutter bees) occur. Cuckoo bees are cleptoparasites, laying their eggs in nests of other bees. *See profile p. 61.*

PURPLE PRAIRIE CLOVER ~ *Dalea purpurea*

FLOWERING PERIOD

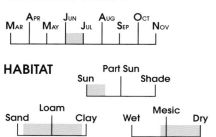

HABITAT

RANGE

HEIGHT 12 - 36" tall

FLOWER	**LEAF**
Pink - Purple	Pinnately Divided
5-Parted	Leaflets: 13 - 20 Pairs
Raceme	Silver - Green

FRUIT	**ROOT**
Seed Pod	Taproot
Does Not Split Open	

PLANT NOTES
Purple prairie clover is tolerant of almost all soil types. Use in masses in boulevards or garden borders and combined with shorter prairie grasses. This fine-textured medium-sized perennial complements larger-leaved plants such as wild petunia.

Note: The plants need to be protected from rabbits until established.

COMPLEMENTARY PLANTS
Butterfly Milkweed   Spotted Bee Balm
Fragrant Hyssop   False Sunflower
Wild Petunia

INSECT NOTES
The numerous, shallow tubular flowers attract bees with all tongue lengths. Flowers develop from the bottom of the raceme upward offering pollen and nectar to visiting insects for close to a month. The flowers are protandrous (anthers dehisce before the stigmas become receptive).

PLANT - INSECT INTERACTIONS

 HONEY BEES

LARVAL HOST PLANT

Southern Dogface Butterfly, *Zerene cesonia*

SPECIALIST BEES

Cellophane Bees, *Colletes albescens,*
C. robertsonii, C. susannae, C. wilmattae

Many types of bees visit the flowers where most female bees collect pollen. The pollen has an oily coating that makes it bright orange in color. As bees collect the pollen, they circle around the flowers on the raceme. Purple prairie clover flowers when many bees, both social and solitary, are provisioning their nests.

Green Sweat Bees, *Agapostemon* spp. *left*
Augochlorella spp. *right*

Bumble Bees, *Bombus* spp. *left*
Leafcutter Bees, *Megachile* spp. *right*

Sweat Bees, *Halictus* spp. *left*
Cuckoo Bees, *Coelioxys* spp. *right*
These cuckoo bees visit only for nectar because they do not provision their own nests; they lay their eggs in leafcutter bee, *Megachile* sp., nests.

Syrphid Flies
***Chrysotoxum* sp.** *above*
***Toxomerus* sp.** *below*
Syrphid flies visit the flowers for nectar and pollen.

Soldier Beetles
***Chauliognathus* spp.**
Banded Long-Horned Beetles,
***Typocerus* spp.**
Beetles feed on nectar. Look for blister beetles, *Epicauta* spp., and cucumber beetles, *Diabrotica* spp., as well.

PALE PURPLE CONEFLOWER ~ *Echinacea pallida*

FLOWERING PERIOD

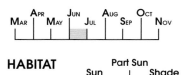

HABITAT

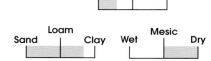

RANGE

HEIGHT 30 - 60" tall

FLOWER
Pale Pink - Pink
Narrow Ray Florets
Rays Grow Upward,
    Fall Outward, then
    Droop Downward
Many Disc Florets
Large Central Cone
Long Hairy Stalks

LEAF
Mostly Basal
Linear - Lanceolate

FRUIT
Achene

ROOT
Taproot

PLANT NOTES
One of the tallest coneflower species. Combine with prairie grasses or medium-height forbs such as little bluestem or butterfly milkweed. The pale pink petals dangle below the large cone and flutter in the wind. Goldfinches feed on the seeds.

COMPLEMENTARY PLANTS
Little Bluestem
Beard Tongues

Thimble Anemone
Ohio Spiderwort

INSECT NOTES
A preferred nectar plant of bees and butterflies. The numerous disc florets on the large central cone offer nectar to visitors with short and long tongues. Bees circle around the cone to feed on nectar and collect pollen.

Pollinators of Native Plants

PLANT - INSECT INTERACTIONS

SPECIALIST BEE

Mining Bee, *Andrena helianthiformis*

Most small- and medium-sized bees visit pale purple coneflower for both pollen and nectar. Rewards are offered for a long time as the florets mature in succession on the central cone.

Long-Horned Bees, *Melissodes* spp.
Male (left), female (right)

Sweat Bees, *Halictus* spp. *left*
Green Sweat Bees, *Agapostemon* spp. *right*

Leafcutter Bees, *Megachile* spp.

Brown-Belted Bumble Bee *Bombus griseocollis*
Female worker bumble bees are major transporters of pollen and effective pollinators. *Male pictured left.*

FLOWER DEVELOPMENT

Anthers develop before the stigmas on the flower head. The central cone is comprised of a single whorl of ray florets around the outside edge; the rest are disc florets. Most or all of the florets are self-incompatible. Ray florets develop first, followed by the inner, neighboring disc florets that continue development toward the center of the cone. In the disc florets, stamens elongate beyond the edge of the corolla; the anthers then dehisce. On the following day the style elongates in the anther tube and, as it pushes upward, hairs on the style pick up pollen grains. The stigma then reflexes and becomes receptive and nectar rewards peak.

Nectar, held in a reservoir formed by fused filament bases, is offered until the fourth day. More nectar is produced by female phase florets located next to the pollen-laden male phase florets on the cone. Bees visiting solely for nectar on the female phase florets are likely to pick up pollen grains from the nearby male phase florets and transfer those grains to the next pale purple coneflower visited. This flower head development sequence controls visitor movements and ultimately aids in the cross-pollination of pale purple coneflowers.

PALE PURPLE CONEFLOWER ~ *Echinacea pallida*

POLLINATOR PROFILE

American Lady Butterfly
Vanessa virginiensis

The American lady butterfly migrates northward in the spring from the southern United States, Mexico and as far south as Central America. Feeding on nectar, adults are common in the North and Northeast from May to July and are regular visitors of pale purple coneflower.

As soon as they arrive in the North, females seek out host plants for their eggs. Eggs are laid near the center of the host plant leaf. Host plants include pussytoes, *Antennaria* spp., and pearly everlasting, *Anaphalis* sp. Caterpillars hatch and form a feeding shelter by webbing a folded leaf together.

An American lady butterfly lays an egg on field pussytoes, *Antennaria neglecta*.

PLANT - INSECT INTERACTIONS

Red Admiral Butterfly
Vanessa atalanta

Butterflies probe the cone disc florets for nectar. Look for red admirals, monarchs, viceroys, skippers, fritillaries and sulphurs.

Great Spangled Fritillary Butterfly
Speyeria cybele

The great spangled fritillary butterfly is a fast-moving butterfly, gliding across prairies and open meadows where its host plants (violets) and nectar plants occur. Adults are abundant from mid-June through July; one generation is produced per year. *See profile p. 59.*

PURPLE CONEFLOWER ~ *Echinacea purpurea* 🐝 HONEY BEES

FLOWERING PERIOD

	Apr	Jun	Aug	Oct	
Mar	May	Jul	Sep	Nov	

HABITAT

Part Sun
Sun | Shade

Loam
Sand | Clay

Mesic
Wet | Dry

RANGE

HEIGHT
30 - 48" tall

INSECT INTERACTIONS

Eastern Tiger Swallowtail Butterfly, *Papilio glaucus*
Like pale purple coneflowers, purple coneflower attracts many types of butterflies including monarchs, red admirals, sulphurs, fritillaries and swallowtails.

Banded Long-Horn Beetle
Typocerus velutinus above
Common on coneflowers, this beetle feeds on pollen and nectar. Eggs are laid on decaying hardwood trees; larvae bore into wood and begin feeding.

Straight Native Species vs Cultivars or Hybrids
Plant breeding and selection can change flower color and shape (double blooms) and the amount of pollen or nectar offered to visiting pollinators, all potential limitations. To provide the most beneficial plants for pollinators, choose straight native species over cultivars or hybrids whenever possible. *See p. 30 for more information.*

Bumble Bees, *Bombus* spp. *left*
Leafcutter Bees, *Megachile* spp. *right*
Short- and long-tongued bees including small carpenter, sweat, long-horned, digger and mining bees visit the flowers for nectar and pollen.

RATTLESNAKE MASTER ~ *Eryngium yuccifolium*

FLOWERING PERIOD

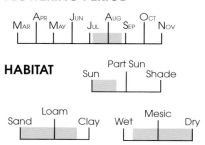

HABITAT

RANGE

HEIGHT 36 - 60" tall

FLOWER	**LEAF**
5-Parted	Mostly Basal
White - Light Pink	Clasping
Round, Congested,	Yucca-Like
Terminal Flower Head	Gray - Green
Branched Clusters	Parallel Veined
Sharp Bracts	Spiny Edges

FRUIT	**ROOT**
Dry	Fibrous
Splits into Two Seeds	

PLANT NOTES

Rattlesnake master has unique round flowers that are held above long, sturdy flower stalks. To feature the yucca-like, spiny, gray foliage, plant rattlesnake master next to shorter grasses such as prairie dropseed.

COMPLEMENTARY PLANTS

Common Ironweed   Meadow Blazingstar
Blue Vervain   Wild Bergamot

INSECT NOTES

The numerous small, white flowers are preferred by wasps that feed on nectar. Butterflies such as monarchs, viceroys, hairstreaks, crescents, sulphurs and fritillaries occasionally visit the flowers for nectar.

PLANT - INSECT INTERACTIONS

HONEY BEES

LARVAL HOST PLANT

Eryngium Stem-Borer Moth,
Papaipema eryngii
Flower Feeding Moth, *Coleotechnites eryngiella*

Red-Shouldered Pine Beetle *left*
Stictoleptura canadensis
Banded Long-Horn Beetles, *Typocerus* spp.
These beetles visit the flowers for nectar.

Wedge-Shaped Beetles *left*
***Macrosiagon* spp.** *See profile p. 99.*
Soldier Beetles, *Chauliognathus* spp. *right*
See profile p. 96.

Soldier Flies
***Odontomyia* spp.**
Soldier fly larvae in this genus are aquatic, breathing through snorkel-like tubes called spiracles attached to the rear of their abdomen. Eggs are laid near the edges of water bodies. Larvae feed on algae.

Yellow-Faced Bees
***Hylaeus* spp.**
Most bee visits are for nectar only, including the visits of yellow-faced bees. Males and females feed on nectar, accessed from the numerous, shallow white flowers.

Bumble Bees, *Bombus* spp.
Common eastern bumble bees, *Bombus impatiens* are a frequent visitor of rattlesnake master. They travel across the flower heads collecting pollen and occasionally slow down to feed on nectar. Their visits are typically hurried and brief.

RATTLESNAKE MASTER ~ *Eryngium yuccifolium*

FLOWER DEVELOPMENT

One stalk on a rattlesnake master plant can have anywhere between ten and forty flower heads. Each flower head is comprised on average of one hundred and six individual, five-petalled white flowers and green sepals. The central flower head develops first, followed by the lateral flower heads.

Flowers open starting at the base and continue development toward the apex. Each flower has two styles that elongate and separate by bending outward during the first week. Stigmas remain unreceptive as filaments start to develop inside the closed petals. Anthers are held inside the flowers until the petals open. When first emerging, the anthers are green, then turn light pink or white before dehiscing. Two to three days later, the two separated stigmas become receptive.

Even though anthers are dehiscing above the newly developing stigmas, receptivity of the stigmas occurs several days after dehiscence; this limits self-pollination and maximizing cross-pollination by the numerous floral visitors.

PLANT - INSECT INTERACTIONS

WASP FAVORITE

The majority of rattlesnake master floral visitors are wasps. The long-lasting numerous white flowers with shallow corollas and abundant nectar are attractive floral traits for wasps. Most social and solitary wasps feed on nectar during the adult stage of their life cycle. Nectar is a source of hydration and sugar (carbohydrates) for both male and female wasps. It also provides females with energy needed for prey foraging, nest construction and provisioning.

Carrot Wasps, *Gasteruption* spp. *left*
Thynnid Wasp, *Myzinum quinquecinctum*

Grass-Carrying Wasps, *Isodontia* spp. *left*
Beewolf, *Philanthus gibbosus* *right*

PLANT - INSECT INTERACTIONS

HONEY
BEES

Paper Wasp, *Polistes fuscatus* *left*
A frequent visitor of rattlesnake master, paper
wasps feed on nectar. *See profile p. 196.*

Great Golden Digger Wasp *right*
Sphex ichneumoneus
This brightly colored wasp hunts true crickets and
katydids to provision nests in the ground.
See profile p. 232.

Beetle Wasps, *Cerceris* spp.
Beetle wasps prey on beetles including weevils, darkling beetles,
bean weevils, leaf-feeding beetles
and flat-headed and metallic wood-
borers. One species, *C. fumipennis,*
is being studied for its use in the biological control of the emerald ash
borer beetle, *Agrilus planipennis*, an
introduced beetle to North America
that kills ash trees, *Fraxinus* spp.

These wasps are solitary, ground-
nesting species that excavate nests
in clay or sand. Nest depths can
range from a few inches to over
three feet. Unlike many other solitary wasps, beetles are cached in
the nest before individual cells have
been constructed.

Mason Wasps, *Ancistrocerus* spp. *left*
Mason wasps nest in above ground, preexisting
cavities. Female mason wasps hunt and provision
nests with caterpillars.

Thread-Waisted Wasps, *Prionyx* spp. *right*

Great Black Wasp, *Sphex pensylvanicus*

Females typically land on top of
their beetle prey, grab the prey's
thorax with their mandibles and insert their stinger in the beetle's leg
where there is a gap in its armor.
The paralyzed prey is then flown
back to the nest. Nests are mass
provisioned with several beetles
and an egg is laid when enough
beetles are cached for one larva to
feed upon.

PRAIRIE SMOKE ~ *Geum triflorum*

FLOWERING PERIOD

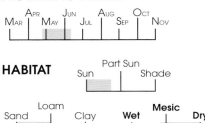

HABITAT

RANGE

HEIGHT 4 - 12" tall

FLOWER	**LEAF**
5-Parted	Basal
Pink Sepals	Pinnately Divided
White Petals	7 - 17 Leaflets
Umbel: 3 Flowers	

FRUIT	**ROOT**
Achene	Fibrous, Rhizome

PLANT NOTES

Prairie smoke is best known by the pink, feathery seed heads that flutter in the wind. This is an excellent native perennial for massing along the front edge of a landscape planting or boulevard, in medium to dry, well-drained soils. The foliage remains green under snow cover.

COMPLEMENTARY PLANTS

Wild Lupine	Wild Petunia
Prairie Phlox	Side Oats Grama
Blue Grama	

INSECT NOTES

Bumble bees buzz pollinate prairie smoke flowers and are the primary pollinators.

PLANT - INSECT INTERACTIONS

Small Sweat Bees, *Lasioglossum* spp.
Small sweat bees feed on pollen grains near the opening of prairie smoke flowers.

Nectar Thievery
Ants search prairie smoke flowers for opportunistic openings created by nectar thieves. These thieves, including wasps, beetles and bees, chew through the side of the flower to access nectar. Ants use this portal to crawl inside the flower to feed on nectar as well.

Bumble Bees, *Bombus* spp.
When female bumble bees shake flowers at the appropriate frequency using buzz pollination, the fine, powdery pollen grains puff out of the anther pores and dust the bumble bee's abdomen. Bumble bees then comb the pollen to pollen baskets, where it is combined with nectar and compressed. Some pollen is inaccessible for grooming and remains on the bumble bee to cross-pollinate the next prairie smoke flower visited.

Bumble Bees, *Bombus* spp.
Some of the first emerging queen bumble bees visit prairie smoke flowers. Holding onto the nodding flowers by the sepals, they insert their heads into the flower grasping the anthers with their forelegs or mouthparts. Using their flight muscles, bumble bees vibrate their thorax to shake pollen from the anthers. This shaking creates an audible buzzing sound.

Buzz pollination is typically used in flowering plants that have a pore or slit at the tip or side of the anther. The pollen is only released from this small opening. Buzz pollination unlocks a substantial amount of pollen in one visit, increasing foraging efficiency for bumble bees. Examples of other native bees that can buzz pollinate flowers include mining, sweat and leafcutter bees.

MAXIMILIAN'S SUNFLOWER ~ *Helianthus maximilanii*

FLOWERING PERIOD

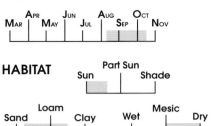

Mar | Apr | May | Jun | Jul | Aug | Sep | Oct | Nov

HABITAT

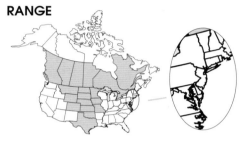

Sun | Part Sun | Shade

Sand | Loam | Clay | Wet | Mesic | Dry

RANGE

HEIGHT 3 - 8' tall

FLOWER	LEAF
Yellow - Orange	Lanceolate
20 - 40 Ray Florets	Stalkless
Narrow Clusters	Folds Upward &
Spreading Bracts,	Curls Downward
White Hairs	Stem: White Hairs

FRUIT	ROOT
Achene	Fibrous
Pair of Awns	Rhizome

PLANT NOTES

Maximilian sunflower flowers late in the fall. Its tall stems and large flowers are complemented by prairie grasses. It has a very tall, narrow upright form combined with leaves that fold inward from the central vein and curve downward resembling water spouts.

COMPLEMENTARY PLANTS

Heath Aster	Big Bluestem
Indian Grass	Showy Goldenrod

INSECT NOTES

Disc florets develop from the outside inward, providing many small tubular florets filled with nectar for pollinators. Nectar is secreted from the base of the style and rises upward in the corolla. Predominantly male bumble bees visit for nectar; other bees (long-horned and sweat) feed on nectar and collect pollen.

PLANT - INSECT INTERACTIONS

 HONEY BEES

LARVAL HOST PLANT

Silvery Checkerspot, *Chlosyne nycteis*
Bordered Patch, *Chlosyne lacinia*

Bumble Bees *upper left*
***Bombus* spp.**
Long-Horned Bees
***Melissodes* spp.** *right*
Sweat Bee *left*
Halictus ligatus
Bees visit the flowers for both nectar and pollen.

Spotted Cucumber Beetle *left*
Diabrotica undecimpunctata
This beetle feeds on the foliage and flowers.
Soldier Beetles, *Chauliognathus* spp. *right*

Syrphid Flies, *Eristalis* spp. *left*
Syrphid Flies, *Allograpta* spp. *right*

Monarch Butterfly
Danaus plexippus
Some of the last monarch butterflies to migrate south in the upper Midwest can be found nectaring on Maximilian sunflower in October.

Garden Webworm Moth
Achyra rantalis
Adults visit a variety of flowers in mid- to late summer for nectar. The larvae of this moth feed at night on the undersides of leaves causing skeletonizing damage. Host plants include alfalfa, beans, peas and strawberries. If caterpillars are a problem, choose native plants that attract their predators or parasitoids such as wasps or tachinid flies.

FALSE SUNFLOWER ~ *Heliopsis helianthoides*

FLOWERING PERIOD

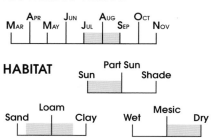

HABITAT

RANGE

HEIGHT 24 - 60" tall

FLOWER	LEAF
Flat Cone, Disc Florets	Ovate, Pointed Tip
8 - 16 Yellow Rays	Opposite
Tubular	Stalked, Toothed
Hairy Bracts	

FRUIT	ROOT
Seed	Fibrous

PLANT NOTES

False sunflower is easy to grow and tolerates partial sun and medium soils. Incorporate native plants that attract beneficial insects (syrphid flies and soldier beetles). These beneficial insects help control aphids that can aggregate on the flower stems.

COMPLEMENTARY PLANTS

Wild Bergamot
Fragrant Hyssop
Purple Prairie Clover
Hoary Vervain

INSECT NOTES

Both nectar and pollen offered by false sunflower attract a variety of visitors including butterflies, bees and flies. With a high frequency of visits, pollen presented daily can be depleted by mid-day. Both the ray and disc florets are fertile and produce seed.

PLANT - INSECT INTERACTIONS

 HONEY BEES

LARVAL HOST PLANT
Rigid Sunflower Borer, *Papaipema rigida*

Crescent Butterflies, *Phyciodes* spp. *above*
Common in sunny habitats where nectar and host plants (asters) occur, pearl, *P. tharos,* and northern crescent, *P. cocyta,* butterflies are very similar in appearance and have overlapping ranges.

Common Ringlet Butterfly *right*
Coenonympha tullia
Adults are active from May to July nectaring on plants in moist prairies or along wetland edges. Larvae feed on grasses and overwinter in sedge mats in wetlands.

Ground Beetles, *Calleida* spp. *left*
Soldier Beetles, *Chauliognathus* spp. *right*
Both of these beetles feed on nectar; soldier beetles are very common visitors of false sunflower.

Sinuous Bee Fly
Hemipenthes sinuosa
Feeding on pollen and nectar, bee flies are common visitors to false sunflower and other open flower heads. This fly is a hyperparasitoid, parasitizing other insect parasites inside host caterpillars. Many of their hosts are parasitic wasp larvae.

The common name *sinuous* refers to the wavy black pattern on the edge of the wings. Look for this sinuous bee fly in open, sunny areas with well-drained, sandy soils flying low to the ground and resting on vegetation or rocks.

Syrphid Flies, *Eristalis* spp.

Pollinators of Native Plants

FALSE SUNFLOWER ~ *Heliopsis helianthoides*

POLLINATOR PROFILE

Leafcutter Bees
Megachile spp.
Male leafcutter bees (above) are regular visitors to false sunflower for nectar. Females (below) also feed on nectar and collect pollen by brushing it onto their abdominal scopae.

Females have large, sharp mandibles used to cut circular or oval leaf pieces from plant leaves or petals; selected leaf pieces are often smooth on one side. Several leaf pieces are rolled into an overlapping cylinder to line brood cells. Leaf pieces are also used to divide brood cells within the cavity.

PLANT - INSECT INTERACTIONS

Medium-sized bees (above) visit flowers to feed on nectar. Some large bumble bee species have been observed collecting pollen on the flowers.
Long-Horned Bees, *Melissodes* spp. *left*
Bumble Bees, *Bombus* spp. *right*

Green Sweat Bees, Augochlorini Tribe *left*
Small Carpenter Bees, *Ceratina* spp. *right*
Small bee species (above) collect pollen. Pollen is presented to pollinators on hairs attached to the style when the style elongates.

Cuckoo Bees
Coelioxys spp.
These cuckoo bees visit the flowers of false sunflower for nectar. They are common where their host, leafcutter bees, *Megachile* spp., occurs.

Pollinators of Native Plants

PLANT - INSECT INTERACTIONS

Clearwing Moths, *Synanthedon* spp. *left*
Clearwing moths are common, day-flying flower visitors in late summer. They nectar on a variety of flower types. Some have wasp-like coloration and are very good wasp mimics. Caterpillars feed on the roots and stems of woody and herbaceous plants including maples, birch, dogwood, Virginia creeper and *Clematis*.

Camouflaged Loopers, *Synchlora* spp. *right*
As they feed on plants, camouflaged looper caterpillars acquire pieces of plant material, including leaves and petals to help them avoid detection by predators. *See profile p. 114.*

**Braconid Wasps
Subfamily Agathidinae**
Braconid wasps crawl over the top of flower heads of false sunflower to find moth caterpillars that develop inside (*see photos bottom left*).

The female carefully maneuvers her long ovipositor through the disc florets to pierce into the caterpillars below, parasitizing them. The braconid wasp eggs hatch and the wasp larvae begin feeding on the caterpillar. One caterpillar can have several braconid wasp larvae developing inside it. The larvae continue to feed on their host until pupation when the host then dies.

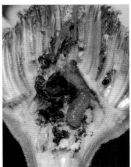 

Moth Caterpillar Flower Head Borers *above*
There are several moth caterpillars that bore into the flower heads and stems of false sunflower. A portion or all of the disc florets on a flower head turn brown from feeding and damage caused by these caterpillars, significantly reducing the number of viable seeds.

PRAIRIE ALUMROOT ~ *Heuchera richardsonii*

FLOWERING PERIOD

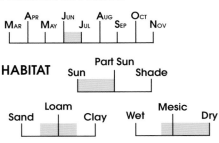

HABITAT

RANGE

HEIGHT 12 - 36" tall

FLOWER	**LEAF**
Green - Cream	Basal Rosette
5-Parted	Long Stalked
Panicle	Palmately-Lobed
Hairs on Stem	7 - 9 Lobes

FRUIT	**ROOT**
Capsule	Stout
Winged Seeds	Coarse

PLANT NOTES

Prairie alumroot is one of a few *Heuchera* species native to North America. The flowers and foliage are not as boldly colored as some of the horticultural introductions but it still excels when used massed in borders, boulevards of formal landscapes or used informally in prairie plantings.

COMPLEMENTARY PLANTS

Harebell	Prairie Phlox
Wild Lupine	Ohio Spiderwort

INSECT NOTES

Both nectar and pollen are offered by prairie alumroot flowers. It is primarily visited by small bee species, especially green sweat bees. The bright orange anthers extend past the corolla where these small bees collect and feed on pollen. Nectar is located at the top of the nodding flower.

PLANT - INSECT INTERACTIONS

FLOWER DEVELOPMENT

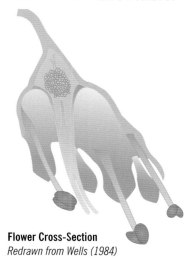

Flower Cross-Section
Redrawn from Wells (1984)

Although the flower is lime-green in color and not very noticeable, it contrasts well with the bright orange anthers - the best visual attractant for bees. An oily film on the pollen grains creates the bright orange coloration but pollen grains lose the ability to germinate as the orange fades, approximately two days after anther dehiscence.

During flower development, the styles emerge first tilting outward in the corolla away from the flower stalk. The stigma remains unreceptive until after the third (last) anther has dehisced. Anthers mature one at a time extending just past the edge of the corolla. The stigmas are receptive for about three days and the styles turn red once the stigmas are no longer receptive. Flowers hang downward on the flower stem helping to protect the floral rewards from rain.

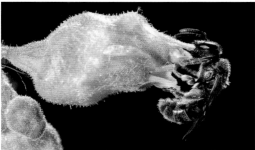

Small Sweat Bees, *Lasioglossum* spp.
Sweat bees are frequent visitors feeding on nectar and collecting pollen. They crawl inside the corolla to feed on pollen from anthers that have not extended past the corolla.

Green Sweat Bees
***Augochlorella* spp.**
Green sweat bees are the most common bee to visit prairie alumroot flowers. They hang underneath the flowers grasping onto the edges of the petals or filaments then chew the anthers with their mandibles to release pollen for collection.

MEADOW BLAZINGSTAR ~ *Liatris ligulistylis*

FLOWERING PERIOD

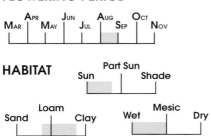

HABITAT

RANGE

HEIGHT 36 - 60" tall

FLOWER	LEAF
Pink - Purple	Alternate
30 - 70 Disc Florets	Linear
3 - 10 Flower Heads	Lower: Stalked
Spike-Like Cluster	

FRUIT	ROOT
Dry Seed, Fluffy Pappus	Corm, Fibrous

PLANT NOTES

Meadow blazingstar is a highly sought-after nectar plant of monarch butterflies in late summer. This plant performs poorly in dry, sandy soils, especially soils prone to periods of drought. For best results, plant in rich, moist soils in full sun. Combine with medium-height prairie grasses. Rough blazingstar, *Liatris aspera* is a very similar-looking blazingstar tolerant of dry sites.

COMPLEMENTARY PLANTS

Blue Lobelia   Common Boneset

INSECT NOTES

Anthers release pollen in a closed cylinder surrounding the style. As the style elongates, tiny hairs on the style collect pollen in the cylinder presenting it to pollinators. The disc florets open from the outside inward on the flower heads. Nectar, preferred by butterflies, is secreted at the base of the style.

PLANT - INSECT INTERACTIONS

 HONEY BEES

Common Wood Nymph Butterfly *left*
Cercyonis pegala
Adult common wood nymph butterflies nectar on flowers in July and August in open prairies and woodland edges. The eastern form has a large yellow patch surrounding the two eye spots on the outer forewing. Larvae feed on grasses.

Great Spangled Fritillary Butterfly *right*
Speyeria cybele See profile p. 59.

Peck's Skipper, *Polites peckius* *left*
Painted Lady Butterfly, *Vanessa cardui*

Bumble Bees *upper left*
Bombus **spp.**
Green Sweat Bees
Agapostemon **spp.**
upper right
Leafcutter Bees *left*
Megachile **spp.**

MONARCH MAGNET

Monarch Butterfly
Danaus plexippus
Meadow blazingstar is a nectar favorite of the monarch butterfly. A small patch of five plants can attract 20 - 30 monarchs at one time. The numerous flowers on each flower head produce an ongoing supply of nectar as they develop on the spike. Meadow blazingstar is short-lived if planted in soils that are too dry. Use rough blazingstar, *Liatris aspera,* instead.

Syrphid Flies, *Helophilus* **spp.**
Bee Flies, *Villa* **spp.** *right*
Both of these flies, regular visitors of meadow blazingstar, feed on nectar and pollen.

WILD LUPINE ~ *Lupinus perennis*

FLOWERING PERIOD

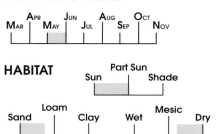

HABITAT

RANGE

HEIGHT 12 - 24" tall

FLOWER	**LEAF**
Blue - Purple	Palmately Divided
5-Parted	7 - 11 Leaflets
Carinate, Raceme	

FRUIT	**ROOT**
Hairy Pod	Taproot

PLANT NOTES

An excellent plant for sandy soils and along landscape edges. To grow from seed, cold stratify for at least ten days and scarify (scratch) the seed coat before planting. Wild lupine is an important larval host plant for several species of butterflies including the endangered karner blue butterfly. This plant is a good alternative to the garden lupine, *Lupinus polyphyllus* that is prevalent in landscapes outside its native range.

COMPLEMENTARY PLANTS

Prairie Smoke	Prairie Phlox
Butterfly Milkweed	Wild Petunia

INSECT NOTES

Wild lupine flowers lack nectar. Many insect visitors look for nectar in vain including butterflies, moths and syrphid flies. The color of the banner petal changes on the flowers signalling to pollinators a depletion in pollen resources.

PLANT - INSECT INTERACTIONS

LARVAL HOST PLANT

Karner Blue Butterfly, *Lycaeides melissa*
Wild Indigo Duskywing, *Erynnis baptisiae*
Persius Duskywing, *Erynnis persius*
Frosted Elfin, *Callophrys irus (Incisalia)*
Orange Sulphur, *Colias eurytheme*
Clouded Sulphur, *Colias philodice*
Painted Lady, *Vanessa cardui*
Clover Looper Moth, *Caenurgina crassiuscula*

Bumble Bees, *Bombus* spp.

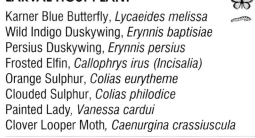

Bumble bees' large size and strength allow them to easily open wild lupine flowers. As the keel (bottom petal) and wings are pressed down, pollen is ejected through the slit at the tip of the keel petals. Activated flowers remain open with the keel depressed and the anthers and stigma exposed. *See Canada tick trefoil, p. 192 for a description of how this type of flower ejects pollen.*

Mining Bees
Andrena spp.

Small Carpenter Bees
Ceratina spp.

Syrphid Flies
Toxomerus spp.
Syrphid flies access pollen on flowers activated by other pollinators.

Mason Bees, *Osmia* spp.

Mason bees are a medium-sized bee, blue, green or metallic in color and hairy. Common in early spring, they are frequent visitors of wild lupine. Mason bees nest in cavities in wood, hollow stems and supplementary bee nests. They are used as an alternative managed pollinator to honey bees of spring-flowering fruit and nut crops such as almonds.

Mason bees use their hind legs to start depressing the keel, then their middle legs and finally their forelegs to keep it depressed. Pollen is ejected onto the underside of their abdomen where their pollen-collecting hairs are located.

WILD BERGAMOT ~ *Monarda fistulosa*

FLOWERING PERIOD

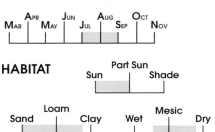

HABITAT

RANGE

HEIGHT 24 - 60" tall

FLOWER	LEAF
Pale Pink - Purple	Opposite
5-Parted	Lanceolate
Tubular	Toothed
Circular Cluster	Aromatic
Upper Lip: White Hairs	Square Stem
Lower Lip: Fine Hairs	

FRUIT	ROOT
Brown Seed	Rhizome

PLANT NOTES

Wild bergamot is a great candidate for mesic, loamy soils and is moderately drought tolerant. Because the foliage can be susceptible to powdery mildew, plant where there is sufficient air circulation and full sun to eliminate moisture on the leaves.

COMPLEMENTARY PLANTS

Black-Eyed Susan   Fragrant Hyssop
Hoary Vervain   Wild Petunia
Butterfly Milkweed

INSECT NOTES

Wild bergamot is one of the best forage plants for bumble bees. Its flowers open continuously throughout the day, providing ongoing nectar rewards as older flowers are depleted and replaced by newly opened flowers.

PLANT - INSECT INTERACTIONS

LARVAL HOST PLANT

Hermit Sphinx Moth, *Lintneria eremitus*
Snout Moths, *Pyrausta generosa, P. signatalis*

SPECIALIST BEE

Black Sweat Bee, *Dufourea monardae*

NECTAR THIEVERY

Mason Wasp, *Parazumia symmorpha*

Short-tongued bees and most wasps cannot legitimately reach the nectar of wild bergamot. For access, a hole (perforation) is chewed at the base of the tubular flowers near the nectary. Nectar is then easily extracted through the hole. Small- to medium-sized bees such as leafcutter, sweat and mining bees feed on nectar through these holes.

Great Black Wasp, *Sphex pensylvanicus*

Great black wasps feed on nectar. They are predators of crickets and katydids. They cache their prey in ground nests for the larvae to feed upon.
See profile p. 184.

PARASITOID PROFILE

Bee Flies, *Bombylius* spp.

With their long, modified mouthparts, bee flies can access nectar in wild bergamot flowers. Similar to syrphid flies, they can hover, darting back and forth. Their hairy bodies keep them warm in early spring and inadvertently pick up pollen grains. Look for bee flies in March, investigating the first bloodroot flowers for nectar, as well as in the summer months nectaring on a variety of plants.

Female bee flies follow their hosts (bees and wasps) back to the hosts' ground nests and lay their eggs at the nest entrance. Bee flies have a modified abdomen used to scoop sand into their abdominal chamber; eggs are coated with sand to provide protection from the elements. Bee flies also lay their eggs on grasshopper eggs, beetles, flies and butterfly and moth caterpillars. Larvae can be both internal and external parasites, feeding on hosts and eventually killing them.

WILD BERGAMOT ~ *Monarda fistulosa*

PREDATOR PROFILE

Soldier Beetles
Chauliognathus spp.

Soldier beetles visit wild bergamot flowers for nectar that is accessed through perforations made by wasps (*see p. 95*). They are common flower visitors in mid- to late summer. Their narrow head, thorax and maxillary palps allow them to feed on and exploit flower nectar and pollen. Considered a **beneficial insect**, soldier beetle larvae feed on aphids, fly larvae, small caterpillars, beetle larvae and grasshopper eggs. Some adults in this family also feed on aphids. One defense mechanism of soldier beetles is to secrete a chemical compound that makes them unpalatable to predators.

Banded Long-Horned Beetle
Typocerus velutinus

The elytra of this beetle is reddish brown with four yellow bands. Larvae are wood-boring, feeding on decaying trees.

PLANT - INSECT INTERACTIONS

Butterflies & Moths

The nectar of wild bergamot flowers is accessed by butterflies and moths with their long proboscis.

Eastern Tiger Swallowtail Butterfly
Papilio glaucus

Silver Spotted Skipper Butterfly
Epargyreus clarus

Monarch Butterfly
Danaus plexippus

Great Spangled Fritillary Butterfly
Speyeria cybele

Moths
Anagrapha spp.

Snout Moths
Pyrausta spp.

Hummingbird Clearwing Moths
Hemaris spp.
Very common daily visitors of wild bergamot.

PLANT - INSECT INTERACTIONS

HONEY BEES

Bumble Bees, *Bombus* spp.

Bumble bees prefer wild bergamot for nectar over many other native plants flowering at the same time. Pollen is deposited on their wings when they brush the flower's anthers.

| *B. auricomus* | *B. ternarius* | *B. perplexus* | *B. bimaculatus* |

FORAGING BEHAVIOR

When large bees visit wild bergamot flowers for nectar, they stay below the anthers and stigma avoiding contact with both. If the bees intend to collect pollen, they hover in front of the anthers and brush them with their mid and hind legs.

Medium-sized bees (*Anthophora, Megachile* and *Melissodes* spp.) have been observed discriminating between staminate and pistillate flowers, avoiding maturing pistillate flowers. Small bees (*Lasioglossum* and *Agapostemon* spp.) forage only for pollen and rarely visit pistillate phase flowers; their tongues are not long enough to reach nectar. Medium and small bees occasionally feed on nectar through perforations made by wasps. *See p. 95.*

Long-Horned Bees **Cuckoo Bees** **Green Sweat Bees** **Wool Carder Bees**
Melissodes spp. *Coelioxys* spp. *Agapostemon* spp. *Anthidium* spp.

Small Resin Bees **Leafcutter Bees** **Sweat Bees** **Sweat Bees**
Heriades spp. *Megachile* spp. *Lasioglossum* spp. *Lasioglossum* spp.

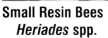

SPOTTED BEE BALM ~ *Monarda punctata*

FLOWERING PERIOD

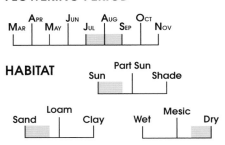

HABITAT

RANGE

HEIGHT 12 - 30" tall

FLOWER	LEAF
5-Parted	Lanceolate
Yellow, Maroon Spots	Pointed Tips
5 - 10 Pinkish Bracts	Hairy Underneath
Whorls	

FRUIT	ROOT
Oval Nutlets	Fibrous

PLANT NOTES
Spotted bee balm is a short-lived perennial that reseeds in sandy, well-drained soils. The whorled tiers of flowers and long petal-like bracts contrast well with other flower forms. Mass for best effect along landscape borders or in boulevards. This is a great plant for a moon garden because the light-colored bracts glow after sunset.

COMPLEMENTARY PLANTS
Prairie Phlox	Side Oats Grama
Wild Lupine	Stiff Goldenrod

INSECT NOTES
The primary visitors of this native perennial are wasps, especially great black, great golden digger and paper wasps. When nectaring on male phase flowers, large bees and wasps have pollen deposited onto their upper thorax.

PLANT - INSECT INTERACTIONS

LARVAL HOST PLANT

Gray Marvel Moth, *Anterastria teratophora*
Snout Moth, *Pyrausta generosa, P. signatalis*

SPECIALIST BEE

Black Sweat Bee, *Dufourea monardae*

These large wasps feed on nectar. Pollen is deposited onto their upper thorax from anthers held in the upper lip.

Great Black Wasp, *Sphex pensylvanicus* *left*
Great Golden Digger Wasp *right*
Sphex ichneumoneus

Sweat Bees
Lasioglossum spp.

Sweat bees cling to the flower's upper lip where the anthers extend, collecting and feeding on pollen. They do not visit for nectar.

Long-Horned Bees, *Melissodes* spp. *left*
Common visitors, these bees make rapid visits to the flowers for nectar.
Bumble Bees, *Bombus* spp. *right*
Small, appropriately-sized bumble bees visit the flowers for nectar.

Wedge-Shaped Beetle
Macrosiagon limbatum

A distinctive orange and black, triangular-shaped small beetle, both male and female wedge-shaped beetles are common on spotted bee balm. Female beetles lay eggs on the foliage. When an egg hatches, the tiny first instar larva attaches itself to a wasp or bee visiting flowers.

The host transports the larva back to its nest where the beetle larva then burrows into the host larva and feeds as an internal parasite. The developing beetle larva continues to consume its host from the inside and eventually emerges from the host. It then proceeds to feed on the host from the outside until the host dies. Look for wedge-shaped beetles on plants with white flowers primarily visited by wasps such as rattlesnake master, *Eryngium yuccifolium* (p. 76), or mountain mint, *Pycnanthemum* spp., (p. 212).

Soldier Beetles
Chauliognathus spp.

Soldier beetles feed on nectar.

WILD QUININE ~ *Parthenium integrifolium*

FLOWERING PERIOD

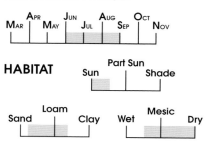

HABITAT

RANGE

HEIGHT 18 - 40" tall

FLOWER
White
5 Ray Florets
Numerous Disc Florets
Flat-Topped Cluster

LEAF
Basal, Toothed
Stem: Alternate,
 Clasping

FRUIT
Achene

ROOT
Taproot
Rhizome

PLANT NOTES
Wild quinine flowers have a fuzzy, soft appearance. They are bright white and remain so for several months. The flowers eventually fade and turn brown when the achenes begin to develop. This native perennial works well in any formal or informal landscape with its upright stature, large blue-gray leaves, long-lasting flower heads and drought tolerance.

COMPLEMENTARY PLANTS
Ohio Spiderwort
Smooth Beard Tongue
Prairie Phlox
Prairie Coreopsis

INSECT NOTES
Bees, wasps, butterflies, moths, ants and flies feed on nectar from the inconspicuous ray florets around the outside of the flower heads. Anthers develop from the outside inward covering the flower head with white pollen that is transferred onto visiting insects. Sweat bees are the most common bee to collect pollen; beetles also feed on pollen.

PLANT - INSECT INTERACTIONS

Bees

Many types of bees visit for nectar or to collect pollen. Not pictured below but also frequent are leafcutter, *Megachile* spp., small resin bees, *Heriades* spp., and sweat bees, *Lasioglossum* spp.

Sweat Bees, *Halictus* spp. *left*
Green Sweat Bees, *Agapostemon* spp. *right*

Mining Bees, *Andrena* spp. *left*
Cuckoo Bees, *Sphecodes* spp. *right*

Small Carpenter Bees, *Ceratina* spp. *left*
Yellow-Faced Bees, *Hylaeus* spp. *right*

Potter Wasps, *Eumenes* spp.

Mason Wasps,
***Parancistrocerus* spp.**

Thread-Waisted Wasps,
***Ammophila* spp.**

Paper Wasps, *Polistes* spp.

WILD QUININE ~ *Parthenium integrifolium*

POLLINATOR PROFILE

Soldier Flies
***Stratiomys* spp.** *above*
***Odontomyia* spp.** *below*
These flies are convincing mimics of bees or wasps. In the *Stratiomys* genus, soldier flies often have yellow coloring on their abdomens. Their common name is derived from their appearance, with some having markings resembling a military jacket. They are common flower visitors in late spring feeding on pollen and nectar.

The larvae of these flies are aquatic, eating algae and tiny aquatic organisms. They breathe through a snorkel-like tube on their last abdominal segment that is surrounded by fine, water-repellent hairs. Larvae pupate enclosed in a rough skin made of calcium carbonate.

PLANT - INSECT INTERACTIONS

Syrphid Flies, Family Syprhidae
Many types of syrphid flies visit the flowers of wild quinine including *Eristalis*, *Toxomerus* and *Syritta* spp. They feed on both pollen and nectar.

Frit Flies, *Malloewia* spp. *left*
Tachinid Flies, Family Tachinidae *right*

Ants, Family Formicidae *left*
Ants are regular visitors of the flowers for nectar.
Crab Spiders, Family Thomisidae *right*
A perfect camouflage to catch unsuspecting prey.

PLANT - INSECT INTERACTIONS

Common Wood Nymph Butterfly *left*
Cercyonis pegala
Great Spangled Fritillary Butterfly *right*
Speyeria cybele See profile p. 59.

Mint Moth, *Pyrausta generosa* *left*
Ebony Bug, *Corimelaena* spp. *right*
These tiny bugs look like beetles because their thorax extends over their abdomen resembling a beetle's elytra. Common on flowers from May through July, they feed on nectar of wild quinine.

Wedge-Shaped Beetles *left*
Macrosiagon spp. See profile p. 99.
Banded Long-Horned Beetle *right*
Typocerus velutinus More information p. 96.

Grapeleaf Skeletonizer Moth
Harrisina americana
This moth visits wild quinine for nectar in late spring. Adults are all black with an orange or red collar. Their range covers the eastern United States from central Minnesota southward to Texas and east. Caterpillars feed on grape leaves, *Vitis* spp. as well as Virginia creeper and woodbine, *Parthenocissus* spp.

The long hairs, and bright yellow and black warning coloration help protect the caterpillars from predators. If the caterpillars are handled, these hairs can cause a skin rash. Pupae overwinter in a spun cocoon in leaves on the ground near host plants.

SMOOTH BEARD TONGUE ~ *Penstemon digitalis*

FLOWERING PERIOD

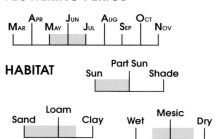

HABITAT

RANGE

HEIGHT 24 - 36" tall

FLOWER	LEAF
White, Purple Lines	Lanceolate
5-Parted, Tubular	Stem: Stalkless
Lower Lip: 3 Lobes	Basal: Stalked
Upper Lip: 2 Lobes	Opposite
Panicle	

FRUIT	ROOT
Oval Capsule	Fibrous

PLANT NOTES
Smooth beard tongue is an upright, bold perennial providing color and interest in the landscape in early spring. Seedlings germinate around the parent plant and are shallow-rooted rosettes that transplant easily.

COMPLEMENTARY PLANTS
June Grass	Harebell
Butterfly Milkweed	Prairie Phlox

INSECT NOTES
Smooth beard tongue flowers have a large, hairy staminode (sterile stamen) on the lower half of the tubular flower. This staminode restricts access to the flower and helps in pollen deposition. Small- and medium-sized bees are the most frequent visitors of smooth beard tongue.

PLANT - INSECT INTERACTIONS

HONEY
BEES

SPECIALIST
BEE

Mason Bee
Osmia distincta

SPECIALIST WASP
Pollen-Collecting Wasp
*Pseudomasaris
occidentalis*

POLLINATOR PROFILE

Small Carpenter Bees, *Ceratina* spp.

Small carpenter bees typically visit tall beard tongue flowers to feed on pollen. As they feed on pollen, they often inadvertently contact the stigma. The hairs on the staminode force them closer to the stigma, resulting in more contact, pollen deposition and pollination.

Digger Bees, *Anthophora* spp.

Digger bees are regular visitors of tall beard tongue flowers. They are ground-nesting and line their brood cells with oil secreted by plants. They resemble long-horned bees with their robust shape and long pollen-collecting scopae on the lower hind legs.

European Wool Carder Bee
Anthidium manicatum

This introduced bee is a common visitor of smooth beard tongue. Females forage for nectar while males patrol the territory and look for an opportunity to mate with the females. Males attack other bees entering their territory with sharp spines on the rear of their abdomens.

Their medium-sized bodies and long tongues enable them to enter the tubular flower to reach nectar. As they enter the flower, anthers held at the top of the corolla deposit pollen onto their head, thorax and abdomen. They are fast-moving and their flower visits are very rapid compared to small carpenter bees and bumble bees.

SMOOTH BEARD TONGUE ~ *Penstemon digitalis*

FLOWER DEVELOPMENT

While smooth beard tongue flowers are self-compatible, its flowers are protandrous to help minimize self-pollination. When the flowers first open, the anthers dehisce and the style is held horizontally. The flowers have four fertile stamens and one sterile stamen (**staminode**). The staminode is covered with bristles on the upper surface, pointing toward the center of the tubular flower.

The day after anther dehiscence, the style elongates, curves downward, then the stigma becomes receptive. It remains receptive to pollen for two more days. Flowers last for about three days, longer in cooler temperatures and shorter in warmer temperatures.

Flower heads are arranged in panicles with each individual tubular flower held perpendicular to the flower stalk. Light pink or purple lines in the flower corolla act as nectar guides for visiting bees. Under ultraviolet light, the only part of the flower that is not highly UV reflective are the nectar guides.

PLANT - INSECT INTERACTIONS

Sweat Bees
Lasioglossum spp. *left, right*

Sweat bees visit the flowers to feed on pollen. They hang underneath the anthers grasping the filaments or style. As they feed, pollen is deposited onto the underside of their abdomen. The bristles on the staminode keep them close to the receptive stigma increasing the probability of pollen transfer on the next smooth beard tongue flower visited.

Leafcutter Bees, *Megachile* spp. *male right*

Another effective pollinator, medium-sized leafcutter bees visit flowers for nectar. The curved filaments hold the anthers near the top of the corolla tube. As bees enter and exit the flower, pollen is deposited onto their thorax and head. If they visit a flower in the female phase, the stigma, curved downward, receives pollen from their thorax.

PLANT - INSECT INTERACTIONS

HONEY
BEES

Bumble Bees, *Bombus* spp.

As bumble bees approach the flower heads, they land and forage first on the lowest open flower, similar to the foraging behavior of bumble bees on wild white indigo (*see p. 64*). Moving upward on the flower panicle, they visit female-phase flowers then male-phase flowers. Pollen is deposited onto bumble bees when the last (male-phase) flowers are visited. Bumble bees transport pollen to the next plant.

Worker bumble bees visit flowers for nectar and if appropriately sized, squeeze their abdomens into the flowers in order to reach nectar rewards. Grasping onto the outer petals when landing, they pull their head and thorax up into the flower. Their forelegs fold down along their abdomen when they are partially inside the flower. Finally, their hind legs push them farther until they can reach the nectaries with their tongues. As they exit, their head and upper thorax rub against the anthers on the top of the flower resulting in pollen deposition on the upper thorax and abdomen. Queen bumble bees, with long tongues, do not insert their thorax into the corolla.

Syrphid Flies, *Toxomerus* spp. *left, middle* *Tropidia* spp. *right*

Syrphid flies visit flowers to feed on pollen which has often fallen to the bottom of the flower corolla. They typically do not attempt to enter the corolla tube; instead, they forage near the entrance on staminate flowers. For this reason, they are not considered effective pollinators. Little pollen is transferred onto their thorax or abdomen and they do not get as close to receptive stigmas as small pollen-foraging bees.

Pollinators of Native Plants

PRAIRIE (Downy) PHLOX ~ *Phlox pilosa*

FLOWERING PERIOD

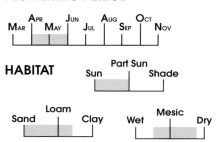

HABITAT

RANGE

HEIGHT 6 - 24" tall

FLOWER
5-Parted, Tubular
White - Light Purple
Cyme

LEAF
Linear
Pointed
Mostly Opposite

FRUIT
Brown Seed Capsule

ROOT
Fibrous

PLANT NOTES
Prairie phlox performs best in well-drained soils in full sun. Use massed on the edges of small prairie plantings or in a boulevard planting. The short, upright stature and thin leaves contrast well with larger-leaved prairie perennials such as prairie alumroot. The flowers are fragrant and long-lasting.

COMPLEMENTARY PLANTS
Prairie Alumroot   Harebell
Thimbleweed   Beard Tongue

INSECT NOTES
Nectaries are located at the base of the long, narrow corolla tube, allowing only long-tongued bees, butterflies and moths to access nectar. Anthers near the top of the corolla are sought out by small bees that feed on or collect pollen. Anthers dehisce first; the style elongates and the stigma becomes receptive afterward. Prairie phlox is self-incompatible.

PLANT - INSECT INTERACTIONS

LARVAL HOST PLANT

Phlox Moth, *Schinia indiana*

Clearwing Moth, *Hemaris thysbe* *left*
Hummingbird clearwing moths feed on nectar. Look for these day-flying moths nectaring on wild bergamot in July. They often have a daily routine (trapline) visiting flowers in a sequential order.

Peck's Skipper, *Polites peckius* *right*
Peck's skippers visit prairie phlox for nectar. Adults are common in June and August.

Green Sweat Bees, *Augochlorella* spp. *left*
Small Carpenter Bees, *Ceratina* spp. *right*

Yellow-Faced Bees, *Hylaeus* spp. *left*
Leafcutter Bees, *Megachile* spp. *right*
The four bee species above do not have tongues long enough to reach nectar in the flower corolla. They are regular visitors, however, inserting their heads into the corolla opening to pull out anthers located nearby. They feed on pollen by perching on the flat surface of the flower.

POLLEN TRANSFER

Butterflies are the primary pollinator of prairie phlox; they are attracted to the floral fragrance and nectar guides (dark pink marks around the corolla opening). Nectar is accessed from a disc at the base of the stigma. As they insert their proboscis into the flowers, it contacts the anthers.

Pollen attaches to the proboscis as the butterfly nectars. Moving on to the next prairie phlox plant, the proboscis coils back into its resting position. Although most of the pollen falls off the coiled proboscis, a small amount of pollen remains to be transferred to a receptive stigma on another prairie phlox flower probed for nectar.

Syrphid Flies, *Pipiza* spp. *left*
***Toxomerus* spp.** *right*

Bumble Bees, *Bombus* spp.

Larger bumble bees access nectar with their long tongues; smaller bumble bees investigate the flowers.

Pollinators of Native Plants

PRAIRIE (Tall) CINQUEFOIL ~ *Potentilla arguta*

FLOWERING PERIOD

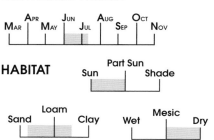

HABITAT

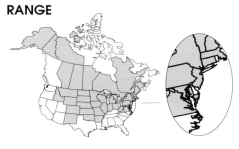

RANGE

HEIGHT 12 - 40" tall

FLOWER
5-Parted,
White - Cream
Cyme

LEAF
Pinnately Divided
Basal: 7 - 11 Leaflets
Stem: 5 Leaflets

FRUIT
Small Seed

ROOT
Central Taproot
Rhizome

PLANT NOTES
Prairie cinquefoil has an upright, narrow form. Arranged in a tight cluster, the bright white strawberry-like flowers with yellow centers are crisp and long-lasting. Plant with shorter grasses such as June grass. Prairie cinquefoil commonly grows along woodland openings and dry prairies in well-drained soil.

COMPLEMENTARY PLANTS
Ohio Spiderwort   Harebell
Pale Purple Coneflower
Butterfly Milkweed

INSECT NOTES
A popular plant of small, short-tongued bees and flies. Nectar, secreted from a ring that surrounds the ovary is accessible to all visitors. Pollen is also accessible and abundant from the large anthers that extend above the petals.

PLANT - INSECT INTERACTIONS

Yellow-Faced Bees, *Hylaeus* spp. *left*
Female yellow-faced bees are attracted to the bright yellow anthers which they chew to collect pollen for nest provisioning.

Mining Bees, *Andrena* spp. *right*
While probing for nectar on the outer edge of the ovary, mining bees crawl across anthers picking up pollen grains.

Two Moon Beewolf
Philanthus bilunatus
Beewolves visit prairie cinquefoil flowers for nectar. These solitary wasps nest in the ground caching their nests with bees, sweat bees, *Halictus* spp., in particular.

Syrphid Flies, *Toxomerus* spp. *left*
Syrphid flies feed on pollen and nectar.
Ants, Family Formicidae Ants feed on nectar.

Small Carpenter Bees
Ceratina spp.

Small carpenter bees have shiny, blue or green metallic bodies; the majority also have white or cream markings on their face. They are sparsely haired compared to sweat bees, *Lasioglossum* spp., that are similar in size.

Small carpenter bees nest in cavities, chewing holes in decaying wood or in pith inside stems. Pith and saliva are used to separate brood cells within the cavity. Perennial stems left lying on the ground make excellent nesting habitat for these bees. One of the earliest bees to emerge in spring, look for them visiting woodland native plants such as bloodroot, hepatica and violets.

YELLOW CONEFLOWER ~ *Ratibida pinnata*

FLOWERING PERIOD

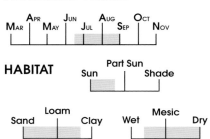

HABITAT

RANGE

HEIGHT 36 - 72" tall

FLOWER	**LEAF**
Drooping Yellow Rays	Pinnately Divided
Many Disc Florets	3 - 7 Segments
Tall Central Cone	Lower: Stalked
Cone: Green - Brown	Stem: Stalkless

FRUIT	**ROOT**
Achene	Rhizome

PLANT NOTES

Yellow coneflower has sturdy, long flower stalks and large, drooping flowers. Combine with short prairie grasses such as June grass, side oats grama or little bluestem to complement and soften the tall flowers.

COMPLEMENTARY PLANTS

Butterfly Milkweed	Wild Bergamot
Rattlesnake Master	Little Bluestem
Spotted Beebalm	Nodding Onion

INSECT NOTES

Yellow coneflower is highly rated for attracting beneficial insects (predators and parasitoids) that keep problem insect populations in balance. These beneficial insects include chalcid wasps, syrphid flies and minute pirate bugs. Disc florets develop from the bottom upward offering pollen first.

PLANT - INSECT INTERACTIONS

 HONEY BEES

LARVAL HOST PLANT
Wavy-Lined Emerald Moth
(Camouflaged Looper) *Synchlora aerata*

SPECIALIST BEE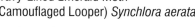
Mining Bee, *Andrena rudbeckiae*

Bumble Bees | **Leafcutter Bees**
Bombus **spp.** | *Megachile* **spp.**

Long-Horned Bees, *Melissodes* **spp.**
Female *(left),* Male *(right)*
One of the most common visitors of yellow cone-flower, females collect pollen. Males feed on nec-tar that is accessible from the short disc florets.

Sweat Bees, *Halictus* spp. *left*
Green Sweat Bees, *Agapostemon* spp. *right*

Cuckoo Bees, *Triepeolus* spp.
These boldly striped black and white bees are regular visitors of yellow coneflower and other mid- to late summer flowering plants. Like other cuckoo bees, they lack pollen-collecting structures on their legs or abdomen because they do not pro-vision their own nests.

Instead, females lay eggs in the nests of long-horned bees, *Melissodes* spp., a ground-nesting bee. When the female host bee leaves the nest, a female cuckoo bee slips in and lays an egg on the wall of a brood cell in the process of be-ing provisioned. When the cuckoo bee larva hatches, it kills the long-horned bee larva, then feeds and develops on the pollen and nectar (bee bread) provided by the host.

YELLOW CONEFLOWER ~ *Ratibida pinnata*

DISGUISED FEEDING

Wavy-Lined Emerald Moth (Camouflaged Looper)
Synchlora aerata

Yellow coneflower is a larval host plant for the wavy-lined emerald moth (along with many other plants in the Asteraceae family). Caterpillars attach small plant fragments (petals and leaves) from the host plant to their backs.

This simple but ingenious camouflage strategy lowers their risk of predation. Look for these caterpillars in July feeding on their host plants. Active in June, adult moths are light green with white wavy lines on their wings (below).

PLANT - INSECT INTERACTIONS

Mint Moths, *Pyrausta* spp. *left*
Azure Butterflies, *Celastrina* spp. *left*

Butterflies probe the disc florets to feed on nectar. Look for viceroy, sulphur, eastern tailed-blue, crescent and hairstreak butterflies.

Ichneumon Wasps *left*
Subfamily Campopleginae

Ichneumon wasps can be found searching for prey inside the flower heads of yellow coneflowers. They prey on caterpillars, sawfly larvae and occasionally beetles.

Chalcid Wasps, Family Chalcididae *right*

These tiny wasps often visit the flower heads of yellow coneflower searching for prey. They are parasitoids of butterfly, moth, fly and beetle larvae or pupae.

Soldier Beetles
Chauliognathus spp.

Soldier beetles visit some of the last yellow coneflower plants to bloom in late summer feeding on pollen and nectar.
See profile p. 96.

PLANT - INSECT INTERACTIONS

HONEY BEES

Lance Flies, Family Lonchaeidae *left*
Leaf Miner Flies, Family Agromyzidae *right*
Several types of small flies including lance and leaf miner flies either lay their eggs in undeveloped flower heads of yellow coneflower or use their ovipositors to puncture the flower heads to feed upon the resulting sap flows.

Lance flies typically lay their eggs in dead or damaged plants where larvae hatch and feed on fungi and decaying plant material. Some lay their eggs in healthy plants. Leaf miner fly larvae develop in the stems, roots or flower heads of plants.

Sap flowing from cone caused by flies *left*
Ants, Family Formicidae *right*
Ants are attracted to the sap flows created by the flies (above) that puncture the undeveloped cones with their ovipositors.

Syrphid Flies, *Toxomerus* spp.
Syrphid flies are common flower visitors of yellow coneflower. Their distinct black and yellow coloration makes them very convincing bee or wasp mimics. They visit flowers for both pollen and nectar and have the ability to hover and rapidly dart back and forth.

Syrphid fly larvae in the subfamily Syrphinae are voracious predators, predominantly feeding on aphids and other soft-bodied insects. Often feeding at night, the larvae have hooks on their mouthparts that they use to impale their victims that they then consume. Considered an excellent beneficial insect, they help keep aphid populations in balance.

BLACK-EYED SUSAN ~ *Rudbeckia hirta*

FLOWERING PERIOD

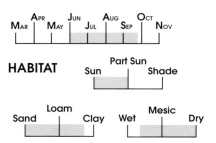

HABITAT

RANGE

HEIGHT 12 - 36" tall

FLOWER	LEAF
Biennial - Perennial	Base: Lanceolate
Yellow - Orange	Stalk: Linear
8 - 21 Ray Florets	Coarse
Many Disc Florets	Hairy
Brown Central Cone	

FRUIT	ROOT
Achene	Fibrous

PLANT NOTES
A very versatile plant for dry to moderately moist, sunny locations. It is a short-lived perennial that often reseeds and does not require replanting. The bright yellow ray florets persist and remain attractive long after the central disc florets have finished flowering, providing a long season of interest.

COMPLEMENTARY PLANTS
Wild Bergamot   Wild Petunia
Butterfly Milkweed   Hoary Vervain

INSECT NOTES
Black-eyed Susan flowers are a great source of pollen and nectar for bees, the primary pollinators. Disc florets mature from the bottom of the cone upward. Some bees, primarily long-horned bees, collect pollen by circling around the cones. Butterflies, flies and beetles are other common visitors.

PLANT - INSECT INTERACTIONS

  HONEY BEES

LARVAL HOST PLANT

Wavy-Lined & Southern Emerald Moth, *Synchlora aerata* and *S. frondaria;* Common Eupithecia, *Eupithecia miserulata;* Silvery Checkerspot Butterfly, *Chlosyne nycteis*

SPECIALIST BEE Mining Bee, *Andrena rudbeckiae*

ULTRAVIOLET ABSORBANCE & REFLECTANCE OF FLOWER PARTS

Black-eyed Susan flowers look very different to bees than to humans. The central disc florets on the cones and the bases of the ray florets absorb ultraviolet light. The outer tips of the ray florets reflect ultraviolet light.

The overall appearance to bees is two contrasting colors with the outer parts of the rays light and the inner parts dark. This color contrast is believed to act as a visual guide for visiting bees, orienting them toward the floral rewards in the center of the flower head.

Photograph Illustrating the Two-Ringed Pattern Revealed Under Ultraviolet Light.
Illustrated from results of McCrea & Morris, 1983.

| Long-Horned Bees
Melissodes spp. | Leafcutter Bees
Megachile spp. | Cuckoo Bees
Coelioxys spp. | Bumble Bees
Bombus spp. |

| Mining Bees
Andrena spp. | Green Sweat Bees
Agapostemon spp. | Green Sweat Bees
Augochlorini Tribe | Small Carpenter
Bees, *Ceratina* spp. |

BLACK-EYED SUSAN ~ *Rudbeckia hirta*

CLEPTOPARASITE PROFILE

Blister Beetles
Nemognatha spp.

These blister beetles are common on black-eyed Susan, often feeding on nectar alongside soldier beetles. They have strange-looking mouth-parts consisting of long maxillae that they use to suck nectar. They feed on pollen with their mandibles.

Females lay eggs on the flowers. When a larva hatches, it attaches itself to a visiting bee and is trans-ported back to the bee's nest. The beetle larva finds a bee brood cell fully provisioned with bee bread and egg. The larva eats the egg then feeds on the bee bread.

PLANT - INSECT INTERACTIONS

Two Moons Beewolf, *Philanthus bilunatus*

Many wasp species visit black-eyed Susan flowers for nectar including sand wasps, mason wasps, thread-waisted wasps and Beewolves (above). Beewolves provision their nests with bees (sweat bees in particular) and wasps. Females construct solitary ground nests excavated in soil banks. To prevent parasitoids from entering, nest entrances are closed while the females are away hunting for prey. When females return, flying with their prey held beneath them, they set the prey aside and re-open the nest entrance.

Soldier Beetles, *Chauliognathus* spp.

Numerous soldier beetles can be found on black-eyed Susan flowers in open, sunny prairies or openings along woodland edges. They feed on pollen and nectar. Pollen collects on their head and forelegs, but most is groomed off so they are not considered effective pollinators.
See profile p. 96.

PLANT - INSECT INTERACTIONS

 HONEY BEES

Bee Flies, Family Bombyliidae
***Exoprosopa* spp.** *left*   ***Villa* spp.** *right*

Feeding on pollen and nectar, bee flies are regular visitors of black-eyed Susan flowers. Bee flies are parasitoids of insect larvae including moths, bees, wasps, grasshoppers and flies. The majority of bee fly larvae attach themselves to their host and feed on them from the outside. Some feed on hosts internally, including *Villa* spp., while others are cleptoparasites feeding on the host's provisions. Bee flies hover over the nests of their hosts and drop eggs down the opening. The newly hatched larvae are mobile and crawl to their hosts.

Syrphid Flies, *Eristalis* spp.
Common on black-eyed Susan flowers, syrphid flies feed on pollen and nectar. On close inspection, syrphid flies are very dextrous while visiting flowers. They often use their forelegs to grasp the anthers so they can lap up the pollen with their sponge-like mouthparts.

PREDATOR PROFILE

Jagged Ambush Bugs
***Phymata* spp.**

Look for jagged ambush bugs perched on flower heads or foliage in full sun on summer days.

Jagged ambush bugs are formidable predators: they have enlarged forelegs and menacing sickle-like tibiae. As their victims come to nectar on flowers (usually bees and flies), these bugs grab them with their forelegs and impale them with their piercing, sucking mouthparts.

Their straw-like mouthparts are usually tucked underneath their bodies when not in use.

WILD PETUNIA ~ *Ruellia humilis*

FLOWERING PERIOD

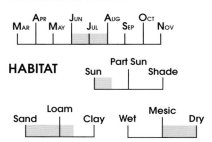

HABITAT

RANGE

HEIGHT 12 - 24" tall

FLOWER	LEAF
5-Parted	Opposite
Pink - Purple	Lanceolate
Funnel-Shaped	Mostly Stalkless
Stalkless	Entire, Long Hairs

FRUIT	ROOT
Smooth Capsule	Taproot

PLANT NOTES

Wild petunia has large, showy flowers that open from the leaf axils. Use at the edge of plantings or boulevards where its short stature is not overpowered by tall plants. Plant in gaps between rocks or similar tight spaces. Plants reseed around parent plant.

COMPLEMENTARY PLANTS

Wild Bergamot	Hoary Vervain
Butterfly Milkweed	Spotted Bee Balm

INSECT NOTES

Nectar is secreted at the base of the ovary. Dark purple lines act as nectar guides on the flower. Large bees are the most effective pollinators, brushing pollen from anthers as they insert their thoraxes and abdomens into the corolla for nectar.

PLANT - INSECT INTERACTIONS

LARVAL HOST PLANT
Common Buckeye, *Junonia coenia* (p. 222) (p. 222)

Small-sized bees, including sweat bees and small carpenter bees (below), visit the flowers for both nectar and pollen. They crawl down the corolla toward the nectary passing by the anthers without making contact. The four anthers are held in the upper part of the corolla where these small bees also grasp the filaments and feed on pollen. The stigma, spatially separated from the anthers, receives little pollen deposited by these small bees when they visit to feed on pollen or nectar.

Leafcutter Bees
Megachile **spp.**
These medium-sized, long-tongued bees visit wild petunia flowers for both pollen and nectar. When they insert their head into the flower corolla, pollen is deposited on the top of their head and thorax. Due to their size and contact with the anthers, they pick up and transfer more pollen than small bees and are likely an effective pollinator.

Sweat Bees, *Lasioglossum* **spp.**

Small Carpenter Bees, *Ceratina* **spp.**

Cabbage White Butterfly
Pieris rapae
Butterflies and day-flying moths occasionally visit wild petunia flowers to feed on nectar. The cabbage white butterfly is an introduced species from Europe that is now common throughout North America. Caterpillars feed on plants in the Brassicaceae family which includes cabbage, broccoli and cauliflower.

Green Sweat Bee,
Agapostemon **spp.**
Green sweat bees visit wild petunia flowers to collect pollen.

Syrphid Flies,
Toxomerus **spp.**
Syrphid flies feed on stray pollen from the stigma as well as pollen from the anthers.

STIFF GOLDENROD ~ *Solidago rigida* (*Oligoneuron*)

FLOWERING PERIOD

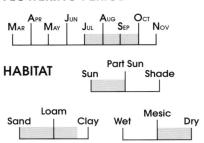

HABITAT

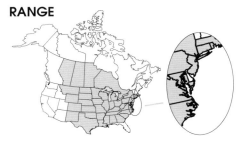

RANGE

HEIGHT 30 - 60" tall

FLOWER	LEAF
Flat-Topped Cluster	Gray - Green
6 - 14 Yellow	Basal: Lanceolate
Ray Florets	Stem: Ovate
Central Disc Florets	Mostly Stalkless
	Alternate

FRUIT	ROOT
Achene with Hairs	Fibrous, Deep

PLANT NOTES

Stiff goldenrod has bold, bright yellow flat-topped flowers. It is suitable for any sunny, dry location. Flowers are long-lasting and the glaucous foliage contrasts nicely with other native prairie plants. The root system is fibrous so stiff goldenrod does not spread rapidly like some of the rhizomatous goldenrods.

COMPLEMENTARY PLANTS

Little Bluestem   Rough Blazingstar
Heart-Leaved Aster

INSECT NOTES

With its abundant pollen and nectar rewards, this native plant attracts a diversity of insects including many types of beetles, syrphid flies, butterflies and wasps. The shallow flowers provide access to nectar for both large and small bees. Specialist bees in particular and occasionally bumble bees collect pollen.

PLANT - INSECT INTERACTIONS

LARVAL HOST PLANT

Dart Moth, *Tricholita notata*

Stiff goldenrod attracts many types of bees. Most feed on nectar from the shallow flowers.

Long-Horned Bees
Melissodes **spp.**

Sweat Bees
Lasioglossum **spp.**

Green Sweat Bees
Agapostemon **spp.**

Sweat Bees
Halictus **spp.**

Bumble Bees
Bombus **spp.**

Leafcutter Bees
Megachile **spp.**

Yellow-Faced Bees
Hylaeus **spp.**

Small Carpenter Bees
Ceratina **spp.**

SPECIALIST MINING BEES ~ *Andrena* spp.

Andrena hirticincta

Most bees are polylectic, feeding on and collecting pollen from many different types of plants. Pollen specialist bees, **oligolectic bees**, feed on and collect pollen from a narrow range of plants, often from one plant family or genus. Some specialist bees have pollen-collecting structures tailored to the size of the pollen grains that they collect. A study on specialist bees (Praz et al., 2008) found that larvae failed to develop on non-host pollen and, in some cases, females ceased nesting if offered non-host pollen.

Along with visual cues, the oily coating on pollen grains contains volatile compounds that help guide bees to host plants. When oligolectic bees raise their larvae on this pollen, the newly emerged bees, as inexperienced foragers, are believed to rely initially on these olfactory cues to find host plants. Several mining bees are specialists of goldenrods and asters such as *Andrena nubecula*, *A. hirticincta* (above), *A. placata,* and *A. simplex.*

STIFF GOLDENROD ~ *Solidago rigida* (*Oligoneuron*)

PREDATOR PROFILE

Yellowjacket Wasps
Vespula spp.

In late summer, yellowjacket wasps switch from a carnivorous diet of insects to carbohydrates (flower nectar) provided by plants such as stiff goldenrod. They are common visitors to picnics, attracted to sugary soda, fruit and meat. Adults are predators hunting beetles, flies, true bugs and wasps. Prey is chewed, regurgitated and fed to larvae. Yellowjacket wasps, Vespula spp., are colony-nesting in paper nests below ground. They aggressively protect their nests. *Dolichovespula* spp. nest in paper nests above ground.

Square-Headed Wasps
Ectemnius spp.

Square-headed wasps are predators of adult flies. Look for them perched on foliage, scouting for prey to fly by. Females construct solitary nests in hollow stems, in cavities in decaying or live wood, or in the ground.

PLANT - INSECT INTERACTIONS

Paper Wasp, *Polistes fuscatus* *left*
Great Golden Digger Wasp *right*
Sphex ichneumoneus *See profile p. 232.*

Potter Wasp, *Eumenes fraternus*. *left*
Potter wasps construct mud nests, often pot-shaped, attached to man-made structures as well plant stems or leaves. Their nests are provisioned with caterpillars. *See profile p. 197.*
Mason Wasp, *Ancistrocerus adiabatus* *right*

Grass-Carrying Wasp, *Isodontia mexicana*
See profile and image of nest, p. 197.
Thread-Waisted Wasps, *Prionyx* spp.

Monarch Butterfly, *Danaus plexippus*
Crescent Butterflies, *Phyciodes* spp.
Stiff goldenrod is a reliable source of late-summer nectar for butterflies, especially migrating species such as monarchs. Look for monarchs, whites, sulphurs, viceroys and buckeyes visiting flowers.

Locust Borer Beetle, *Megacyllene robiniae*
The locust borer beetle feeds on pollen and can be found on many goldenrod species in late summer. Its black and yellow coloring, mimicking a yellow-jacket wasp, provides protection from predators. Larvae excavate tunnels in the wood of black locust trees, *Robinia pseudoacacia*.

Syrphid Flies, *Spilomyia* spp.
With yellow markings on their eyes, thorax and abdomen, these syrphid flies are convincing mimics of wasps. Common in late summer, they feed on nectar and pollen. Larvae develop in water-filled holes in trees.

Tachinid Flies, *Archytas* spp.
A parasitoid of many insects including beetles, butterfly and moth caterpillars and true bugs. Female tachinid flies typically lay their eggs on the host or inject their eggs into the host with their ovipositor. When the larva hatches on the surface, it burrows into the host, consuming the host internally during development. The entry point on the host often does not heal over completely and provides the fly larva with a breathing hole; others use the host's air supply. Tachinid flies have long bristles on the end of their abdomen. They visit flowers for nectar, especially in late summer.

Syrphid Flies, *Eristalis* spp.
Syrphid flies feed on nectar and pollen. Many are convincing mimics of bees with black and yellow coloring and abundant hairs.

OHIO SPIDERWORT ~ *Tradescantia ohiensis*

FLOWERING PERIOD

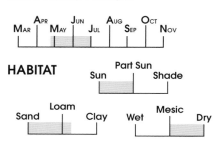

HABITAT

RANGE

HEIGHT 24 - 48" tall

FLOWER	**LEAF**
Blue - Violet	Long
3-Parted	Linear
Cyme	Clasping

FRUIT	**ROOT**
Capsule: 3 Sections	Fibrous, Fleshy
3 - 6 Seeds	

PLANT NOTES

Unique features of Ohio spiderwort flowers include the bright blue color, three-parted form and hairy, upright filaments. The spreading, linear leaves contrast nicely with any broad-leaved prairie plant. Use Ohio spiderwort near the edge of plantings for best effect. Flowers open in the morning and close during the heat of the day.

COMPLEMENTARY PLANTS

Pale Purple Coneflower   Harebell
Golden Alexanders

INSECT NOTES

Ohio spiderwort flowers do not have any nectaries, so insect visits are for pollen feeding and collection only. Large bees are primarily responsible for pollination; their size and foraging behavior deposits more pollen onto receptive stigmas than small bees. Flies feed on pollen but transfer little pollen to stigmas of other spiderwort flowers. Butterflies and moths are occasional visitors, investigating the flowers for nectar.

HONEY BEES

Sweat Bees
Lasioglossum spp.

Green Sweat Bees
Agapostemon spp.

Mason Bees
Osmia spp.

Small Carpenter Bees, *Ceratina* spp.

Bumble Bees, *Bombus* spp. *left*
Bumble bees are the primary pollinators of Ohio spiderwort. After landing on a flower, bumble bees gather anthers together with their legs, collecting pollen for nest provisioning.

Narcissus Bulb Fly *right*
Merodon equestris
This syrphid fly is an introduced species from Europe. Larvae live in, and feed on, the bulbs of *Narcissus* plants including daffodils and jonquils.

Syrphid Flies, *Toxomerus* spp. *left*
Bee Flies, *Hemipenthes* spp. *right*

POLLINATOR PROFILE

European Wool Carder Bee
Anthidium manicatum
A European species introduced for pollination of commercial crops, this bee has spread rapidly across the continent and is becoming a common visitor of flowers in urban and suburban landscapes.

Female wool carder bees use their sharp mandibles to cut and harvest hairs from plants; these plant hairs are used to line or form their brood cells. Females often visit Ohio spiderwort during the day when the flowers are closed to collect hairs from the flower stems and buds. The combative, territorial males defend areas where females are foraging. The males often chase other bees from their patrolled area.

Eastern Tiger Swallowtail Butterfly, *Papilio glaucus*
Butterflies occasionally investigate the flowers for nectar.

HOARY VERVAIN ~ *Verbena stricta*

FLOWERING PERIOD

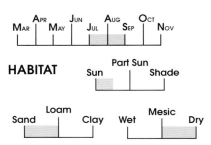

HABITAT

RANGE

HEIGHT 24 - 48" tall

FLOWER	LEAF
Blue - Purple	Ovate, Pointed Tips
5-Parted	Opposite
Tubular	Toothed, Stalkless
Narrow Spikes	Coarse, White Hairs

FRUIT	ROOT
Brown Nutlets	Fibrous

PLANT NOTES

Hoary vervain is common in disturbed, dry sites such as old fields, grazed pastures or railways. With its long flowering period and high drought tolerance, it is an excellent perennial for sandy, well-drained soils.

COMPLEMENTARY PLANTS

Wild Bergamot	Spotted Bee Balm
Little Bluestem	Black-Eyed Susan
Fragrant Hyssop	Stiff Goldenrod
Butterfly Milkweed	

INSECT NOTES

Hoary vervain is a preferred nectar plant of butterflies and bees. Most insects visit the flowers for nectar, except for a few bee species, some specialists, that collect pollen.

LARVAL HOST PLANT

Verbena Moth, *Crambodes talidiformis*
Fine-Lined Sallow Moth, *Catabena lineolata*

SPECIALIST BEE

Calliopsis nebraskensis

Long-Horned Bees, *Melissodes* spp.

Leafcutter Bees, *Megachile* spp. left
Green Sweat Bees, *Agapostemon* spp. right

Cuckoo Bees, *Triepeolus* spp. left
Cuckoo Bees, *Coelioxys* spp. right

POLLINATOR PROFILE

Bumble Bees, *Bombus* spp.

An overwintering queen bumble bee emerges in early spring and begins nest initiation; the queen constructs a nest, forages for nest provisions and lays eggs. She lays several fertilized eggs onto pollen balls to produce female offspring that become workers. In all bees, unfertilized eggs become males and fertilized eggs become females.

In their eusocial nest, female workers handle the majority of foraging, provisioning and brood care while the queen remains in the nest creating wax cups (nectar pots) and laying and incubating eggs. The queen secretes a wax to cover the eggs on the pollen ball. Several generations of offspring are produced each season, providing the continuous presence of bumble bees foraging and nectaring throughout the summer months.

In the fall, males and new queens are produced. All males and females perish except for mated females. These females (queens) overwinter and emerge in spring to begin construction of a new nest.

HOARY VERVAIN ~ *Verbena stricta*

FLOWER DEVELOPMENT

Flowers develop from the bottom upward on the flower spikes. The flower corolla is curved and horizontal near the opening where anthers are attached. When anthers dehisce, pollen remains in the corolla tube near the anthers. It does not fall toward the receptive stigma below because of the horizontal corolla position and hairs within the corolla tube. Anthers dehisce one day before the flowers open and continue to dehisce until the corolla falls away two days later.

Pollen is accessible for short- and long-tongued bees in the corolla tube. Once the flower opens, the stigmas develop progressively, starting near the base of the stigmatic lobes and spreading across the stigmatic surface. Nectar, secreted at the base of the ovary, is the main attractant for floral visitors. A few bee genera have been observed collecting pollen including *Melissodes*, *Hoplitis*, *Ceratina* and the specialist *Calliopsis verbenae*.

PLANT - INSECT INTERACTIONS

Feeding from one flower head for several minutes, butterflies probe each flower for nectar then fly to a neighboring flower head. Skipper butterflies are frequent visitors. In addition to the butterflies below, look for the monarch, little yellow, great spangled fritillary and painted lady butterflies.

Peck's Skipper, *Polites peckius* *left*
Fiery Skipper, *Hylephila phyleus* *right*

Silver Spotted Skipper, *Epargyreus clarus*
Eastern Tailed-Blue, *Everes comyntas* *right*

Common Wood Nymph, *Cercyonis pegala*
Cabbage White Butterfly, *Pieris rapae* *right*

PLANT - INSECT INTERACTIONS

HONEY BEES

Syrphid Flies, *Eristalis* spp.

These stout-bodied flies visit hoary vervain flowers to feed on nectar. They are considered a honey bee mimic; their bee-like disguise and buzzing are believed to help deter predators. Mated females overwinter as adults instead of larvae, unlike many other syrphid fly species. Larvae are aquatic and feed on small aquatic organisms. They breathe through a long, retractable tube on the end their abdomens.

Bee Flies, *Bombylius* spp.

With long mouthparts and the ability to hover, bee flies are efficient foragers of nectar on hoary vervain flowers. Common in spring through summer, females lay eggs at the opening of bee nests, especially those that nest in the spring such as mining bees, *Andrena* spp. A bee fly larva feeds on the host bee larva in the nest, pupates, then emerges the following spring or early summer from the nest as an adult. Male and female bee flies nectar on plants. *See profile p. 95.*

Syrphid Flies, *Toxomerus* spp.

Syrphid Flies, *Tropidia* spp. *See profile p. 181.*

Goldenrod Soldier Beetle
Chauliognathus pensylvanicus

GOLDEN ALEXANDERS ~ *Zizia aurea*

FLOWERING PERIOD

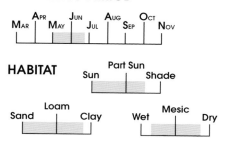

HABITAT

RANGE

HEIGHT 20 - 40" tall

FLOWER	**LEAF**
Yellow	Pinnately Divided
5-Parted	Lobed Leaflets
Compound Umbel	Long-Stalked
10 - 20 Umbellets	Toothed

FRUIT	**ROOT**
Oblong Seed	Dense, Fibrous

PLANT NOTES
A very adaptable native perennial for average soils and moisture. Golden alexanders provide bright color in restored landscapes or gardens in early spring. The flowers are an important source of nectar and pollen for insects just emerging from pupation.

COMPLEMENTARY PLANTS
Wild Lupine   Ohio Spiderwort
Wild Geranium
Smooth Beard Tongue

INSECT NOTES
The small, numerous, shallow flowers provide nectar for short- and long-tongued bees throughout the flower development. A disc at the top of the ovary secretes nectar. Flowers develop from the outside of the umbel toward the center; stigmas are receptive first followed by anthers dehiscing. Small bees that collect pollen such as mining bees, *Andrena* spp., are primarily responsible for pollination; large bees visit the flowers for nectar.

PLANT - INSECT INTERACTIONS

LARVAL HOST PLANT

Black Swallowtail, *Papilio polyxenes*
Ozark Swallowtail, *Papilio joanae*
Rigid Sunflower Borer, *Papaipema rigida*

SPECIALIST BEE

Mining Bee, *Andrena ziziae*

Azure Butterflies, *Celastrina* spp.

Azure butterflies visit native plants for nectar that flower in the spring including golden alexanders. These small, dusky gray butterflies often go unnoticed despite their eye-catching, light blue coloring on the inside of their wings.

Ebony Bugs, *Corimelaena* spp. *left*

Found in aggregations on the flower heads, these bugs are regular visitors of golden alexanders.

Soldier Beetles, *Rhagonycha* spp. *right*

These beetles are common in the spring and feed on nectar of golden alexanders.

Ladybird Beetle
Cycloneda munda

Both adults and larvae feed on soft-bodied insects and are utilized in the biological control of aphids. Females consume hundreds of aphids before laying eggs.

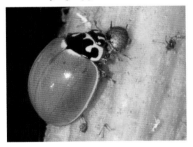

This beetle overwinters as an adult in aggregations, emerging in spring. Look for ladybird beetle eggs laid near aphid clusters, often under the flower heads of golden Alexanders.

EGGS

LARVA

GOLDEN ALEXANDERS ~ *Zizia aurea*

POLLINATOR PROFILE

Mining Bees, *Andrena* spp.

Mining bees are small- to medium-sized and typically short-tongued. They are moderately hairy and often have stripes of pale hair on their abdomens. Mining bees are one of the first bees to emerge in the spring, common in woodlands flying around spring wildflowers searching for nectar and pollen. *See bloodroot, p. 164.* One way to visually identify mining bees is by their two distinctive facial depressions (foveae) between the compound eyes (see light-colored hair on the face in photo above). Females have pollen-collecting hairs on the upper part of their hind legs and on the side of their thorax.

They nest in sandy or loose loamy soil in the ground, often in lawns. They are solitary with each female caring for her own young.

PLANT - INSECT INTERACTIONS

Mason Bees, *Osmia* spp. *left*

Golden alexanders' flowering often coincides with mason bee nest construction. Males and females feed on nectar; females collect pollen.

Bumble Bees, *Bombus* spp. *right*

Bumble bees visit the flowers of golden alexanders typically for nectar but may also collect pollen.

Sweat Bees, *Lasioglossum* spp.

Taking advantage of the easy access to floral rewards, sweat bees feed on nectar and collect pollen.

Yellow-Faced Bees, *Hylaeus* spp. *left*
Small Carpenter Bees, *Ceratina* spp. *right*

Potter Wasp, *Eumenes fraternus* *left*
Paper Wasp, *Polistes fuscatus* *right*
Paper wasps feed on nectar which helps fuel nest construction, foraging and hunting activities in early spring.

Syrphid Flies, *Toxomerus* spp. *left*
Tachinid Flies, *Siphona* spp. *right*

Crab Spiders, Family Thomisidae
Look for crab spiders waiting on or hidden in golden alexanders' flowers for prey. Some species are able to change color so they blend in with the flower. *See profile p. 171.*

PREDATOR PROFILE

Wood-boring Mason Wasp
Euodynerus foraminatus
Mason wasps nest in abandoned mud nests, cavities in twigs or wood. They are predators of caterpillars (moth larvae). Female mason wasps search for prey on foliage, then sting it multiple times to cause paralysis. The caterpillars are carried back to their nests where they are placed in prepared cells in the nest cavity, and several caterpillars are cached in each cell. Rather than laying an egg on one of the prey cached in the cell, before hunting for prey, the female lays an egg suspended from a silk thread from the roof of the empty cell.

Mason wasps visit golden alexanders for nectar. For plants with long tubular flowers and inaccessible nectar such as *Penstemon* spp., mason wasps often chew holes (perforations) on the outside of flowers near the nectaries to access nectar. *More information. p. 9.*

CHAPTER FIVE
Native Plant - Insect Interactions
WOODLAND EDGE

WHITE BANEBERRY ~ *Actaea pachypoda*

FLOWERING PERIOD

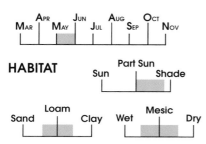

HABITAT

RANGE

HEIGHT 18 - 36" tall

FLOWER	LEAF
White	Alternate
4- to 10-Parted	2 - 3 Pinnately Divided
10 - 28 Flowers	3-Parted Leaflets
Raceme	Sharply Toothed

FRUIT	ROOT
White Berry	Fibrous
Brown Seed	Rhizome

PLANT NOTES

White baneberry is a large woodland perennial that works well as a backdrop to small, more delicate woodland natives. Another common name for this plant is "doll's eyes" because of the black spots on the white berries. Sow seeds immediately when the berries mature in early September or, alternatively, keep them moist and cold-stratified in damp sand for spring sowing.

COMPLEMENTARY PLANTS

Blue Cohosh   Wild Geranium

INSECT NOTES

Sweat bees and green sweat bees are the most common visitors of white baneberry. They investigate the flowers for nectar and when not finding any reward, feed on and collect pollen. Syrphid flies are occasional visitors feeding on pollen. The European snout beetle, *Phyllobius oblongus*, an introduced species into North America, has been observed visiting baneberry flowers to copulate.

PLANT - INSECT INTERACTIONS

FLOWER DEVELOPMENT

The flowers of white baneberry are protogynous; the two-lobed stigmas become receptive when flowers begin to open. Anthers elongate following stigma receptivity and dehisce on average four days after flower opening. The flowers do not produce any nectar but are strongly fragrant. Fragrance is produced in the staminodia (sterile stamens) and production begins with flower opening. White baneberry flowers typically have between four and nine staminodia located in the outer whorl. The white petals do not last until anther dehiscence, falling off to leave white filaments and staminodia exposed. White berries mature in late August to mid-September, the fleshy, soft exterior encapsulating six brown seeds.

Similar to other native plants such as bloodroot, *Sanguinaria canadensis,* white baneberry is self-compatible. Pollinator visitation can be variable with the absence of a nectar reward, less visually attractive white flowers and differences from year to year of flowering onset due to seasonal temperatures. The initial floral attractant for pollinators is likely the fragrance exuded from the staminodia. An abundant supply of pollen is the only reward.

Small Sweat Bees, *Lasioglossum* spp.

Grasping several anthers together to collect pollen, female sweat bees deposit pollen grains on their abdomen and legs. The receptive stigmas are often brushed with pollen as sweat bees forage and climb across them.

Sweat bees are one of the few floral visitors of white baneberry so they are considered a pollinator even though white baneberry is self-compatible. In a study by (Pellmyr 1985), sweat bees did not demonstrate floral constancy and switched between dandelions and white baneberry.

SHARP-LOBED HEPATICA ~ *Anemone acutiloba*

FLOWERING PERIOD

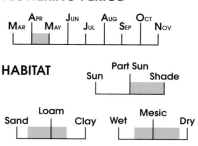

HABITAT

RANGE

HEIGHT 2-6" tall

FLOWER	LEAF
White - Lavender	Basal
5- to 12-Parted	3-Lobed
Hairy Stalk	Pointed

FRUIT	ROOT
Beaked Achene	Fibrous

PLANT NOTES
Sharp-lobed hepatica needs a good layer of leaf litter to protect the roots from freeze-thaw cycles of late winter. Where large populations of introduced earthworms occur, the leaf litter can be entirely consumed putting these and other delicate woodland plants at risk. The leaves of hepatica persist through the winter. They are bronze-colored in spring and are replaced with new green leaves that unfurl after flowering finishes in May.

COMPLEMENTARY PLANTS
Bloodroot	Bishop's Cap
Downy Yellow Violet	Wild Ginger

INSECT NOTES
Hepatica flowers are nectarless. Many small bees that have just emerged from nests search for nectar in vain. The flowers offer an abundant amount of white pollen that is collected by solitary bees for nest provisioning. The open flower form and exposed anthers are ideal for attracting small bees providing them with a flat landing platform for feeding and pollen collection.

PLANT - INSECT INTERACTIONS

Small Carpenter Bees, *Ceratina* spp.
Small carpenter bees visit the flowers, searching and probing for nectar. Once the anthers dehisce, bees return to feed on and collect pollen.

Small Sweat Bees, *Lasioglossum* spp.
Small sweat bees and small carpenter bees (above) are the most frequent visitors of hepatica flowers. They actively collect and feed on pollen and are considered, out of all the recorded visitors, the most effective pollinators.

**Mining Bees
Andrena spp.**
Large mining bees investigate the flowers for nectar. Females occasionally collect pollen but have demonstrated a preference for nectar-producing plants flowering at the same time such as trout lilies, *Erythronium* spp.

NECTARLESS FLOWERS

Flowering so early in the spring, hepatica is self-compatible when pollinators are absent. Studies have shown that self-pollination in hepatica flowers results in lower seed germination compared to flowers cross-pollinated by insects (Bernhardt, 1976; Motten, 1982).

Some of the earliest queen bumble bees emerge when flowers open but no historical observations have been made of bumble bees visiting hepatica flowers. Their preference for more complex, nectar-producing flowers, such as Dutchman's breeches, may be the reason hepatica flowers are overlooked.

Medium-sized bees, such as mining bees, *Andrena* spp., have also shown a preference for nectar-producing plants (*Erythronium* spp.) that flower concurrently. Hepatica therefore tends to receive fewer visits from mining bees and relies on sweat and carpenter bees for pollination. Butterflies, moths and hummingbirds are also absent this early in the spring; their migratory arrival or emergence from diapause (hibernation) occurs after hepatica has finished flowering.

WILD COLUMBINE ~ *Aquilegia canadensis*

FLOWERING PERIOD

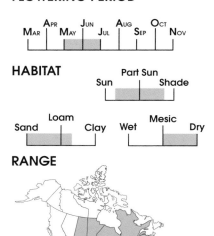

HABITAT

RANGE

HEIGHT 12 - 36" tall

FLOWER	LEAF
5-Parted	2 - 3 Times, 3-Parted
Red Sepals	Rounded, Lobed
5 Spurs	Alternate
Yellow Laminae	

FRUIT	ROOT
5 Follicles	Fibrous
Small Black Seed	

PLANT NOTES

The flowering period of wild columbine coincides with the return of migrating hummingbirds. The flower's nectar provides an important source of energy for hummingbirds when few other plants are in flower. This native plant is very adaptable growing in sunny, dry, rocky terrain, partly shaded woodlands and poor gravelly soils.

COMPLEMENTARY PLANTS

Field Pussytoes   Wild Lupine
Prairie Smoke

INSECT NOTES

Sweat bees climb up the flowers to feed on nectar. With nectar secreted in the spurs, long-tongued bumble bees or hummingbirds are required for pollination. During unseasonably cool temperatures when there is a scarcity of pollinators, wild columbine is self-compatible.

PLANT - INSECT INTERACTIONS

  HONEY BEES

LARVAL HOST PLANT Columbine Duskywing Butterfly, *Erynnis lucilius*
Columbine Borer Moth, *Papaipema leucostigma*

FORAGING BEHAVIOR OF BUMBLE BEES

Bumble bee queens and workers forage for nectar on wild columbine by either grasping onto the stamens and forcing their head into the spur or crawling up the stamens and pushing their head and thorax into the mouth of the spur. They typically visit several spurs on an individual flower before moving on to another flower.

The rusty patched bumble bee, *Bombus affinis*, is the only observed bumble bee species to create nectar perforations at the top of the spurs (Robertson 1895; Macior 1966). They initially probe the outside of the spurs using their antennae and tongues. The antennae are possibly used to detect volatile compounds emitted from the nectar. They then quickly make a perforation in the spur, insert their tongues and feed on nectar.

Queen bumble bees collect pollen usually by hanging upside down and grasping the filaments. Using their mid and hind legs, they scrape pollen from the anthers. Pollen falls on their legs and, after the bee leaves the flower, is combed and pressed into pollen baskets. Anthers dehisce for about five days and, following dehiscence, the sepals widen and nectar production increases.

Small Sweat Bees, *Lasioglossum* spp.

Small sweat bees crawl up into the nectar spurs to feed on nectar. They also feed on and collect pollen and likely transfer some pollen to receptive stigmas on another wild columbine flower.

Columbine Sawfly, *Pristophora aquiligae*

The columbine sawfly is an introduced sawfly, not native to North America. Although the larvae resemble caterpillars (larvae of butterflies and moths), they mature to a non-stinging wasp. Larvae actively feed on wild columbine foliage in May, often devouring all the leaves on a plant except the leaf mid-veins and petioles. They can be easily hand-picked from the plant if causing considerable damage, or left for wasps or birds that predate and feed on them.

GOAT'S BEARD ~ *Aruncus dioicus*

FLOWERING PERIOD

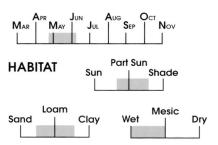

HABITAT

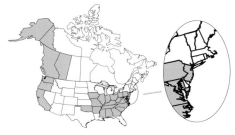

RANGE

HEIGHT 36 - 72" tall

FLOWER	**LEAF**
5-Parted	Ovate - Lanceolate
White - Cream	2 - 3 Times
Branching Spikes	Pinnately Divided
	Toothed

FRUIT	**ROOT**
Small	Taproot

PLANT NOTES

An excellent alternative to non-native *Astilbe* species in the woodland garden, goat's beard performs best in a humus-rich, medium to moist location. Use as a backdrop to short, late spring-flowering native plants such as Virginia bluebells or wild geranium.

COMPLEMENTARY PLANTS

Wild Geranium
White Baneberry
Virginia Waterleaf

INSECT NOTES

Beetles show a preference for goat's beard, visiting the male and female flowers for nectar and transferring pollen from the male flowers. Small- and medium-sized bees collect pollen, especially mining bees, *Andrena* spp. However, the majority of visitors - butterflies, moths, flies, beetles, ants - feed on nectar.

PLANT - INSECT INTERACTIONS

 HONEY BEES

LARVAL HOST PLANT

Dusky Azure Butterfly, *Celastrina nigra*

Long-Horned Beetles
***Strangalepta* spp.** *left* ***Strangalia* spp.** *right*

Long-Horned Beetles, *Leptura* spp. *left*
Fire-Colored Beetle, *Pedilus labiatus* *right*
The larvae of this beetle feed on fungi in decaying wood. Look for this beetle on flowers near woodlands. *See profile p. 155.*

Mining Bees, *Andrena* spp. *left*
Small Carpenter Bees, *Ceratina* spp. *right*

PARASITOID PROFILE

Carrot (Gasteruption) Wasps
Gasteruption spp.
Adult carrot wasps visit goat's beard flowers for nectar. They have a distinctive form, holding their long, narrow abdomen high above their bodies. Females either lay their eggs in the cavity nests of solitary bees such as yellow-faced and leafcutter bees, or cavity-nesting mason wasps. Look for carrot wasps in late summer on plants near wooded areas including zigzag goldenrod, *Solidago flexicaulis,* see p. 168.

Green Bottle Flies, *Lucilia* spp.
Syrphid Flies, *Toxomerus spp.*
Many types of flies visit the flowers for nectar. Look for thick-headed, soldier and leaf-miner flies.

DUTCHMAN'S BREECHES ~ *Dicentra cucullaria*

FLOWERING PERIOD

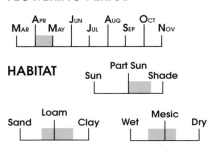

HABITAT

RANGE

HEIGHT 4 - 12" tall

FLOWER	LEAF
White - Cream	Basal
2 Spurred Petals	Pinnately Divided
2 Inner Petals	Long Stalked
Raceme	Hairless

FRUIT	ROOT
Oval Seed Capsule	Bulbous, Fleshy

PLANT NOTES

Dutchman's breeches flowers very early in the spring. The bright white flowers look like tiny trousers (breeches) hanging on a clothesline. Small plants take a few years to establish and flower but it is worth the wait. Foliage yellows and dies back by mid-June. Inter-plant with later flowering woodland plants such as false Solomon's seal to replace the void left after dormancy.

COMPLEMENTARY PLANTS

Sharp-Lobed Hepatica	Bloodroot
Trout Lily	Wild Ginger

INSECT NOTES

The flowering of Dutchman's breeches coincides with the emergence of over-wintering queen bumble bees. Small worker bumble bees chew holes (perforations) in the two nectar spurs to steal nectar - they are not strong enough to pry open the petals and have shorter tongues than queen bumble bees. Small bees, including cuckoo bees, *Nomada* spp., investigate the flowers for nectar and feed on nectar through perforations. The seeds of Dutchman's breeches are dispersed by ants.

PLANT - INSECT INTERACTIONS

FORAGING BEHAVIOR

Dutchman's breeches flowers are visited by queen bumble bees that have the tongue length, size and strength to pry open the petals. As the flower develops, the bottom of the outer petals reflexes revealing the yellow coloration near the opening. This coloration acts as a visual attractant to queen bumble bees.

Bumble bees land on the side of the flowers and grasp onto the outer petals and often clutch onto adjacent flowers with their rear legs (see top photo). Once they have a good hold, they rotate their bodies in order to access the flower opening, directing their head toward one of the nectar spurs. They push their tongues, then heads between the outer and inner petals to reach the nectar in the spurs. Pollen is brushed onto their head and thorax as the inner petals are deflected, revealing the anthers. Their forelegs often grasp the inner petals, exposing the anthers and stigma and ultimately depositing pollen onto their forelegs.

Pollen also accumulates on the bottom edges of the petals. The inner petals are hinged and when the bee removes its head from the flower, the petals return to their original position. Pollen that has dropped to the edges of the petals is deposited onto the middle legs of the bee. The most important placement of pollen for pollination of the next flower visited is on the head and thorax of the bumble bee.

The flowers of Dutchman's breeches are self-compatible and often self-pollinate in the absence of queen bumble bees. Anthers and stigmas are held closely together in the inner petals and therefore come into direct contact.

As queen bumble bees emerge from hibernation, they fly low to the ground in woodlands searching for appropriate nesting sites in abandoned rodent holes, leaf piles or other dry locations. The low-growing, Dutchman's breeches' flowers provide an important nectar source for the initial provisioning of the bumble bees' nests.

LARGE-LEAVED ASTER ~ *Eurybia macrophylla*

FLOWERING PERIOD

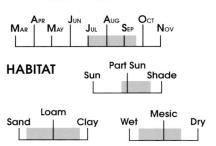

HABITAT

RANGE

HEIGHT 12 - 48" tall

FLOWER	LEAF
White - Light Purple	Basal Rosette
9 - 20 Ray Florets	Toothed, Large
Flat-Topped Panicle	Ovate - Cordate
Branched Cluster	Stem: Stalkless

FRUIT	ROOT
Achene	Fibrous
Cylinder-Shaped	Rhizome

PLANT NOTES
Large-leaved aster is one of a few native woodland perennials to flower in late summer. It works well massed in mesic woodlands along the edges of plantings or in partly shaded bioswales or ditches. Combine with ferns for a great contrast in foliage textures.

COMPLEMENTARY PLANTS
American Spikenard   Native Ferns
Zigzag Goldenrod

INSECT NOTES
Anthers release pollen in a closed cylinder surrounding the style. As the style elongates, tiny hairs collect the pollen and push it up through the cylinder making it available to pollinators. Nectar is secreted at the base of the style.

PLANT - INSECT INTERACTIONS

  HONEY BEES

LARVAL HOST PLANT

Silvery Checkerspot, *Chlosyne nycteis*
Pearl Crescent Butterfly, *Phyciodes tharos*
Goldenrod Hooded Owlet, *Cucullia asteroides*

Bumble Bees, *Bombus* spp. *left*
Yellow-Faced Bees, *Hylaeus* spp. *right*

Long-Horned Bees, *Melissodes* spp. *left*
Green Sweat Bees, *Augochloropsis* *right*
Both of these sweat bee species feed on nectar and occasionally collect pollen.

Small Sweat Bees *Lasioglossum* spp.
Look for small sweat bees and cuckoo bees, *Sphecodes* spp., in the same family. *Sphecodes* bees lay their eggs in the nests of sweat bees. They often have a distinctive red abdomen.
See photo p. 101.

SPECIALIST BEE

Mining Bee *male above*
Andrena hirticincta
This oligolectic bee is a specialist of goldenrods and asters, foraging in late-summer through fall when its host plants such as large-leaved aster are flowering.
See profile p. 123.

Syrphid Flies, *Toxomerus* spp.
Syrphid flies feed on pollen and nectar and are common visitors of large-leaved aster.
See profile p. 115.

Pollinators of Native Plants

149

WILD GERANIUM ~ *Geranium maculatum*

FLOWERING PERIOD

HABITAT

RANGE

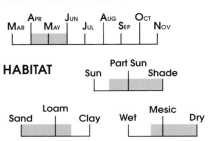

HEIGHT   12 - 36" tall

FLOWER	**LEAF**
Pink - Purple	Palmately Divided
5-Parted	5 - 7 Segments
Corymb	Hairy

FRUIT	**ROOT**
5 Pistils	Rhizome
Small Black Seed	Thick, Fleshy

PLANT NOTES

Wild geranium rivals cultivated geraniums with its numerous, large pink flowers. It flowers profusely in springs with high rainfall. An excellent plant to mass under trees, interplant with ferns or late-summer flowering woodland natives. The foliage typically turns bright red in fall for another season of interest.

COMPLEMENTARY PLANTS

Woodland Phlox	White Baneberry
Virginia Waterleaf	Long-Styled Cicely

INSECT NOTES

Wild geranium flowers develop to ensure cross-pollination, although self-pollination is possible. The row of outer anthers develop first, followed by the inner row (A). The stigma becomes receptive after anthers have dehisced (B). Nectar is secreted from five glands located between the stamens and sepals. Bees foraging for nectar deposit more pollen on stigmas than bees collecting pollen. Dark lines on the flowers act as nectar guides.

PLANT - INSECT INTERACTIONS

 HONEY BEES

LARVAL HOST PLANT

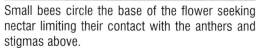

Leafmining Moth, *Parectopa geraniella*
White-Marked Tussock Moth, *Orgyia leucostigma*

SPECIALIST BEE

Mining Bee, *Andrena distans*

Small bees circle the base of the flower seeking nectar limiting their contact with the anthers and stigmas above.

Small Carpenter Bees, *Ceratina* spp. *left*
Small Sweat Bees, *Lasioglossum* spp. *right*

Orchard Mason Bees, *Osmia lignaria* *left*
Mason bees visit wild geranium for both pollen and nectar. Females collect nest provisions at the same time this native plant flowers.
Mining Bees, *Andrena* spp. *right*

Bumble Bees, *Bombus* spp. *left*
Sweat Bees, *Halictus* spp. *right*

CLEPTOPARASITE PROFILE

Cuckoo Bees, *Nomada* spp.

Wild geranium is a nectar source for this cuckoo bee in early spring. Female *Nomada* bees lay their eggs in nests of ground-nesting bees, especially mining bees, *Andrena* spp. The cuckoo bee eggs hatch and the larvae kill the host bee larvae and consume the provisions provided by the host. *Nomada* bees are reddish-brown to black with yellow or white markings.

Syrphid Flies, *Pipiza* spp. *left*
Thick-Headed Flies
***Myopa* spp.** *right*

Fruitworm Beetle
Byturus unicolor

 Mating on the flowers, this beetle also feeds on nectar and pollen. *See profile p. 180.*

VIRGINIA WATERLEAF ~ *Hydrophyllum virginianum*

FLOWERING PERIOD

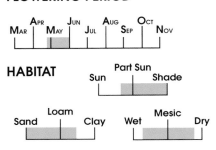

HABITAT

RANGE

HEIGHT 6 - 24" tall

FLOWER	LEAF
Pink - Purple	Alternate
5-Parted	Pinnately Divided
Tubular	Lower: Long Petioles
Stamens Hairy	Silver - White Spots
Branched Cyme	

FRUIT	ROOT
Capsule, Seeds	Fibrous, Rhizome

PLANT NOTES
The silver-spotted leaves are prominent before the flower heads develop; they then turn dark green. Mass plants together near the edge of a woodland for a colorful display. Virginia waterleaf is also a great plant to utilize in drier sites under trees or to combine with Pennsylvania sedge.

COMPLEMENTARY PLANTS
Downy Yellow Violet	Wild Geranium
False Solomon's Seal	Early Meadowrue

INSECT NOTES
Queen bumble bees visit the flowers for pollen and nectar. Short-tongued bees have difficulty reaching nectar because of hairs on the stamens. These hairs also help slow down the evaporation of nectar. The stamens and style protrude past the flower petals. Anthers mature first and the stigma becomes receptive afterward to increase the probability of cross-pollination.

PLANT - INSECT INTERACTIONS

SPECIALIST BEE
Mining Bee, *Andrena geranii*

Small bees feed on pollen from anthers that extend past the corolla opening. They also climb into the flower to access nectar.

Sweat Bees, *Lasioglossum* spp. *left*
Small Carpenter Bees, *Ceratina* spp. *right*

Both of these bees provision nests in the early spring and visit the flowers for nectar and pollen.
Orchard Mason Bee, *Osmia lignaria* *left*
Mining Bees, *Andrena* spp. *right*

Syrphid Flies, *Toxomerus* spp.
Syrphid flies feed on pollen and nectar.
Ants, Family Formicidae
Ants frequently feed on nectar but the hairs on the stamens help restrict ants from stealing it.

Black Weevil
Idiostethus tubulatus
This small black weevil is common in Virginia waterleaf flowers feeding on pollen.

Bumble Bees, *Bombus* spp.
One of the primary bees responsible for pollination, bumble bees visit Virginia waterleaf to feed on nectar. They hang upside down on the flowers while foraging for nectar, contacting the anthers with their legs and abdomen. Pollen grains not groomed from their legs and abdomen are transferred to receptive stigmas on another Virginia waterleaf plant. Green sweat bees, *Augochlorella* spp., and cuckoo bees, *Nomada* spp., are other common visitors of Virginia waterleaf.

FALSE SOLOMON'S SEAL ~ *Maianthemum racemosum*

FLOWERING PERIOD

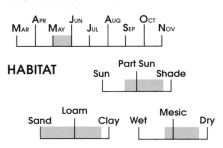

Mar	Apr May	Jun Jul	Aug Sep	Oct Nov

HABITAT

Part Sun

Sun — Shade

Loam

Sand — Clay Wet Mesic — Dry

RANGE

HEIGHT 12 - 24" tall

FLOWER	LEAF
White - Cream	5 - 12
6-Parted	Oblong, Stalkless
Branched,	Alternate
Terminal Cluster	Zigzagging Stem

FRUIT	ROOT
Red Berry	Rhizome

PLANT NOTES

This woodland perennial is rhizomatous and forms a low-growing mass once established from a new planting. This is an exceptional native plant for shaded woodland landscapes because of the bright red fruit, large white flower clusters, arching form and massing habit.

COMPLEMENTARY PLANTS

| Native Ferns | Virginia Bluebells |
| Woodland Phlox | Wild Geranium |

INSECT NOTES

The majority of insects visit the flowers for pollen including small bees, flies and beetles. Small septal nectaries on the ovary at the base of the flower attract moths and butterflies. The flowers are self-incompatible and rely on insects for cross-pollination.

Pollinators of Native Plants

PLANT - INSECT INTERACTIONS

HONEY BEES

Azure Butterflies, *Celastrina* **spp.** *left*
Azure butterflies visit false Solomon's seal for nectar in early spring, especially near woodland edges or openings.

Moth, *Neoheliodines cliffordi* *right*
This tiny moth visits flowers for nectar. Four o'clock plants, *Mirabilis* spp. are the larval host plant of this specialist moth. Larvae are pale green with a dark head and typically feed on the undersides of leaves. They are leaf skeletonizers so turn over leaves to look for webbing.

Lily of the Valley Weevil, *Hormorus* **spp.** *left*
These weevils are common on *Maianthemum* spp. feeding on the foliage. They chew the edges of leaves resulting in an undulating leaf edge.

Long-Horned Beetle, *Euderces picipes* *right*
This colorful ant-like beetle feeds on pollen of false Solomon's seal. Look for this beetle near woodlands visiting the white flowers of native shrubs such as downy arrowwood viburnum, *Viburnum rafinesquianum,* and nannyberry viburnum, *Viburnum lentago*.

POLLINATOR PROFILE

Fire-Colored Beetles
Pedilus **spp.**
Fire-colored beetles visit false Solomon's seal flowers to feed on pollen. Larvae develop in decaying wood and feed on fungi. These beetles are common on flowers near woodlands where decaying wood and blister beetles occur.

Male fire-colored beetles climb onto blister beetles, prompting the blister beetles to release cantharidin, a chemical that fire-colored beetles lick off. Male fire-colored beetles use this chemical as an olfactory attractant for females. When male beetles mate with females, cantharidin is transferred to females. The females' eggs are coated with the chemical helping protect the eggs from predation.

Small Sweat Bees
Lasioglossum **spp.**

Female sweat bees, including *Lasioglossum* spp. and *Augochlora* pura feed on and collect pollen from the flowers.

BISHOP'S CAP (MITERWORT) ~ *Mitella diphylla*

FLOWERING PERIOD

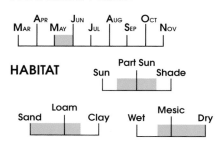

HABITAT

RANGE

HEIGHT 4 - 16" tall

FLOWER	LEAF
White, Tiny	Basal: Long Stalked
Snowflake-Like	Cordate
Fringed Petals	Stem: Stalkless
Tall Raceme	3 Lobes

FRUIT	ROOT
Black Seed, Tiny	Rhizome

PLANT NOTES

Bishop's cap is an excellent alternative to non-native coral bells, *Heuchera* spp., and works well planted under trees. The plants spread by rhizomes forming a compact mass. To appreciate the tiny, snowflake-like flowers, use near the edge of a woodland garden or shady landscape.

COMPLEMENTARY PLANTS

Downy Yellow Violet   Rue Anemone
Woodland Phlox   Wild Ginger

INSECT NOTES

Bishop's cap attracts small bees including green sweat, *Augochlorella* spp., and sweat, *Lasioglossum* spp., bees. Many types of flies visit the flowers for pollen or nectar. The flowers are largely ignored by medium and large bees that prefer to forage on other woodland native plants offering more nectar rewards.

Pollinators of Native Plants

PLANT - INSECT INTERACTIONS

Vinegar Flies, Family Drosophilidae *left*
Tachinid Flies, *Siphona* spp. *right*
These flies feed on the nectar of bishop's cap.

Syrphid Flies
***Sphegina* spp.** *left*
See profile p. 159.

***Allograpta* spp.** *right*
Syrphid flies feed on both nectar and pollen.

Sweat Bees, *Lasioglossum* spp.
Sweat bees are the most common bee visitors of bishop's cap; their tiny size allows them to cling to the flowers, accessing both pollen and nectar. With several woodland plants flowering at the same time, visits to bishop's cap flowers by large pollinators are low. On wild geranium flowers, large bees have a landing platform and easy access to nectar compared to bishop's cap flowers.

RAIN-DISPERSED SEEDS

Fertilized seeds of bishop's cap develop attached inside the curved, cup-shaped sepals. As the seeds approach maturity, the flower stalk becomes vertical in order to face the open cups upward. The shiny black seeds held inside are splashed out and dispersed during rainfall.

In one experiment, water drops falling between 3'4" and 3'8" dispersed the seeds an average of 11.6" away from the plant. It was presumed that regular rainfall can disperse seeds much greater distances from the plant (Savile, 1953).

Ants, Family Formicidae
Ants crawl up the flower stalks and into the flowers to feed on nectar.

LONG-STYLED SWEET CICELY ~ *Osmorhiza longistylis*

FLOWERING PERIOD

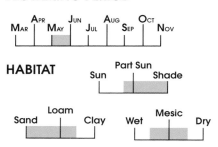

HABITAT

RANGE

HEIGHT 12 - 36" tall

FLOWER
White, 5-Parted
Compound Umbel
Styles Longer
    Than Petals

LEAF
Two Times
    Pinnately Divided
Lower: Stalked
Upper: Stalkless

FRUIT
Bristly, Curved
Seed

ROOT
Anise Scented
Taproot

PLANT NOTES
Long-styled and hairy sweet cicely (*O. clay-tonii*) are very similar. Long-styled has styles longer than the petals, burgundy to wine colored stems that are anise scented and curved bristled seed pods. The bristled seed pod is straight on hairy sweet cicely. The seed clings to clothing or animals.

COMPLEMENTARY PLANTS
Wild Geranium   Woodland Phlox
Early Meadowrue   Virginia Bluebells

INSECT NOTES
The small shallow flowers attract bees, flies and moths. Nectar is secreted from a disc at the top of the ovary and is accessible to short-tongued bees. The umbelliferous flowers contain both staminate and hermaphrodite flowers. The staminate flowers secrete nectar from the stylopodia.

Pollinators of Native Plants

PLANT - INSECT INTERACTIONS

Small Sweat Bees, *Lasioglossum* spp. *left*
Sweat bees are frequent visitors of long-styled sweet cicely flowers. They collect pollen and feed on nectar.
Mining Bees, *Andrena* spp. *right*

Medium-Sized Bees
Medium-sized bees, including digger bees, *Anthophora* spp. and mason bees, *Osmia* spp., visit the flowers for nectar. Pollen collection is typically only by sweat bees (above) and green sweat bees, *Agapostemon* spp.

Tachinid Flies, *Siphona* spp. *left*
These tachinid flies are regular visitors of long-styled sweet cicely to feed on nectar. They have long, elbowed mouthparts, longer than many other fly species and can reach nectar in complex flowers with deep corollas. Most are parasitoids of caterpillars.
Syrphid Flies, *Toxomerus* spp. *right*
Syrphid flies feed on pollen and nectar.

POLLINATOR PROFILE

Syrphid Flies, *Sphegina* spp.
These flies, typically found visiting shallow flowers, are common in, or near, woodlands in early spring. They feed on both nectar and pollen of long-styled sweet cicely. With their over-sized hind femurs and narrow waists, these flies resemble thread-waisted wasps. Larvae develop in water-logged wood as well as under wet bark. Look for these syrphid flies on bishop's cap, tall meadowrue, marsh marigold, golden Alexanders and goat's beard in the spring.

SEED DISPERSAL

Long-styled sweet cicely reproduces by seed; the curved, narrow seeds are covered in short spines. When an animal such as a raccoon or deer passes by the plant, the spines on the seeds attach to their fur. Eventually, the seeds drop off the animal away from the plant.

Pollinators of Native Plants

JACOB'S LADDER ~ *Polemonium reptans*

FLOWERING PERIOD

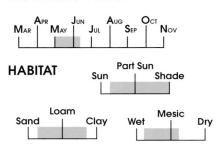

HABITAT

RANGE

HEIGHT 10 - 20" tall

FLOWER	**LEAF**
Light Blue	Oval, Alternate
5-Parted	Pinnately Divided
Corymb	7 - 17 Leaflets

FRUIT	**ROOT**
Rounded Capsule	Taproot
3 Cells, Seed	

PLANT NOTES

A very versatile native plant, Jacob's ladder performs best in partial shade and mesic soils. It can tolerate full sun but needs a location that remains moist. When planted in woodlands, it flowers between the early spring ephemerals such as bloodroot and the second flush of flowers from false Solomon's seal and Virginia waterleaf.

COMPLEMENTARY PLANTS
Wild Geranium   Native Ferns
Long-Styled Sweet Cicely   White Baneberry

INSECT NOTES
The open flowers attract long- and short-tongued bees that visit for both pollen and nectar. Syrphid flies and beetles feed on pollen but butterflies and moths visit for nectar. Nectar is secreted from a disc around the base of the ovary.

PLANT - INSECT INTERACTIONS

HONEY BEES

Fire-Colored Beetle, *Pedilus lugubris* *left*
This fire-colored beetle feeds on pollen of Jacob's ladder flowers. It is common in early spring in woodlands. *See profile p. 155.*

Syrphid Flies, *Toxomerus spp.* *right*
This female syrphid fly is feeding on pollen, a great source of protein to nourish egg development. Syrphid flies also feed on nectar.

Sweat Bees, *Lasioglossum* spp.
Sweat bees visit the flowers to feed on nectar which becomes available after the anthers dehisce and when the stigma is receptive. In the image on the left, the sweat bee is searching for nectar in the flower but none is offered yet. Nectar is offered in the right image; the flowers are in the female phase with the stigma receptive.

Other bees that visit Jacob's ladder flowers include mason bees, *Osmia* spp.; small carpenter bees, *Ceratina* spp.; mining bees, *Andrena* spp.; digger bees, *Anthophora* spp.; and bumble bees, *Bombus* spp.

FLOWER DEVELOPMENT & FORAGING BEHAVIOR

Anthers typically develop first in Jacob's ladder flowers. The style elongates below the anthers and the stigma becomes receptive once anthers dehisce. With this separation between the two reproductive parts, self-pollination is limited. Self-compatibility in other *Polemonium* species is low; therefore, Jacob's ladder likely depends on cross-pollination by insects.

Nectar secretion begins when the style elongates and the three stigma lobes open attracting both small and large bees. Pollen is transferred onto their heads and thoraxes as they climb into the flower to feed on nectar. Large bees are the most effective pollinators of Jacob's ladder because they come into contact with pollen-laden anthers more often than small bees.

Syrphid flies and beetles are ineffective pollinators. Visiting the flowers to feed on pollen, they do not transport significant amounts of pollen to other Jacob's ladder flowers. Foraging behavior is not plant-specific - they may visit Jacob's ladder but the next plant visited is an entirely different species. The result is limited cross-pollination of Jacob's ladder by flies and beetles.

SMOOTH SOLOMON'S SEAL ~ *Polygonatum biflorum*

FLOWERING PERIOD

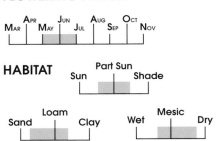

HABITAT

RANGE

HEIGHT 12 - 48" tall

FLOWER	**LEAF**
White - Light Yellow	Oblong
6-Parted	Clasping, Hairless
Tubular, Nodding	Alternate

FRUIT	**ROOT**
Berry, Dark Blue	Rhizome

PLANT NOTES

Solomon's seal has a wonderful arching form that complements other plant forms. The flowers are not always evident because they hang hidden beneath the leaves. The foliage is robust, however, and remains green throughout the summer months as the berries mature. This plant spreads forming small clusters due to its rhizomatous root system. **Note:** Deer browse the shoots in early spring.

COMPLEMENTARY PLANTS

Wild Geranium   Virginia Waterleaf
Downy Yellow Violet

INSECT NOTES

The flowers are buzz-pollinated by bumble bees, usually small workers that can fit their head and thorax into the flower corolla to grasp anthers. Look for medium-sized digger bees, *Anthophora* spp. also visiting the flowers. Small bees climb up the corolla to access nectar accumulating at the top of the flowers and are probably ineffective pollinators.

Pollinators of Native Plants

PLANT - INSECT INTERACTIONS

Small Carpenter Bees, *Ceratina* spp. *left*
Sweat Bees, *Lasioglossum* spp. *right*
Due to their small size, these bees can access both nectar and pollen on Solomon's seal flowers. Inserting their head into the flower opening, they feed on pollen.

Anthers curve inward and touch each other and can obstruct large bees from entering the flower; small bees climb past the anthers along the outer edge of the tubular flowers. Nectar is secreted from the wall of the ovary (septal nectary) and accumulates at the top of the flower. Pollen is released into the center of the flower.

Other bees that visit Solomon's seal flowers include digger bees, *Anthophora* spp., and green sweat bees, *Augochlorella* spp.

FLOWER DEVELOPMENT

Flowers develop proximally (closest to the stem) to distally (farthest from the stem) on the arching flower stalk. The style is shorter than the anthers but elongates to the top of them. The stigma is slightly three-lobed and held in the center of the filaments. The flowers on the proximal end of the flower stalk tend to be larger in size and produce more seeds. The plant puts fewer resources into the development of flowers on the distal end since those flowers open later, are smaller and potentially restrict access and offer fewer rewards to pollinators.

BUZZ POLLINATION (SONICATION)

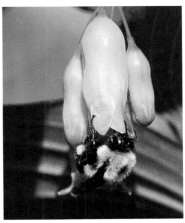

Bumble Bees, *Bombus* spp.
Bumble bees visit the flowers of Solomon's seal to feed on nectar and collect pollen. Nectar can be reached by bumble bees with long tongues when they insert their head and thorax into the corolla opening.

Pollen, held in six anthers, is vibrated out of anther openings by bumble bees. They grasp the anthers, either with their forelegs or mouthparts, close their wings then vibrate their flight muscles at a high frequency. The resulting sound is a low-pitched buzzing noise.

The small pollen grains are released in puffs and dust the abdomen and head of the bumble bee. Bumble bees often fly to a flat surface to brush and press the pollen into their pollen baskets. Other bees that buzz-pollinate flowers include mining bees, *Andrena* spp.; sweat bees, Halictidae family; and leafcutter bees, Megachilidae family.

BLOODROOT ~ *Sanguinaria canadensis*

FLOWERING PERIOD

HABITAT

RANGE

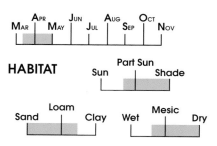

HEIGHT 3 - 6" tall

FLOWER	**LEAF**
White, 7 or More Petals	One, Basal
Single Flower Per Stalk	3 - 9 Lobes

FRUIT	**ROOT**
Long Capsule, Seeds	Rhizome

PLANT NOTES

Bloodroot is one of the first spring ephemerals to flower. Its showy white petals are over two inches in width and open fully on sunny days. Flowers close at night as temperatures drop and resemble white candles: the solitary blue-gray leaf wrapped around the stem resembles a candle holder. The rhizome releases red juice when crushed or broken.

COMPLEMENTARY PLANTS

Spring Beauty
Sharp-Lobed Hepatica
Dutchman's Breeches
False Solomon's Seal

INSECT NOTES

Flies and bees circle around open bloodroot flowers on warm spring afternoons. They try in vain to feed on nectar but none is offered. Female bees collect pollen, the only reward. In colder, unseasonable weather, when pollinators are unavailable, bloodroot flowers self-pollinate around the third day of flowering.

PLANT - INSECT INTERACTIONS

 HONEY BEES

LARVAL HOST PLANT

Southern Armyworm, *Spodoptera eridania*
Tufted Apple Bud Moth, *Platynota idaeusalis*

Mining Bees, *Andrena* spp.

Mining bees are the primary pollinators of bloodroot. Pollen collects on the underside of their abdomens before being combed to their upper hind legs. They crawl over the receptive stigma when visiting flowers to collect pollen.

FLOWER DEVELOPMENT

To initially limit self-pollination, the stigma becomes receptive before the anthers dehisce. This strategy limits pollen from the same flower coming into contact with the receptive stigma. The anthers, during the first few days of the flower opening, bend downward toward the outside of the flower to separate from the receptive stigma.

If temperatures are warm enough for pollinators to fly, pollen from other bloodroot plants is deposited onto the receptive stigma when pollinators visit the flower. If no pollinating visits by insects occur by the third day of flowering, anthers bend inward contacting the stigma, self-pollinating the flowers.

Cuckoo Bees, *Nomada* spp. *left*
Bee Flies, *Bombylius* spp. *right*
Both of these floral visitors investigate the flowers for nectar.

ANT-DISPERSED SEEDS

Long, narrow seed pods form after fertilization and split open in mid-June. Inside are rows of dark brown seeds with a caterpillar-like fleshy elaiosome attached. The protein-rich elaiosome attracts ants that carry the seeds back to their nests. Ants consume the elaiosome and put the seed in their nest 'trash pile.' Dispersed and planted away from the parent plant, the seeds are safe from rodents.

Sweat Bees
Lasioglossum spp.
When the flowers first open, sweat bees crawl around the base of the ovary searching for nectar (left). Once anthers dehisce, they return to collect pollen (right). Small carpenter bees, *Ceratina* spp., also investigate the flowers for nectar. Since bloodroot flowers earlier than other plants, there is no competition for insect visitors. Bloodroot plants can therefore afford to preserve valuable resources by not offering a nectar reward.

ZIGZAG GOLDENROD ~ *Solidago flexicaulis*

FLOWERING PERIOD

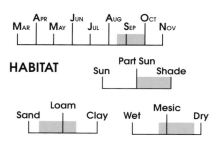

	Apr	Jun	Aug	Oct	
Mar	May	Jul	Sep	Nov

HABITAT

Part Sun
Sun / Shade

Loam
Sand / Clay   Wet   Mesic   Dry

RANGE

HEIGHT 8 - 48" tall

FLOWER
Yellow Florets
Terminal & Leaf Axils
Raceme or Panicle
Stem: Zigzags

LEAF
Ovate
Alternate
Winged Stalk
Toothed

FRUIT
Achene With Hairs
Cylindrical

ROOT
Rhizome
Fibrous

PLANT NOTES
A very shade-tolerant plant, zigzag goldenrod spreads by rhizomes and forms a mass in the woodland landscape. The zigzagging stems, coarsely toothed leaves and bright yellow flowers are some of the best features of this plant.

COMPLEMENTARY PLANTS
Large-Leaved Aster
Heart-Leaved Aster   American Spikenard

INSECT NOTES
The flowers are an important source of nectar for many types of insects including bees, flies and wasps. Look for a variety of wasps whose visits to flowers increase in late summer. Nectar is accessible to short- and long-tongued bees from the shallow florets.

PLANT - INSECT INTERACTIONS

LARVAL HOST PLANT

Bilobed Dichomeris, *Dichomeris bilobella*
Brown Hooded Owlet, *Cucullia convexipennis*
Twirler Moth, *Gnorimoschema gallaeasterella*

SPECIALIST BEES

Mining Bees, *Andrena hirticincta;*
Andrena placata; Andrena simplex

Sweat Bees, *Lasioglossum* spp. *left*
Yellow-Faced Bees, *Hylaeus* spp. *right*
These small bees are frequent visitors of zigzag goldenrod flowers and feed on nectar.

Green Sweat Bees, *Agapostemon* spp. *left*
Green sweat bees and sweat bees, *Halictus* spp., visit the flowers for nectar.

Mining Bee, *Andrena hirticincta* *right*
One of the few bee species that collects pollen from the flowers, the mining bee pictured above is a pollen-collecting specialist of goldenrods and asters. Nests are provisioned in early fall.
See profile p. 123.

Brown Hooded Owlet Moth
Cucullia convexipennis

This caterpillar feeds on zigzag goldenrod foliage in August, just before flowers begin to bud. The bright red, yellow and black warning coloration helps protect them from predation. This moth's host plants include goldenrod and aster species. Caterpillars are preyed upon by tachinid flies that lay white eggs on their bodies. Fly larvae burrow inside the caterpillars and feed internally until the caterpillars die.

Bumble Bees, *Bombus* spp.

Bumble bees, mostly males, visit zigzag goldenrod for nectar. Males look for a female (future queen) to mate with while active in early fall.

ZIGZAG GOLDENROD ~ *Solidago flexicaulis*

PREDATOR PROFILE

Mason Wasps
Ancistrocerus spp.

Mason wasps visit zigzag goldenrod for nectar along with other nectar-producing plants flowering in late summer. Males have been shown to spend more time at flowers nectaring than females, searching for females to mate with as they forage. Females construct nests in pre-existing cavities in wood, hollow stems or abandoned nests of other mud or potter wasps. After finding a suitable nest cavity, females lay an egg in the first brood cell. They then search for caterpillars on foliage. When prey is found they are stung multiple times to cause paralysis; immobilized prey are carried back to the nest.

When enough caterpillars are hunted and cached for one larva, the cavity is sealed with a mud partition. Females repeat this process in the nesting cavity several times, creating multiple brood cells. The developing wasp larvae feed on the caterpillars provided, pupate then emerge as adults the following year.

PLANT - INSECT INTERACTIONS

Thread-Waisted Wasp *left*
Eremnophila aureonotata

Look for the white (silver) spots on the thorax of this solitary wasp.

Carrot Wasp, *Gasteruption* spp. *right*

Common on flowers from late spring until fall, these tiny solitary wasps feed on nectar.
See profile p. 145.

Both of these social wasps visit goldenrods and other plants flowering in late-summer for nectar. They chew on exposed wood to produce a wood pulp. The resulting paper-like material is used for nest construction. Males are common nectar feeders, waiting to mate with a female that overwinters and becomes a queen the following spring.
See profile for paper wasps p. 196 and yellowjacket wasps p. 124.

Paper Wasp, *Polistes fuscatus* *left*
Yellowjacket, *Vespula maculifrons* *right*

PLANT - INSECT INTERACTIONS

INSECT MIMICRY

Syrphid Flies, *Ocyptamus* spp. *left*
With a long, narrow, curving abdomen, these syrphid flies are one of the easier syrphids to identify. They are regular visitors of goldenrods in late summer. The larvae of these beneficial insects are predators of aphids and mealy bugs.

Syrphid Flies, *Toxomerus* spp *right*
These syrphids feed on pollen and nectar; their larvae feed on aphids. Adult females lay eggs on plants near aphid populations.

Syrphid Fly, *Spilomyia sayi*
This fly is a convincing mimic of mason wasps, a feature that provides the fly protection from avian predation. With the threat of being stung, birds are more likely to leave this fly alone rather than risk a counterattack. Other syrphid flies in this genus mimic bald-faced hornets, *Dolichovespula* spp., and yellowjacket wasps, *Vespula* spp.

Syrphid Flies, *Eristalis* spp. *left*
Many syrphid flies in the *Eristalis* genus are mimics of bees including bumble and honey bees.
***Tropidia* spp.** *right*
The larvae of this syrphid fly develop in dung or other rotting organic material. They are common throughout the summer, feeding on nectar and pollen from a variety of flower types. *See profile p. 181.*

Goldenrod Soldier Beetle
Chauliognathus pensylvanicus

RUE ANEMONE ~ *Thalictrum thalictroides*

FLOWERING PERIOD

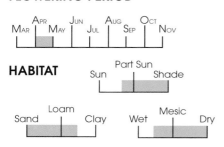

HABITAT

RANGE

HEIGHT 3 - 8" tall

FLOWER	**LEAF**
White - Pink	Basal, Hairless
5 - 10 Sepals	2 - 3 Times Parted, Rounded Leaflets

FRUIT	**ROOT**
Achene	Fibrous, Fleshy

PLANT NOTES
A delicate woodland native, rue anemone is very suitable for medium to dry woodlands. This plant resembles false rue anemone, *Enemion biternatum*, which has five sepals. Rue anemone spreads by seed and forms small clusters in the woodland.

Note: It may be difficult to find plants for sale from native plant nurseries.

COMPLEMENTARY PLANTS
Wild Ginger   Bishop's Cap
Downy Yellow Violet
Large-Flowered Bellwort

INSECT NOTES
Rue anemone is self-incompatible and relies on insect pollination. The flowers are nectarless so most visiting insects collect and feed on pollen or investigate the flowers for nectar. Look for sweat and mining bees and syrphid and bee flies visiting the flowers.

PLANT - INSECT INTERACTIONS

Sweat Bees, *Lasioglossum* spp. *left*
Sweat bees investigate the flowers for nectar; females feed on and collect pollen.

Large Mining Bees, *Andrena* spp. *right*
Large mining bees collect pollen for nest provisioning by landing on top of the anthers gathering them together with their legs. Pollen is transferred onto the legs and abdomen then groomed to the pollen-collecting hairs on their rear legs. Mining bees' medium size, foraging behavior and location of pollen deposition likely transfers pollen to other rue anemone flowers, pollinating the plants.

Other Visiting Bee Species
Small carpenter bees, *Ceratina* spp., cuckoo bees, *Nomada* spp., mason bees, *Osmia* spp., and sweat bees, *Halictus* spp., also visit the flowers of rue anemone.

FLOWER DEVELOPMENT

Anthers develop first, from the outside inward on the flower and dehisce on average two to four days after the flowers open. Rue anemone has the disadvantage of competing for insect visitors with nectar-producing plants such as large-flowered bellwort, *Uvularia grandiflora*, and violets, *Viola* spp. Pollen is the only reward offered by rue anemone flowers.

PREDATOR PROFILE

Crab Spiders
Family Thomisidae
Look for crab spiders with legs outstretched waiting on or hidden in flowers for prey, usually bees, flies and beetles. Using two large forelegs to snatch prey, they grasp the prey and chew a small hole in the insect's body. The spider regurgitates digestive fluids into the prey to dissolve the insect's internal organs and muscles. The spider then sucks out the liquid meal from the host's shell.

Some crab spiders can change their body color, an excellent camouflage, to match the color of the flower.

Syrphid Flies
Melanostoma spp.
Syrphid flies feed on pollen and are one of the most common visitors to rue anemone flowers. Look for *Tropidia* spp., *Eristalis* spp., and *Brachypalpus* spp.

LARGE-FLOWERED BELLWORT ~ *Uvularia grandiflora*

FLOWERING PERIOD

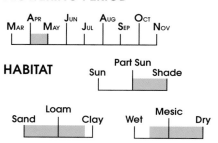

HABITAT

RANGE

HEIGHT 8 - 18" tall

FLOWER	**LEAF**
Nodding, Yellow	Ovate
6-Parted	Hairy Beneath
Twisted	Clasping

FRUIT	**ROOT**
3-Celled Capsule	Rhizome

PLANT NOTES
Large-flowered bellwort grows quickly once soil temperatures warm in spring, flowering within a week of shoots appearing above ground. The large, twisted yellow flowers, tight stem clusters and pierced leaves are unique features of this plant.
Note: This plant is browsed by deer.

COMPLEMENTARY PLANTS
Wild Ginger	Virginia Waterleaf
Bishop's Cap	Wild Geranium
Downy Yellow Violet	

INSECT NOTES
The bright yellow, nectar-producing flowers attract bees and flies. Bees must climb into the flower to access nectar at the top of the nodding flowers. Large bees brush against the anthers while inside the flower and are more effective pollinators than small bees.

PLANT - INSECT INTERACTIONS

Mining Bees, *Andrena* spp.

Unlike other woodland native plants that flower at the same time, large-flowered bellwort offers a nectar reward. The flowers are more attractive than nectarless plants to bees, especially males, that only visit for nectar.

Mining bees are active in the spring and are attracted to large-flowered bellwort flowers. Medium-sized and large mining bees crawl inside the nodding flowers to feed on nectar and pollen.

Sweat Bees
Lasioglossum spp.

Sweat bees crawl inside the flowers to feed on and collect pollen. They also attempt to access nectaries from the outside of the flower through gaps in the flower petals.

More pollen is transferred onto their moderately hairy thorax and head compared to small bees. Mining bees, therefore, are likely one of the most effective pollinators of large-flowered bellwort. Any remaining pollen that cannot be combed off is transferred to a receptive stigma on another bellwort plant.

Male mining bees look for mates as females visit the flower for nest provisions (above).

ANT-DISPERSED SEEDS

Large-flowered bellwort seeds are dispersed by ants. They are attracted to the fleshy, caterpillar-like elaiosome attached to the seeds. Ants crawl inside the flowers to feed on nectar. *See bloodroot, p. 165.*

DOWNY YELLOW VIOLET ~ *Viola pubescens*

FLOWERING PERIOD

HABITAT

RANGE

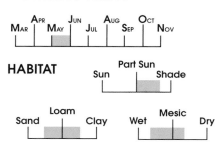

HEIGHT 8 - 16" tall

FLOWER	**LEAF**
Yellow	Basal Rosette
5-Parted	Cordate
Side Petals: Bearded	Long Stalked
Lower Petal: Purple Lines	Stem: Alternate

FRUIT	**ROOT**
Oval Capsule	Rhizome
3 Segments	

PLANT NOTES
Downy yellow violets are wonderful plants for any moist woodland. In richer soils, plants re-seed and form clusters. Use intermixed with other low-growing woodland plants such as wild ginger, or massed under trees on the edge of plantings.

COMPLEMENTARY PLANTS
Wild Ginger	Bishop's Cap
Rue Anemone	Wild Geranium

INSECT NOTES
Nectar is secreted from a gland-like spur on the bottom anthers which are short-ened and form a ring around the ovary. The style is pushed upward as a bee probes for nectar, releasing pollen onto the head and thorax of the bee.

PLANT - INSECT INTERACTIONS

Small Carpenter Bees, *Ceratina* spp.

Sweat Bees, *Lasioglossum* spp.

FEEDING POSITIONS

There are two common feeding positions of visitors to violet flowers: the prone, (right-side up), and supine, (upside-down) positions. Both positions result in the style being pushed upward. When the cone formed by the stamens is opened, pollen releases onto the visitor.

When a prone (right-side up) bee inserts its head into the flower, the style is pushed upward and pollen is released onto the top of the bee's head and thorax. In the supine (upside-down) position, bees land on the front petal and turn themselves upside down. The style is pushed upward and pollen is released on the face and lower abdomen of the visiting bee.

PRONE

SUPINE

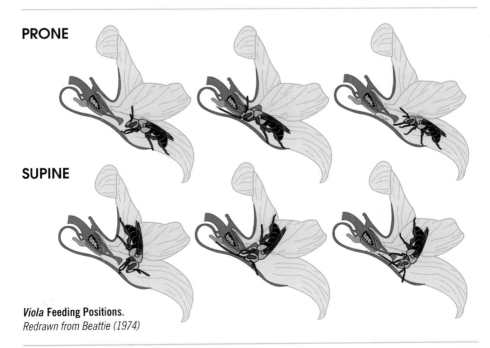

***Viola* Feeding Positions.**
Redrawn from Beattie (1974)

CHAPTER SIX
Native Plant - Insect Interactions
WETLAND EDGE

CANADA ANEMONE ~ *Anemone canadensis*

FLOWERING PERIOD

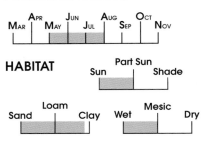

Mar Apr May Jun Jul Aug Sep Oct Nov

HABITAT

Sun Part Sun Shade

Sand Loam Clay Wet Mesic Dry

RANGE

HEIGHT 8 - 30" tall

FLOWER
5-Parted
White, 1 - 1.5" Wide
Numerous Stamens

LEAF
Basal: Stalked
Palmately Divided
3 - 5 Lobes
Stem: Stalkless,
    Opposite

FRUIT
Achene
Flattened

ROOT
Rhizome

PLANT NOTES
Common on sandy lake shores with moist soil, Canada anemone is an excellent plant to use for lakescaping projects or in areas where the soil remains moist. It can spread quickly in humus-rich soils so it is best not to plant Canada anemone in small areas where it could spread to undesirable locations.

COMPLEMENTARY PLANTS
Golden Ragwort   Blue Lobelia
Wingstem   Swamp Milkweed

INSECT NOTES
With no nectar offered, Canada anemone puts all its resources toward pollen production to attract pollinators. The flowers attract many types of bees, beetles and flies that feed on or collect pollen. The flowers are self-incompatible requiring cross-pollination by pollinators.

PLANT - INSECT INTERACTIONS

Mining Bees, *Andrena* spp.

Small Carpenter Bees, *Ceratina* spp.

Small Sweat Bees, *Lasioglossum* spp.

Green Sweat Bees, *Agapostemon* spp. *left*
Leafcutter Bees, *Megachile* spp. *right*

POLLINATOR PROFILE

Yellow-Faced Bees
Hylaeus spp.

Yellow-faced bees are one of the easier bees to identify because of their small size and distinctive coloring. They have black bodies and yellow (sometimes white) markings on the face, thorax and legs.

Females construct nests in hollow stems or preexisting cavities in wood and occasionally in old ground nests of other bees. The brood cells are lined with a silk-like substance that is secreted from salivary glands and spread around the brood cell with their tongues. The lining provides water proofing.

These bees have no pollen collecting structures; instead, female bees collect pollen (and nectar) from flowers and store it in their crop. These ingredients are regurgitated and combined to create provisions for developing larvae. The provisions are runny compared to the dry, cake-like bee bread that many other solitary bees create. Eggs are laid on top of the liquid.

Pollinators of Native Plants

CANADA ANEMONE ~ *Anemone canadensis*

POLLINATOR PROFILE

Fruitworm Beetle
Byturus unicolor

The adult fruitworm beetle feeds on pollen from plants flowering in early spring such as Canada anemone and wild geranium.

Long, dense hairs covering the elytra of this beetle collect pollen grains. Adults emerge from the soil in early spring, feed on host plants (raspberries, blackberries and avens), mate, then lay eggs. Larvae burrow into the flower buds and fruit of the host plants. Buds drop off or decay, or the fruit becomes misshapen and wormy.

PLANT - INSECT INTERACTIONS

Long-Horned Beetles

Long-horned beetles visit Canada anemone flowers to feed on pollen.

Analeptura lineola *left*

The larvae of this beetle are wood-boring and feed on trees including birch, *Betula* sp., ironwood, *Ostrya* sp., and pine, *Pinus* sp.

Anoplodera pubera *right*

Also wood-boring, the larvae of this beetle feed on elm, *Ulmus* spp., walnut and butternut, *Juglans* spp. and pine, *Pinus* spp.

Tumbling Flower Beetles, *Mordella* spp. *left*
Tumbling flower beetles feed on pollen grains that have dropped onto the petals. When disturbed, they fly away or tumble downward.

Long-Horned Beetles, *Euderces* spp. *right*
These small, long-horned beetles resemble ants in their coloration and shape. They visit a variety of flowers including white-flowering shrubs like *Viburnum* spp., in the spring.

PLANT - INSECT INTERACTIONS

Syrphid Flies, *Tropidia* spp. *left*
These flies are common near fresh water where their larvae develop in decomposing plant material and dung. They feed on pollen and are frequent visitors of Canada anemone. A wasp-like characteristic of this fly is the enlarged rear femur.

Syrphid Flies, *Chrysogaster* spp. *right*
These shiny blue flies with large red eyes visit Canada anemone to feed on pollen. Larvae develop in water; they have a modified breathing tube that pierces through aquatic plants for an air supply.

Crab Spiders, Family Thomisidae *left*
An unlucky syrphid fly, *Chrysogaster* sp., has been caught by this crab spider that was hiding camouflaged on the flowers. *See profile p. 171.*

Katydids, Family Tettigoniidae *right*
Katydids feed on the flower petals and foliage of Canada anemone.

FLOWER DEVELOPMENT

Each flower has five white sepals. A domed receptacle in the center is comprised of several spirals of stamens and many single-ovuled pistils. When the flower first opens, the longest filaments' anthers begin to dehisce on the outer edge of the receptacle. For the next four to five days, anthers continue to dehisce progressively toward the center of the receptacle. During the first two or three days of flower opening, the sepals close at night to protect the dehiscing anthers from shedding pollen if it rains. The stamens follow this sepal opening and closing pattern by bending inward over the pistils when the flower closes, then reflexing or bending outward as the sepals open.

When the flowers first open the styles are held straight. The styles begin to reflex toward the center and become receptive as the anthers begin to dehisce. As flowering progresses, the styles bend outward away from the center of the flower. This long female phase is believed to increase the likelihood of pollination, especially during unseasonable weather. The long male phase increases the odds of pollen transfer by insects.

SWAMP MILKWEED ~ *Asclepias incarnata*

FLOWERING PERIOD

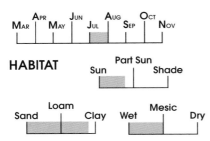

HABITAT

RANGE

HEIGHT 36 - 60" tall

FLOWER	**LEAF**
Light - Dark Pink	Linear
5-Parted with	Hairless
Horn, Hoods Above	Opposite
Petals Below	Pointed

ROOT	**FRUIT**
Fibrous	Seed, White Hairs
	Upright Pods

PLANT NOTES

The flowers of swamp milkweed have a strong, vanilla-like odor. Use on the edge of moist sites where this fragrance can be appreciated. Swamp milkweed is a good candidate for rain gardens, shoreline plantings or any low-lying, moist sunny area. It is an important nectar and larval host plant for the monarch butterfly.

COMPLEMENTARY PLANTS

Common Ironweed	Michigan Lily
Fringed Loosestrife	Cardinal Flower

INSECT NOTES

Swamp milkweed provides only nectar to visiting insects. Pollen is packaged into polliniae (see p. 187). Flowers are visited by a diverse range of insects including bees, wasps, ants, flies, butterflies, moths, beetles and bugs.

PLANT - INSECT INTERACTIONS

LARVAL HOST PLANT

Monarch Butterfly, *Danaus plexippus*
Queen Butterfly, *Danaus gilippus*

Monarch Butterfly, *Danaus plexippus*

Milkweeds, *Asclepias* spp., are the only larval host plant for the monarch butterfly. Plant milkweed species to provide food sources for both larvae (leaves) and adults (nectar). Adult female butterflies lay eggs on the underside of leaves in mid-summer (above right).

Larvae hatch and feed on the new growth of milkweed leaves until pupation. Look for frass (droppings) on the leaves as a sign of larval feeding, or investigate for caterpillars by turning over the leaves. Caterpillars undergo five growth stages (**instars**), molting their outer skin at each stage. Fifth instar caterpillars are approximately two inches (five centimeters) long. When ready to pupate, they crawl to a sheltered spot nearby.

Swamp milkweed and common milkweed (*Asclepias syriaca*) are preferred host plants of monarch butterfly caterpillars. Even though monarch caterpillars sequester toxic compounds from consuming milkweed, they are still predated on and parasitized by birds and insects including soldier bugs, tachinid flies and paper and parasitic wasps.

BUTTERFLIES & MOTHS

Swamp milkweed is an excellent late season butterfly and moth plant, providing an abundant amount of nectar. Look for small skippers, monarchs, fritillaries, red admirals, sulphurs, whites, swallowtails and crescents on the flowers.

Great Spangled Fritillary *left*
Speyeria cybele
Red Admiral Butterfly *right*
Vanessa atalanta

Butterflies alight on top of the flowers probing for nectar with their long proboscis. Their legs may slip into the stigmatic chambers and pull out a pollinarium but bees and wasps are primarily responsible for the transfer of pollen. Butterflies and moths are secondary, less effective pollinators of milkweed plants.

Hummingbird Clearwing Moth
Hemaris spp. *left*
Skipper Butterflies *right*
Family Hesperiidae

SWAMP MILKWEED ~ *Asclepias incarnata*

PREDATOR PROFILE

Great Black Wasp
Sphex pensylvanicus

The great black wasp visits swamp milkweed for nectar. This wasp is also a frequent visitor of spotted bee balm, *Monarda punctata (p. 98)*. Females select a sheltered location to construct solitary ground nests in loose soils. The burrows are dug on an angle with several individual cells. Cells are provisioned with two to six grasshoppers or katydids over the course of one to ten days. After cell provisioning is complete, an egg is laid and the cell is closed. The wasp larva hatches, feeds and eventually pupates, then emerges as an adult.

PLANT - INSECT INTERACTIONS

Green Bottle Flies, *Lucilia* spp. *left*
Tachinid Flies, *Archytas* spp. *right*

Bee Flies, *Bombylius* spp. *left*
These hovering bee flies rarely land on milkweed flowers and therefore do not pick up any pollinia sacs on their legs.

Bee Flies, *Villa* spp. *right*
These flies land and forage for nectar on the flowers rather than hovering. They are parasitoids of bees and wasps. Larvae feed on hosts internally.

Syrphid Flies
Tropidia spp.

The unusual large rear femurs on these syrphid flies are distinctive providing them with a wasp-like appearance. They visit a variety of flowers in the summer months to feed on nectar and pollen. *See profile p. 181.*

PLANT - INSECT INTERACTIONS

HONEY BEES

Yellowjacket Wasps, *Vespula* spp. *left*
Yellowjacket wasps are late-summer visitors of the flowers for nectar. *See profile p. 124.*
Paper Wasp, *Polistes fuscatus* *right*

Great Golden Digger Wasp
Sphex ichneumoneus
A regular visitor of swamp milkweed for nectar, this wasp also visits plants flowering at the same time including purple prairie clover, *Dalea purpurea*; spotted bee balm, *Monarda punctata*; and rattlesnake master, *Eryngium yuccifolium*.
See profile p. 232.

Nest Excavation *left*
Katydid Prey Carried To Nest *right*

PREDATOR PROFILE

Square-Headed Wasps
***Tachytes* spp.**
Square-headed wasps patrol areas where there are sources of nectar or prey. They land on foliage to watch for prey. Males also patrol mating territories close to nest entrances where females emerge.

These solitary wasps are ground-nesting, using abandoned burrows created by other wasps or ants. If females do any excavation of the nest burrow, they loosen soil with their mandibles and forelegs. Small soil pellets are picked up, held between their mouthparts and forelegs, then carried backward and dropped away from the nest entrance.

Females hunt and provision their nests with grasshoppers, crickets and occasionally mantids; grasshoppers are the most common prey. The prey is grasped with their mandibles and carried underneath the abdomen as they fly back to the nest. Cells within the burrow are cached with prey then eggs are laid.

SWAMP MILKWEED ~ *Asclepias incarnata*

MONARCH APOSEMATISM

Milkweed Leaf Beetle
Labidomera clivicollis

When monarch caterpillars consume the foliage of milkweed plants, they build up toxic compounds in their systems including alkaloids and latex. The bright coloring of both caterpillars and adults signal to birds that they are unpalatable, an adaptation known as aposematism. Other insects besides the milkweed beetles (pictured above and below) feed on the leaves, roots and seeds of milkweed plants. Many insects such as milkweed bugs, have coloring similar to the black and orange patterning of adult monarchs.

Red Milkweed Beetles
Tetraopes spp.

Adults interrupt the flow of latex by chewing the leaf midrib to release sap, then feed on the leaves beyond the cut. The larvae of this beetle feed on the roots of milkweed plants.

PLANT - INSECT INTERACTIONS

Soldier Beetles, *Chauliognathus* spp. *left*

Soldier beetles feed on the nectar of swamp milkweed flowers and are common on many late-summer flowering native plants, especially goldenrod. Considered a beneficial insect, some adults and many larvae in this beetle family (Cantharidae) feed on aphids. *See profile p. 96.*

Banded Long-Horned Beetles *right*
Typocerus spp.

Both this long-horned beetle and the soldier beetle above have a narrow thorax and head allowing them access to nectar at the bottom of the hood of milkweed flowers.

Long-Horned Beetles, *Euderces* spp. *left*
Trigonarthris spp. *right*

The larvae of this beetle typically feed on moist or rotting dead wood. Adults are active from May through August visiting a variety of flowers to feed on pollen or nectar.

PLANT - INSECT INTERACTIONS

Yellow-Faced Bees, *Hylaeus* spp. *left*
Swamp milkweed is a preferred nectar plant of yellow-faced bees.

Bumble Bees, *Bombus* spp. *right*
Bumble bees are effective pollinators frequently transferring pollinia sacs from one milkweed plant to the next. They also show a preference for foraging on milkweed, limiting visits to neighboring species also in flower.

Sweat Bees, *Lasioglossum* spp. *left*
Green Sweat Bees, Augochloropsis *right*

Small Resin Bees, *Heriades* spp. *left*
Leafcutter Bees, *Megachile* spp. *right*

POLLEN TRANSFER

Pollinia Stuck to Wasp Legs

Milkweeds, *Asclepias* spp., have an unusual method of transferring pollen from one plant to the next. Pollen is aggregated in sac-like bundles called pollinia, located on either side of the stigmatic chamber. Two bundles are strung together with translator arms and a corpusculum at the top.

When insects seek out nectar in one of the five stigmatic chambers, they risk slipping their leg into the flower and thus removing the sacs when pulling their leg out. The sticky pollinia sacs are carried to other milkweed plants on their legs and, if the insect slips again, a pollinia sac can be inserted into the stigmatic chamber. One successful visit transfers a large amount of pollen and ensures pollination of the flower.

Honey Bee
Apis mellifera
Small- and medium-sized bees can perish when tangled and immobilized by the pollinia.

MARSH MARIGOLD ~ *Caltha palustris*

FLOWERING PERIOD

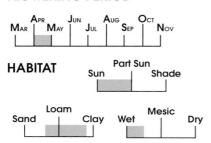

HABITAT

RANGE

HEIGHT 8 - 24" tall

FLOWER	**LEAF**
Yellow Sepals	Cordate
5- to 9-Parted	Palmately Veined
Ring of Stamens	Basal: Long Stalked
Center: Many Pistils	Stem: Alternate

FRUIT	**ROOT**
Seed	Crown, Fibrous

PLANT NOTES
Marsh marigold is a compact, robust plant with bright yellow flowers. This is one of the first wetland plants to flower in the spring. Site marsh marigold where there is ample organic matter and the soil remains moist throughout the summer. Use in rain gardens, ditches or along pond edges.

COMPLEMENTARY PLANTS
Skunk Cabbage	Cardinal Flower
Wild Calla Lily	Touch-Me-Not

INSECT NOTES
Nectar is secreted at the base of the pistils. Anthers on the outer edge of the spiral dehisce first, followed by anthers on the inside, closer to the pistils. The stigmas mature last. Small- and medium-sized bees including mining bees, sweat bees and green sweat bees visit the flowers for nectar and pollen. As the flowers fade, the outer edges of the sepals turn white indicating to pollinators that rewards are no longer offered.

PLANT - INSECT INTERACTIONS

Ants, Family Formicidae *left*
Ants crawl through the dense whorl of stamens to access nectar at the base of the ovary. Both large and small ant species are common on marsh marigold flowers in early spring when other sources of nectar are scarce.

Cuckoo Bees, *Nomada* spp. *right*
Cuckoo bees visit the flowers for nectar only. With no nests to provision (they lay their eggs in ground-nesting bee nests), they have no need to collect pollen.

FLORAL ATTRACTANTS

The flowers of marsh marigold are well equipped to attract pollinators both visually and by scent. Not only does this plant have the advantage of flowering in early spring with less competition from other flowering plants but the flowers also have some unusual visual characteristics to draw pollinators.

Two types of cellular structures are present in the sepals: first, the outer portion of the sepal has a reflective starch layer and a well-defined cuticle. Second, the center of the flower, including the inner part of the sepals, absorbs ultraviolet light and therefore appears darker to pollinators than the outer sepals. The cells in the top portion of the sepals contain flavonols which absorb ultraviolet light. The bright yellow color of marsh marigold flowers visible to humans appears purple to bees.

The pistil clefts secrete small drops of nectar and emit a strong scent.

SYRPHID FLY FAVORITE

The most common and abundant visitors of marsh marigolds are syrphid flies. They use their sponge-like mouthparts to feed on pollen from the numerous anthers. Propping themselves on top of the stamens while feeding, they often get coated in pollen.

Syrphid Flies, *Neoascia* spp.

Syrphid Flies, *Xylota* spp.

Syrphid Flies, *Lejops* spp.

WHITE TURTLEHEAD ~ *Chelone glabra*

FLOWERING PERIOD

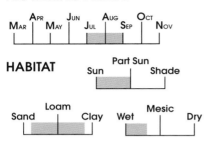

HABITAT

RANGE

HEIGHT 24 - 48" tall

FLOWER	**LEAF**
White - Light Pink	Linear
5-Parted, Spike	Opposite
Upper Lip: 2 Lobes	Hairless
Lower Lip: 3 Lobes	Toothed

FRUIT	**ROOT**
Seed Capsule	Taproot
Flattened, Winged	Rhizome

PLANT NOTES

The long, dark green linear leaves of white turtlehead set off the dense spike of flowers. Plant where soils are moist throughout the summer months, not just seasonably wet in the spring. A low-lying spot in a rain garden or bioswale is a good site for this native plant.

COMPLEMENTARY PLANTS

Common Ironweed   Blue Lobelia
Cardinal Flower   Wingstem

INSECT NOTES

Worker bumble bees and hummingbirds are the most frequent visitors. Bees must push their way into the flower by forcing open the upper and lower lips to access nectar. Nectar is secreted around the base of the ovary rewarding pollinators strong enough to open the flower.

PLANT - INSECT INTERACTIONS

LARVAL HOST PLANT   Baltimore Checkerspot Butterfly, *Euphydryas phaeton*

Two-Spotted Long-Horned Bee, *Melissodes bimaculata*
This long-horned bee is medium-sized and strong enough to pry open the flower lobes to enter down the side. Each visit lasts for around a minute. Turning around in the flower the bee reemerges head first.

Bumble Bees, *Bombus spp.*

Bumble bees are the primary visitors of white turtlehead flowers. A typical visit to the flower to access nectar averages thirty seconds. A large amount of energy is expended to pry open the flower and climb inside. The reward is high, however, as only bumble bees and the occasional medium-sized bee can gain access to the flowers. With lower visitation rates, high nectar rewards and on average over three milligrams of sugar produced daily, the bees' efforts are worthwhile.

As a bumble bee enters a flower, the hairy bristles on the lower lip hold the bee higher in the flower corolla where the anthers and stigmas are located. Pollen collects on the upper abdomen and thorax. When stigmas become receptive, the style has elongated, curving downward from the top of the flower. As a bee with a pollen-laden thorax enters, pollen is transferred to the receptive stigma.

CANADA TICK TREFOIL ~ *Desmodium canadense*

FLOWERING PERIOD

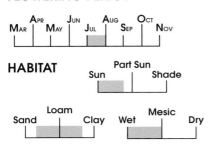

HABITAT

RANGE

HEIGHT 36 - 60" tall

FLOWER	**LEAF**
Pink - Purple	Lanceolate
5-Parted, Carinate	3 Leaflets
Branched Panicle	Stalked, Sheaths

FRUIT	**ROOT**
Segmented Pod	Taproot
Hooked Hairs	Nitrogen-Fixing
	Nodules

PLANT NOTES

This tall, perennial legume has large, branching flower heads and soft-textured foliage. Although it typically grows in moist soils, it can be planted in mesic soils where plants do not grow as tall. The segmented pods are covered in hooked hairs and attach to clothing.
Note: The introduced Japanese beetle, *Popillia japonica*, feeds on the foliage.

COMPLEMENTARY PLANTS

Fragrant Hyssop	Wild Bergamot
Canada Milk Vetch	Little Bluestem

INSECT NOTES

The large upper standard unfolds revealing dark pink nectar guides that act as a visual attractant to pollinators. Medium to large-sized bees trip (activate) the flowers by pressing down the keel while probing for nectar. Small bees and flies feed on floral resources on activated flowers.

PLANT - INSECT INTERACTIONS

LARVAL HOST PLANT   Northern Cloudywing Butterfly, *Thorybes pylades;*
Southern Cloudywing Butterfly, *Thorybes bathyllus;* Hoary Edge, *Achalarus lyciades*

| Unactivated Flower | Keel Depressed | Pollen Ejected | Activated Flower |

Leafcutter Bees, *Megachile* spp.

Large leafcutter bees are regular visitors of Canada tick trefoil. They are one of the bees responsible for tripping (activating) the flowers. As the keel is pressed downward, the column enclosing the stamens and style held under tension rises upward ejecting pollen onto the bee.

The scopae (pollen collecting hairs) on the abdomens of leafcutter bees get coated with pollen and later come into contact with receptive stigmas of the next Canada tick trefoil flowers visited. Once the flower keel has been depressed and activated, the keel remains in the lowered position. Small bees and flies, such as sweat bees and syrphid flies (below), feed on pollen from anthers exposed from activated flowers.

Leafcutter bees also cut pieces of leaves from Canada tick trefoil plants for nest construction.

Sweat Bees, *Lasioglossum* spp. *left*
Small Resin Bees, *Heriades* spp. *right*

Syrphid Flies
***Toxomerus* spp.**
Syrphid flies feed on pollen exposed on activated flowers.

Bumble Bees, *Bombus* spp. *left*
Long-Horned Bees, *Melissodes* spp.
Large bees activate the flowers when foraging for nectar. Flowers fade to a light purple once they have been activated which is a visual cue to pollinators that floral resources have been depleted.

Pollinators of Native Plants

COMMON BONESET ~ *Eupatorium perfoliatum*

FLOWERING PERIOD

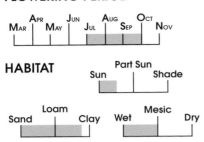

HABITAT

RANGE

HEIGHT 24 - 60" tall

FLOWER	**LEAF**
White	Lanceolate
5 Lobes	Opposite, Clasping
~15 Florets	Toothed
Branched Cluster	Stem: White Hairs

FRUIT	**ROOT**
Achene	Fibrous
Hair Tufts	Rhizome

PLANT NOTES

Common boneset has an upright form with arching, opposite leaves and a soft-textured appearance from the hairy stems. The flowers open from the center of the cluster outward providing a long season of interest and floral resources for pollinators. Plant where the soil remains moist throughout the summer months.

COMPLEMENTARY PLANTS

Swamp Milkweed   Ironweed

INSECT NOTES

Anthers release pollen in a closed cylinder surrounding the style. As the style elongates, tiny hairs collect the pollen and push it up through the cylinder making it available to pollinators. Wasps are frequent visitors to feed on nectar which is secreted at the base of the style.

PLANT - INSECT INTERACTIONS

HONEY BEES

LARVAL HOST PLANT

Clymene Moth, *Haploa clymene*
Three-Lined Flower Moth, *Schinia trifascia*
Boneset Borer Moth, *Carmenta pyralidiformis*

Yellow-Faced Bees, *Hylaeus* spp. *left*
Yellow-faced bees visit common boneset flowers for nectar. *See profile p. 179.*

Mining Bees, *Andrena* spp. *right*
Mining bees are common in the fall, visiting flowers for nectar and pollen. Many are specialists of goldenrod and aster species.

Sweat Bees, *Lasioglossum* spp.

Bumble Bees, *Bombus* spp. *left*
Bumble bees visit common boneset for nectar.
Green Sweat Bees, *Agapostemon* spp. *right*

PREDATOR PROFILE

Assassin Bugs, *Zelus* spp.
Looking for prey on flowers and foliage, these bugs are common in late summer and fall. They have long mouthparts (beaks) tucked under their abdomen and sheathed in a special groove. Slinging their mouthparts forward, they impale their prey, including boll weevils, leafhoppers, butterfly and moth caterpillars, wasps or flies.

From glands on their forelegs, these bugs secrete a sticky substance that is smeared on foreleg hairs. These glands develop when the nymphs reach the second instar. The sticky substance is used to attract and trap prey so it can be easily impaled.

Assassin bugs in this genus have been used as an effective beneficial insect (biological control agent) in several commercial crops including cotton, soybean and alfalfa. These bugs help reduce population outbreaks of butterfly and moth caterpillars that are destructive feeders on the crops.

COMMON BONESET ~ *Eupatorium perfoliatum*

PREDATOR PROFILE

Four-banded Sand Wasp, *Bicyrtes quadrifasciatus*

Sand wasps visit common boneset for nectar. Females build single or multicelled nests in sandy soil. They employ an interesting nest excavation technique: appearing to bob their head up and down at the nest entrance, they use the spines on their forelegs to rake away the soil that has been excavated from the nest burrow.

Nests are provisioned with true bug nymphs and adults from the large suborder Heteroptera. Unlike their close relatives in the *Bembix* genus that progressively-provision their nest cells, *Bicyrtes* mass-provision their nest cells. Females collect a sufficient amount of bugs, place them in the nest cell, lay an egg on the first bug placed in the cell, then seal off the nest.

PLANT - INSECT INTERACTIONS

Paper Wasp, *Polistes fuscatus*

Paper wasps build open-celled, single comb paper nests under protected horizontal surfaces such as a large tree branch or house soffit. Overwintered, reproductive females initiate nest construction in the spring. Like bumble bees, the eusocial nest produces female offspring (workers) to help with foraging, nest provisioning and brood care. Paper wasps prey on caterpillars and beetle larvae; they dismember and pre-chew the prey then feed pieces of the chewed prey to the larvae. Paper wasps are used as a biological control agent for tobacco hornworms in agricultural fields. They are common visitors to plants throughout the summer months. Mated females (reproductives) overwinter and construct new paper nests in the spring.

Bald-Faced Hornet, *Dolichovespula maculata*

Bald-faced hornets are predators of other insects including robber flies. Similar to paper wasps, they feed chewed insects to their larvae. These hornets construct large, conical, paper nests in trees.

PLANT - INSECT INTERACTIONS

Humped-backed Beewolf,
Philanthus gibbosus

Beewolves are wasps that prey on bees which the stock in their nests to feed their larvae. Females excavate solitary nests in the ground, capture and paralyze their prey (often sweat bees), then fly back to the nest carrying it underneath them. The wasp larvae develop and feed on bees. Beewolves visit common boneset flowers for nectar and prey.

Beetle Wasps, *Cerceris* spp. *left*
See profile p. 79.

Potter Wasp, *Eumenes fraternus* *right*
Potter wasps are predators of caterpillars (moth larvae). This potter wasps constructs jug-shaped mud nests attached to plants or structures. The female collects water and mud, combines the two to make mud, then carries clumps of mud clasped in her mandibles back to the nest. Many clumps are required to complete the construction of the nest.

PREDATOR PROFILE

Grass-Carrying Wasp
Isodontia mexicana

Grass-carrying wasps are predators of crickets and katydids. Females sting their prey in the head or thorax which causes paralysis. Females carry the immobile prey back to their nests in cavities in hollow stems, holes bored in wood or openings in rocks. Prey, once stocked in the nests, are food for the developing wasp larvae.

Females collect grass blades carrying strands clasped in their mandibles. They use these blades to divide their nesting cavity into sections or to close the cavity. Grass-carrying wasps often build their nests in bee boards. Look for grass blades stuffed into the ends of the board holes. These wasps feed on nectar of common boneset.

Pollinators of Native Plants

COMMON BONESET ~ *Eupatorium perfoliatum*

PARASITOID PROFILE

Thynnid Wasps, *Myzinum* spp.
Thynnid wasps visit common boneset for nectar. Males have a menacing-looking, curved pseudostinger on the end of their abdomen. Instead of constructing nests, females search for scarab beetle larvae in the ground. When a host is located, they burrow into the ground and lay one egg on the host.

When the wasp larva hatches, it burrows into the host and begins feeding on non-essential tissue first. As the larva grows and develops, it feeds on the internal organs of the host, eventually killing it. Remaining in the soil to pupate, adult wasps emerge the following summer to repeat the life cycle. Look for thynnid wasps nectaring on plants in midsummer including rattlesnake master, *Eryngium yuccifolium* p. 76.

Soldier Beetles
Chauliognathus spp.

PLANT - INSECT INTERACTIONS
PARASITOID PROFILE

Cuckoo Wasps, *Hedychrum* spp.
Shiny and hairless, these wasps are metallic green or blue in color. Cuckoo wasps resemble green sweat bees (Augochlorini tribe). When not visiting flowers for nectar, these wasps investigate the nests of their prey—cavity-nesting bees and wasps. Females lay eggs through a tube-like ovipositor but their sting is greatly reduced in size and ineffective.

Entering the nest of prey can be risky. The one defense mechanism that these wasps employ is to curl into a ball. The cuckoo wasp lays an egg on the host's larva and the wasp larva waits to begin feeding on its host until after the host larva has finished the provisions and started to pupate.

Thread-Waisted Wasp
Eremnophila aureonotata
Predators of moth and butterfly caterpillars, this wasp stings and paralyzes prey but does not sting humans. Look for this wasp visiting flowers near deciduous woodlands in mid-summer.

198

PLANT - INSECT INTERACTIONS

HONEY BEES

Tachinid Flies, *Gymnoclytia* spp. *left*
Parasitoids of adult stink bugs in the family Pentatomidae, tachinid fly females often find their hosts by smell. They lay an egg on the host. The fly larva hatches and burrows into the host feeding internally until eventually the host dies.

Tachinid Flies, *Archytas* spp. *right*
These tachinid flies parasitize moth and butterfly caterpillars.

Syrphid Flies, *Eristalis spp.* *left*
Helophilus spp. *right*

Thick-Headed Flies, *Physocephala* spp. *left*
See profile p. 233.
Bee Flies, *Villa* spp. *right* *See profile p. 119.*

Virginia Creeper Clearwing Moth, *Albuna fraxini*
Many clearwing moths are considered wasp mimics, a survival strategy to avoid predation. As the common name suggests, the larvae of this moth bore into the roots of Virginia creeper, *Parthenocissus quinquefolia*. This moth's range includes the upper Midwest and Northeast states, from Minnesota eastward to New York.

Monarch Butterfly
Danaus plexippus
Monarchs occasionally visit common boneset for nectar.

SPOTTED JOE PYE WEED ~ *Eutrochium maculatum*

FLOWERING PERIOD

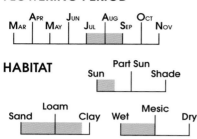

| Mar | Apr May | Jun Jul | Aug Sep | Oct Nov |

HABITAT

Sun | Part Sun | Shade

Sand | Loam | Clay | Wet | Mesic | Dry

RANGE

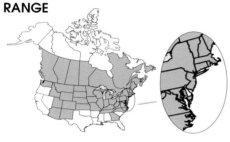

HEIGHT 4 - 10' tall

FLOWER	LEAF
Light - Dark Pink	Whorled,
Disc Florets	Groups of 4 - 5
Tubular, 5 Lobes	Sharply Toothed
Branched Cluster	Short Stalked
Large Flower heads	Stem: Purple Dots

FRUIT	ROOT
Achene, Hair Tufts	Fibrous

PLANT NOTES

Spotted joe pye weed is an extremely colorful and bold native plant. Its large flower heads, tall stature and whorled leaves provide an excellent visual attractant for pollinators. The closely related sweet joe pye weed, *Eutrochium purpureum,* does not have spotted stems and is more tolerant of partial-shade and drier conditions.

COMPLEMENTARY PLANTS

Ironweed	Swamp Milkweed
White Turtlehead	Culver's Root

INSECT NOTES

The numerous tiny disc florets on the large flower heads offer a large quantity of nectar to visiting pollinators. Nectar is secreted at the base of the style. Only a few bees such as bumble bees and long-horned bees collect pollen; most visits by pollinators are for nectar. Sand and thread-waisted wasps, flies and moths are occasional visitors.

PLANT - INSECT INTERACTIONS

 HONEY BEES

LARVAL HOST PLANT

Three-Lined Flower Moth, *Schinia trifascia*
Ruby Tiger Moth, *Phragmatobia fuliginosa*

Azure Butterflies, *Celastrina* spp. *left*
Silver Spotted Skipper Butterfly *right*
Epargyreus clarus

White Admiral Butterfly *left*
Limenitis arthemis arthemis
Milbert's Tortoiseshell Butterfly *right*
Nymphalis urticae

Eastern Tiger Swallowtail Butterfly *left*
Papilio glaucus
Monarch Butterfly, *Danaus plexippus* *right*

POLLINATOR PROFILE

Rusty Patched Bumble Bee
Bombus affinis

The rusty patched bumble bee is listed as a threatened species by the Xerces Society. It was once commonly seen in the upper Midwest and Northeast region of America (also southern Ontario). Since 2000 the population has been in decline.

The rusty patched bumble bee has an orange to rust-colored patch in the middle of the second abdominal segment with yellow hairs surrounding the patch. This bumble bee may visit spotted joe pye weed, wild bergamot and culver's root. Observations should be reported to Bumble Bee Watch.
www.bumblebeewatch.org

Cuckoo Bees, *Coelioxys* spp.
Leafcutter Bees *right*
***Megachile* spp.**
These cuckoo bees and their hosts, leafcutter bees, visit spotted joe pye weed for nectar.

BOTTLE GENTIAN ~ *Gentiana andrewsii*

FLOWERING PERIOD

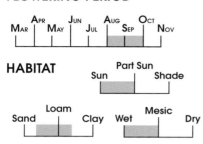

HABITAT

RANGE

HEIGHT 12 - 30" tall

FLOWER	**LEAF**
White - Violet	Lanceolate
5 Lobes	Stalkless
Terminal,	Stem: Opposite
Leaf Axils	Top: Whorled

FRUIT	**ROOT**
Small Seed	Shallow Taproot

PLANT NOTES
Bottle gentian can be one of the last plants to finish flowering in the fall often blooming into mid-October. Found along wetland edges in moist soils, this plant performs best where it does not compete with tall grasses or sedges. Flower color can vary from white to violet but is typically medium blue.

COMPLEMENTARY PLANTS
New England Aster   Sneezeweed
Riddell's Goldenrod

INSECT NOTES
Bottle gentian is pollinated by bumble bees, the only observed insect capable of forcing open the pleated corolla lobes. They climb into the flower to collect pollen and feed on nectar. Nectar is secreted at the base of the ovary. Shorter-tongued bumble bees chew holes near the nectaries to steal nectar. Blister beetles feed on the flowers.

PLANT - INSECT INTERACTIONS

BUMBLE BEE FORAGING BEHAVIOR

The flowers are visited by bumble bees, the primary pollinator of bottle gentian. Landing on top of the flower, bumble bees pry open the pleated lobes with their forelegs and head then crawl inside with their wings facing the outside of the flower (A,B). The pleated lobes close around the bumble bee as their abdomen enters the flower. Making their way down the corolla, they collect pollen by scraping it from the anthers with their legs. Pollen falls onto their sternum as they are positioned upside down. After collecting pollen, they either back out or turn themselves around inside the flower, still facing inward. Crawling back up the corolla they emerge head first (C,D,E). Pollen not combed off is transferred from their sternum to a receptive stigma in the next bottle gentian flower.

Each pollen-collecting visit can last anywhere between two and ten seconds on average; in the sequence of images above, the visit lasted close to a minute. Nectar, not the primary attractant for bumble bees, is offered but is low in sugar concentration. Small worker bumble bees steal nectar through holes (perforations) made at the base of the corolla. The pleated flower lobes remain closed preventing access by flies or small bees.

FLOWER DEVELOPMENT

Bottle gentian flowers are self-compatible although a very low fruit set has been observed (Costelloe, 1988). The flowers are protandrous with anthers dehiscing before the stigma becomes receptive. Filaments are attached to the corolla wall and curve inward toward the middle of the flower. After anthers have dehisced, the style elongates past the anthers to spatially separate the two reproductive organs and limit self-pollination. The stigma then becomes receptive. Flower clusters develop from the outside inward. Once the flower development is complete, flowers change color from blue to white or purple.

GREAT ST. JOHN'S WORT ~ *Hypericum pyramidatum*

FLOWERING PERIOD

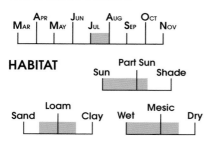

HABITAT

RANGE

HEIGHT 36 - 72" tall

FLOWER	LEAF
Soft - Bright Yellow	Lanceolate
5-Parted	Stalkless
5 Styles, Many Stamens	Often Clasping
Single Or Cymes	

FRUIT	ROOT
Seed Capsule	Rhizome
5 Cells, Many Seeds	

PLANT NOTES
A robust, shrub-like perennial with large, bold flowers (over two inches wide). It performs well in moist sites in part sun and can be used as a herbaceous hedge. The flowering period is shortened dramatically if planted in an upland, sunny, dry site.

COMPLEMENTARY PLANTS

Michigan Lily	Swamp Milkweed
Culver's Root	Tall Meadowrue

INSECT NOTES
With its numerous stamens, great St. John's wort produces a large quantity of pollen. Some insects explore for nectar but the flowers lack nectaries so all visits are for pollen. Female leafcutter bees, *Megachile* spp., cut pieces of leaves from great St. John's wort plants for lining and dividing brood cells.

PLANT - INSECT INTERACTIONS

HONEY BEES

LARVAL HOST PLANT

Black Arches Moth, *Melanchra assimilis*
Gray Half-Spot Moth, *Nedra ramosula*

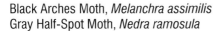

Leafcutter Bees, *Megachile* spp.
Leafcutter bees float across the top of the anthers collecting pollen on their abdomens. Females also cut pieces of the hairless leaves used for lining and dividing their brood cells in cavity nests.

Bumble Bees, *Bombus* spp.
Bumble bees visit great St. John's wort to collect pollen. They work their way across the flower pausing to gather the stamens together with their forelegs. Pollen is transferred onto their mid and hind legs, and abdomen. Bumble bees then comb the grains into their pollen baskets (corbiculae) for transport. Buzz pollination is sometimes utilized; anthers dehisce pollen longitudinally.

Green Sweat Bees, *Agapostemon* spp. *left*
Female green sweat bees collect pollen and explore the flowers for nectar.
Sweat Bees, *Lasioglossum* spp. *right*
Sweat bees feed on pollen.

Banded Long-Horned Beetles
Typocerus spp. *left*
Long-horned beetles crawl across great St. John's wort flowers and feed on pollen.
Beewolf *right*
Philanthus gibbosus
Beewolves investigate the flowers for nectar. *See profile p. 197.*

Many types of syrphid flies visit the flowers to feed on pollen and investigate for nectar.
Syrphid Flies, *Toxomerus* spp. *left*
Tropidia spp. *right See profile p. 181.*

PRAIRIE BLAZINGSTAR ~ *Liatris pycnostachya*

FLOWERING PERIOD

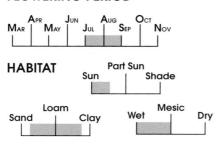

HABITAT

RANGE

HEIGHT 24 - 48" tall

FLOWER
Pink - Purple
5 Lobes
5 - 10 Disc Florets/Head
Terminal Spike
Bracts: Recurved

LEAF
Linear
Alternate
Stem: White Hairs

FRUIT
Achene, Hair Tufts

ROOT
Corm

PLANT NOTES
The tall, linear flower heads open from the top downward providing a long season of color and interest. Prairie blazingstar is found in calcareous fens and moist prairies. Site this plant in a moist location in loam or clay-loam soils for best results. Do not allow seedlings to dry out.

COMPLEMENTARY PLANTS
Swamp Milkweed   Cardinal Flower
Fringed Loosestrife   Common Boneset

INSECT NOTES
Prairie blazingstar florets are self-incompatible and require cross-pollination. Nectar is secreted from a ring at the base of the style. Pollen falls into a cylinder formed by the filaments. When the style elongates after anther dehiscence, hairs pick up the pollen and present it to pollinators. Most insect visits are for nectar although leafcutter bees often collect pollen.

PLANT - INSECT INTERACTIONS

 HONEY BEES

LARVAL HOST PLANT

Bleeding Flower Moth, *Schinia sanguinea*
Blazingstar Borer Moth, *Papaipema beeriana*

Bumble Bees, *Bombus* spp. *left*
Bumble bees primarily visit the flowers for nectar. A few species, *B. impatiens* and *B. pensylvanicus* have been observed collecting pollen. Due to their floral constancy and foraging behavior, they are considered a primary pollinator.

Leafcutter Bees, *Megachile* spp. *right*
Leafcutter bees are frequent visitors to the flowers for both pollen and nectar.

Long-Horned Bees
***Melissodes* spp.** *left*
These bees collect pollen and feed on nectar. Small carpenter bees and sweat bee also visit the flowers for nectar.

Bee Flies, *Exoprosopa* spp. *left*
Many species of bee flies visit the flowers for nectar; *Villa* sp. are regular visitors.

Syrphid Flies, *Syrphus* spp. *right*

Tiger Moth, *Grammia arge*
The bold stripes and coloring on tiger moths act as a warning to predators. This moth has a tympanum (sound-detecting organ) on its thorax that faces backward. It uses this organ to detect the sound of predators above. Larval host plants include prickly pear cactus, *Opuntia* spp., and sunflowers, *Helianthus* spp.

Monarch Butterfly
Danaus plexippus
Many butterflies visit the flowers for nectar. Look for fritillary, painted lady, swallowtail and sulphur butterflies as well as skippers.

Pollinators of Native Plants

GREAT BLUE LOBELIA ~ *Lobelia siphilitica*

FLOWERING PERIOD

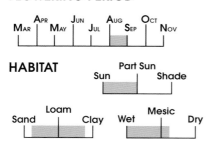

HABITAT

RANGE

HEIGHT 12 - 48" tall

FLOWER	LEAF
Blue - White	Ovate
5-Parted	Alternate
Upper Lip: 2 Lobes	Toothed
Lower Lip: 3 Lobes	Stalkless
Bilabiate, Raceme	

FRUIT	ROOT
Seed, Small	Fibrous

PLANT NOTES
One of the best attributes of this plant is the blue flower color. A short-lived perennial in dry soils, great blue lobelia reseeds in rich soils but rarely forms dense clusters. Seedlings are shallow-rooted and transplant easily.

COMPLEMENTARY PLANTS
Swamp Milkweed	White Turtlehead
Common Ironweed	Mountain Mint

INSECT NOTES
Bumble bees are the most frequent visitor and primary pollinators. Depending on how far bees enter the corolla in search of nectar, pollen is deposited on their upper head, thorax or abdomen. Nectaries are located at the base of the corolla on the ovary. Anthers develop first; pollen is released at the top of the flower.

208

PLANT - INSECT INTERACTIONS

HONEY
BEES

Digger Bee, *Anthophora terminalis*

Medium-sized digger bees can access the nectar but the effort required is greater than that of bumble bees. Using their head and tongue, they push the column holding the style and filaments upward, high enough out of the way to enter the flower corolla. Pollen is deposited on their head.

Small bees feed on pollen from the anthers. They also crawl into the flower to feed on nectar.

Yellow-Faced Bees, *Hylaeus* spp. *left*
Green Sweat Bees, Augochlorini Tribe *right*

Small Carpenter Bees, *Ceratina* spp.

Bumble Bees, *Bombus* spp.

Bumble bees are considered the primary pollinator of great blue lobelia. When landing on the flower, they push the style and filament column out of the way, turn their bodies 180 degrees and enter the flower corolla. The depth of their descent into the corolla determines the amount of pollen deposited on the top of their head, thorax and abdomen. The amount and size of the pollen deposit and their pollen-grooming efficiency determine their effectiveness at transferring pollen to the next flower's receptive stigma, resulting in cross-pollination.

Weevil
Cleopomiarus hispidulus

Common on blue lobelia flowers, this weevil feeds on the seeds.

OBEDIENT PLANT ~ *Physostegia virginiana*

FLOWERING PERIOD

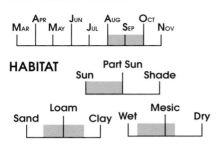

HABITAT

RANGE

HEIGHT 24 - 60" tall

FLOWER
Pink, 5-Parted
2-Lipped, Tubular
Lower Lip: 3 Lobes
Bilabiate, Raceme

LEAF
Lanceolate
Opposite, Toothed
Usually Stalkless
Square Stem

FRUIT
Brown Seed

ROOT
Central Taproot
Rhizome

PLANT NOTES
Gardeners often lament that the common name for this plant is ill-conceived because the plant rapidly spreads in the garden. With its rhizomatous root system, obedient plant is ideal for larger spaces where it can be used in a mass and allowed to interweave through other plants. A moist location in full sun is a good site such as the edge of a water body.

COMPLEMENTARY PLANTS
Swamp Milkweed   White Turtlehead
Common Ironweed   Blue Lobelia

INSECT NOTES
The majority of visitors are bees; small bees make lengthy visits to a flower head climbing in and out of each open flower. Medium-sized bumble bees whose size matches the corolla openings visit frequently but the visits are typically short. Butterflies such as monarchs and sulphurs occasionally visit the flowers for nectar.

PLANT - INSECT INTERACTIONS

Bumble Bees, *Bombus* spp.

The flowers develop from the bottom upward on the raceme; the flowers are protandrous with four stamens attached to the upper lip. When bumble bees enter the flower, pollen is deposited on the top of their thorax and abdomen. After the anthers dehisce, the style bends downward into the center of the corolla and becomes receptive.

Two-Spotted Stink Bug
Cosmopepla lintneriana

Feeding on the flowers and foliage, this stink bug is a very common visitor of obedient plant. Females lay then guard eggs on host plants. Host plants include goldenrods, nettles and mints.

As a defense against predation, this stink bug emits an odor when harassed. This volatile secretion is dispensed from one or two glands located on their thorax. A two-spotted stink bug can not only control the amount secreted from either or both glands, but can reabsorb the secretion into the gland.

Green Sweat Bees, *Agapostemon* spp. *left*
Sweat Bees, *Halictus* spp. *right*

Small- and medium-sized bees crawl into the flowers to feed on nectar but make little contact with the anthers.

Adults emerge in May after overwintering under leaf litter in the late fall. Nymphs also have the aposematic black and orange coloration, another defense mechanism. *Read more about aposematism on p. 186.*

Sweat Bees, *Lasioglossum* spp. *left*
Yellow-Faced Bees, *Hylaeus* spp. *right*

VIRGINIA MOUNTAIN MINT ~ *Pycnanthemum virginianum*

FLOWERING PERIOD

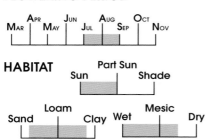

HABITAT

RANGE

HEIGHT 12 - 36" tall

FLOWER
White, 5-Parted
2-Lipped, Tubular
Bilabiate
Branched, Terminal
  Flattened Cluster

LEAF
Linear - Lanceolate
Opposite
Square Stem
Mint Fragrance

FRUIT
Black Seed, Small

ROOT
Rhizome

PLANT NOTES
Virginia mountain mint is a fine-textured perennial. When crushed, the foliage has a strong, clean, mint odor. Sited in a moist location, this plant performs extremely well, flowering for more than a month. Use in low-lying, sunny areas along wetlands, ponds, lake shores or rain gardens.

COMPLEMENTARY PLANTS
Swamp Milkweed   White Turtlehead
Common Ironweed   Blue Lobelia

INSECT NOTES
The flowers attract a diversity of insects including effective pollinators (medium to large bees), predators and parasitoids. A disc secretes nectar near the base of the flower; as an insect probes for nectar, pollen is deposited on their head. Purple spots on the lower lip of the flowers act as a visual attractant.

PLANT - INSECT INTERACTIONS

BEE FORAGING BEHAVIOR

The shallow corollas and numerous flowers clustered on the flower head provide many opportunities for nectar foraging to visiting insects. Even though bees do not typically show a preference for white flowers, the purple spots on the lower lip act as a good visual attractant.

Yellow-faced bees and small resin bees (below) use this lower lip as a landing platform from which they nectar. Medium-sized bees such as the long-horned bee (below), are more likely to contact the stigma and stamens held in the arching upper lip. Most of the visits by these small- and medium-sized bees are for nectar.

Long-Horned Bees, *Melissodes* spp. *left*
Green Sweat Bees, *Agapostemon* spp. *right*

Yellow-Faced Bees, *Hylaeus* spp. *left*
Small Resin Bees, *Heriades* spp. *right*

Bumble Bees, *Bombus* spp.

Bumble bees visit the flowers of Virginia mountain mint for nectar. The flowers are protandrous (anthers dehisce before the stigma become receptive). Similar to other plants in the mint family (Lamiaceae), the anthers and stigmas are held in the arching upper lip. This awning-like upper lip provides some protection to these reproductive parts. The corolla tube is short, enabling short- and long-tongued bees to easily access nectar.

Bumble bees climb across the flower heads, feeding on nectar from each flower. Flowers develop and open from the center of the flower head outward. Bumble bees pick up small amounts of pollen on their legs and abdomen while foraging. Their size and foraging behavior of travelling across the flower heads increase the likelihood of collecting pollen on their abdomens and legs and transporting it to receptive stigmas on other Virginia mountain mint plants.

VIRGINIA MOUNTAIN MINT ~ *Pycnanthemum virginianum*

WASP FAVORITE

Similar to rattlesnake master, *Eryngium yuccifolium* (p. 76), and common boneset, *Eupatorium perfoliatum* (p. 194), Virginia mountain mint nectar is preferred by wasps. The tightly clustered flowers on the terminal flower head, white flower color and access to nectar are some of the attractive floral traits for wasps.

Virginia mountain mint blooms after many of these wasps have completed nest construction and provisioning. Male and female wasps visit the flowers for nectar which provides them with a source of carbohydrates as well as hydration in the middle of the summer. Many wasps are considered beneficial insects, hunting a number of prey including caterpillars, grasshoppers, katydids, crickets and beetles.

Paper Wasp, *Polistes fuscatus*

Thynnid Wasps, *Myzinum* spp.

PLANT - INSECT INTERACTIONS

Great Golden Digger Wasp
Sphex ichneumoneus

Great Black Wasp
Sphex pensylvanicus

Cuckoo Wasp, *Hedychrum* spp. *left*
Beewolves, *Philanthus* spp. *right*

Potter Wasps, *Eumenes* spp. *left*
Grass-Carrying Wasps, *Isodontia* spp. *right*

Pollinators of Native Plants

PLANT - INSECT INTERACTIONS

HONEY BEES

Soldier Flies, *Odontomyia* **spp.** *left*
See profile p. 102.
Syrphid Flies, *Syritta* **spp.** *right*
Visiting a variety of plants for nectar, these syrphid flies are active as adults throughout the summer.

Wedge-Shaped Beetles, *Macrosiagon* **spp.**
Both of these wedge-shaped beetle species are common on Virginia mountain mint, feeding on nectar. Their frequency of visiting the flowers coincides with wasps and bees, their prey, that also visit the flowers for nectar.

Adult female wedge-shaped beetles lay their eggs on flowers visited by their prey. After the eggs hatch, the larvae climb onto unsuspecting hosts and are transported to their hosts' nests. Once in the nest of their prey, the larvae crawl to the host larvae and burrow into their hosts and feed internally. Non-vital parts of the host are consumed first, then vital organs are targeted. This larval feeding ultimately kills the host.

POLLINATOR PROFILE

Banded Hairstreak Butterfly
Satyrium calanus
This butterfly is active as an adult in late June through early August. Common near woodlands or woodland edges, adults nectar on a variety of flowers including Virginia mountain mint. Females lay eggs in the buds of the previous year's growth of their host plants: oak, walnut and hickory trees. Larvae hatch in the spring, the timing coinciding with bud break, and feed on the new tree growth.

Ants, Family Formicidae
Ants are common visitors of Virginia mountain mint feeding on nectar.

Pollinators of Native Plants

215

CUP PLANT ~ *Silphium perfoliatum*

FLOWERING PERIOD

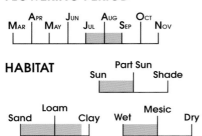

	Apr	Jun	Aug	Oct	
Mar	May	Jul	Sep	Nov

HABITAT

Part Sun
Sun — Shade

Loam — Mesic
Sand — Clay — Wet — Dry

RANGE

HEIGHT 3 - 10' tall

FLOWER	**LEAF**
16 - 35 Ray Florets	Large
Bright Yellow	Opposite
Central Disc Florets	Clasping
Branched Cluster	Toothed

FRUIT	**ROOT**
Winged Achene	Fibrous

PLANT NOTES
Cup plant is best sited in a large garden or landscape; its size can overpower and dominate small gardens.

A NOTE OF CAUTION
Cup plant should not be planted outside of its native range; it has invaded wetlands in the Northeast including Connecticut and New York state and is listed as an invasive plant.

COMPLEMENTARY PLANTS
Spotted Joe Pye Weed   Swamp Milkweed

INSECT NOTES
Cup plant has a high wildlife value. The large leaves surrounding the stem are reservoirs providing birds and invertebrates with drinking water. The sunflower-sized seeds are sought after by finches and sparrows and the flowers attract many bees and beneficial insects.

PLANT - INSECT INTERACTIONS

HONEY BEES

LARVAL HOST PLANT

Silphium Moth, *Tabenna silphiella*
Giant Eucosma Moth, *Eucosma giganteana*

Eastern Tiger Swallowtail Butterfly *left*
Papilio glaucus
Fiery Skipper Butterfly *right*
Hylephila phyleus
Several species of skipper butterflies visit cup plant flowers for nectar. Fiery skipper adults are active in the North in August and early September. Fiery skipper larvae feed on grasses.

Katydids, Family Tettigoniidae

Katydids feed on cup plant leaves in early summer. They lay their eggs in soft stems or leaves with their ovipositor. Katydids are hunted by many wasp species that sting them to cause paralysis. The wasps carry the katydids back to their nests. The katydids are cached alive but immobilized; when the wasp larvae hatch they feed on the katydids. Wasps that prey on katydids include grass-carrying, great black and great golden digger wasps.

CLEPTOPARASITE PROFILE

Cuckoo Bees, *Triepeolus* spp.
This cuckoo bee is a cleptoparasite of long-horned bees (*Melissodes* spp.). Female cuckoo bees wait for female long-horned bees to leave the ground nest, then slip in and lay their eggs in the wall of a brood cell. When the host larva hatches, the cuckoo bee larva kills the host and consumes and develops on the provisions of pollen and nectar (bee bread).

Triepeolus cuckoo bees are black with white or yellow markings. Bees in the *Epeolus* genus look very similar to these cuckoo bees. Cuckoo bees have no pollen-collecting structures; they visit flowers such as cup plant for nectar only. Look for *Triepeolus* cuckoo bees in late summer and early fall.

CUP PLANT ~ *Silphium perfoliatum*

POLLINATOR PROFILE

Green Sweat Bees
Agapostemon spp.

Green sweat bees are some of the most brightly colored bees with black and yellow (or white) striped abdomens and bright green thoraxes. Females of some *Agapostemon* species have entirely green abdomens and closely resemble bees in the Augochlorini tribe. They visit cup plant flowers for both pollen and nectar.

These bees prefer to visit open, shallow flowers because they are typically short-tongued. Nests are deep and excavated vertically in the ground or on slopes. Females may share nest entrances but build and provision their own individual brood cells (communal).

Many *Agapostemon* sp. have more than one generation per year and are therefore active from late spring until fall, visiting harebell, *Campanula rotundifolia,* when they first emerge in the spring and New England aster, *Symphyotrichum novae-angliae,* in the fall.

PLANT - INSECT INTERACTIONS

The open, composite cup plant flowers are visited by all sizes of bees. Only the ray florets around the outer edge of the flower head are fertile, producing a ring of large (sunflower-sized) seeds. Most visits by bees are for nectar; some species of bumble bees, long-horned bees, leafcutter bees, green sweat bees and sweat bees have been observed collecting pollen. Anthers dehisce first and as the style elongates, it collects and presents pollen grains on hairs on the style.

Long-Horned Bees, *Melissodes* spp.

Bumble Bees, *Bombus* spp. *left*
Leafcutter Bees, *Megachile* spp. *right*

Mining Bees
Andrena spp.

Several species of mining bees visit cup plant; many are autumnal species that emerge in the late summer or early fall. They typically visit the flowers for nectar.

PLANT - INSECT INTERACTIONS

HONEY BEES

Brown Ambrosia Aphids, *Uroleucon* spp.

Large aphid populations on the underside of cup plant leaves are common. Aphids, small soft-bodied insects, feed on plants by piercing through the plant tissue with their straw-like mouthparts and sucking out the liquid. Their waste material (honey dew) is sticky and sweet and attracts a number of insects, ants in particular, that feed on it. Brown ambrosia aphids feed on plants in the Asteraceae family.

Instead of laying eggs on plant material, females store eggs internally in late summer, then overwinter. The eggs develop without fertilization; aphids hatch inside the female and are born live the following spring. Newly hatched aphids lack wings; as they mature, some individuals form wings and fly to new host plants to feed.

PREDATOR PROFILES

Ladybird Beetle Larvae, *Cycloneda* spp.

Both the adult and larva of this ladybird beetle are predators of aphids. Adults are spotless with all red or orange elytras. Look for ladybird larvae on the underside of leaves, working their way through an aphid population. They can consume several dozen aphids in one day. Many ladybird beetles such as the Asian lady beetle, *Harmonia axyridis*, have been introduced into North America for the control of aphids. Their numbers and range have quickly increased. They are now considered a serious pest, threatening native biodiversity. They are also pests of fruit including grapes for wine production.

Brown Lacewing Larvae
Family Hemerobiidae

Brown lacewings are common near woodlands and woodland openings. Like the ladybird beetles (above), both the adults and larvae are predacious, feeding on aphids and other small, soft-bodied insects. Females lay their eggs on plants. Brown lacewing larvae are also called aphid wolves for their preference for feeding on aphids. They overwinter as either pupae or adults. Green lacewings, in the family Chrysopidae, lay their eggs suspended from threads attached to leaves.

NEW ENGLAND ASTER ~ *Symphyotrichum novae-angliae*

FLOWERING PERIOD

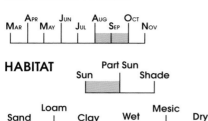

HABITAT

RANGE

HEIGHT 12 - 72" tall

FLOWER	LEAF
Pink - Purple	Lanceolate
45 - 100 Ray Florets	Alternate, Clasping
Orange Disc Florets	Hairy
Branching Cluster	Entire

FRUIT	ROOT
Achene with	Fibrous, Rhizome
Hair Tufts	

PLANT NOTES
New England aster is one of most colorful fall-flowering native plants. Combine with golden-rod species that prefer moist locations such as Riddell's goldenrod, *Solidago riddellii,* for a great color contrast of purple and yellow flower heads. Use in moist swales, ditches or other low-lying areas in the landscape.

COMPLEMENTARY PLANTS
Riddell's Goldenrod	Bottle Gentian
Cup Plant	Common Boneset

INSECT NOTES
The numerous disc florets provide both nectar and pollen to visiting insects. Male bees are common visitors feeding on nectar while waiting to mate with a female. It is also one of the preferred nectar plants of butterflies and moths in the fall.

PLANT - INSECT INTERACTIONS

  HONEY BEES

LARVAL HOST PLANT

Pearl Crescent Butterfly, *Phyciodes tharos*
Canadian Sonia Moth, *Sonia canadana*

SPECIALIST BEE

Mining Bee, *Andrena simplex*

FLOWER DEVELOPMENT & PRESENTATION OF RESOURCES

New England aster flowers are protandrous (anthers develop and dehisce before the stigma becomes receptive). The filaments form a cylinder around the style; after the anthers dehisce, pollen drops and fills this cylinder. The style, located in the center of the cylinder, then begins to develop by elongating. As it pushes upward, hairs on the style pick up pollen grains and expose them to pollinators. Both small and large bees can collect pollen from this presentation mechanism.

Secreted from a ring-shaped nectary around the base of the style, nectar rises up the corolla of the tubular florets and is accessed by all types of pollinators, both short- and long-tongued. The ray florets on the flower head are fertile and develop first, followed by the inner or central disc florets.

Small Carpenter Bees
Ceratina **spp.**

Leafcutter Bees
Megachile **spp.**

Bumble Bees
Bombus **spp.**

Long-Horned Bees
Melissodes **spp.**

Cuckoo Bees
Triepeolus **spp.**

Green Sweat Bees
Agapostemon **spp.**

Pollinators of Native Plants

NEW ENGLAND ASTER ~ *Symphyotrichum novae-angliae*

POLLINATOR PROFILE

Arcigera Flower Moth
Schinina arcigera
The arcigera flower moth is active as an adult from mid-August until October. Caterpillars feed in the fall on flowers, fruit and seeds of their host plants in the Asteraceae family, including asters. Caterpillars pupate in late fall and overwinter as pupae in the ground. Adults emerge in late summer feeding on nectar and mate, to produce one generation per year.

Its range includes eastern North America from Manitoba east to Nova Scotia and south to Florida and Texas.

PLANT - INSECT INTERACTIONS

A BUTTERFLY-PREFERRED FLOWER
New England aster flowers have a number of features that make them attractive to butterflies. The clusters of flowers create an excellent visual attractant combined with the contrasting colors of the ray (purple or pink) and disc (orange or yellow) florets that help guide butterflies to the nectar source. These flowers have open, flat landing platforms for butterflies to perch on as they feed on nectar. They can nectar on the numerous, tightly aggregated, disc florets by remaining on one flower for an extended period of time thus saving the energy to fly to other flowers. Although each floret only offers a small amount of nectar, the combined feeding on many florets of one flower head yields a substantial amount of nectar for butterflies.

Common Buckeye Butterfly *left*
Junonia coenia
The common buckeye butterfly is a year-round resident in Florida and migratory elsewhere. It flies northward in the spring reaching the central United States by April and the northern states such as Illinois and Wisconsin by May. In late summer, adults feed on nectar of New England aster in the North, preparing to migrate southward to Florida for the winter. This butterfly commonly puddles and/or rests on the ground in well-drained soils.
Crescent Butterfly, *Phyciodes* spp. *right*
The northern (*P. selenis*) and pearl (*P. tharos*) crescent butterflies are very similar in appearance and difficult to tell apart. Both choose asters exclusively as larval host plants.

PLANT - INSECT INTERACTIONS

 HONEY BEES

Bee Flies, *Bombylius* spp. *left*

Bee fly adults are common from early spring until fall. Bee fly females follow their hosts (bees) back to the hosts' ground nests and lay eggs at the entrance. Bee fly larvae are parasitic, burrowing into the host to feed and eventually kill it. *See profile p. 131.*

Syrphid Flies, *Syrphus* spp. *right*

Many types of syrphid flies visit New England aster flowers for nectar and pollen. Look for syrphid flies in the *Toxomerus*, *Tropidia*, *Helophilus,* and *Syritta* genera.

Soldier Beetles, *Chauliognathus* spp.

Adult soldier beetles are abundant in late summer, visiting some of their preferred plants such as goldenrods and asters for nectar and pollen. Their black and yellow coloration is a form of wasp mimicry, helping to protect them from predation by birds. *See profile p. 96.*

POLLINATOR PROFILE

Syrphid Flies, *Eristalis* spp.

Visiting flowers for nectar and pollen, these syrphid flies are common from April through October. They are particularly abundant in late summer visiting aster and goldenrod flowers. Waiting to mate, both males and females are active at this time.

With light orange coloration, some *Eristalis* species are considered visual and auditory mimics of honey bees. They make a loud buzzing sound while hovering and have a bee-like appearance and preference for visiting flowers. These convincing forms of mimicry help deter predators that suspect the flies could counterattack by stinging.

Larvae are aquatic, feeding on small organisms in shallow, muddy puddles, ditches or other stagnant water. They breathe through a long, snorkel-like tube (spiracular lobe). The other common name for this fly is rat-tailed maggot.

BLUE (SWAMP) VERVAIN ~ *Verbena hastata*

FLOWERING PERIOD

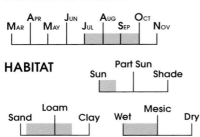

HABITAT

RANGE

HEIGHT 40 - 60" tall

FLOWER	**LEAF**
Blue - Violet	Lanceolate
5-Parted	Opposite
Tubular	Coarsely Toothed
Panicle: Spikes	Short Petioles

FRUIT	**ROOT**
Nutlet	Rhizome, Fibrous

PLANT NOTES
The long, candelabra-like flower spikes of blue vervain provide a striking contrast to the flower forms of neighboring plants. Blue vervain can tolerate flooding and short periods of standing water. It is a good candidate for the wetter parts of a rain garden, on the edge of a pond or creek or other low-lying locations where mid-summer color is needed.

COMPLEMENTARY PLANTS
Swamp Milkweed   Boneset
Common Ironweed   Spotted Joe Pye Weed

INSECT NOTES
Similar to hoary vervain (p. 128), blue vervain produces large quantities of nectar and most insect visits are for nectar only. The flowers attract many types of bees, wasps, flies and butterflies. Flowers develop from the bottom upward on the spike providing a long flowering period and ongoing nectar rewards.

PLANT - INSECT INTERACTIONS

LARVAL HOST PLANT

Verbena Moth, *Crambodes talidiformis*

SPECIALIST BEE

Calliopsis nebraskensis

Syrphid Flies, *Tropidia* spp. *left*
With large, oversized rear femurs and a curved abdomen, these syrphid flies mimic wasps. They visit blue vervain for nectar.

Syrphid Flies, *Eristalis* spp. *right*
Common on flowers in mid-summer, many flies in this genus are excellent bee mimics.
See profile p. 223.

Bee Flies, *Bombylius* spp.
Bee flies nectar on flowers when they first open. Even though their hairy thorax and abdomen are effective at picking up pollen grains, their hovering behavior limits the amount of pollen transported. Instead, when they insert their long mouthparts into the flower, pollen is deposited onto their tongue when they contact the anthers.

PARASITOID PROFILE

Thick-Headed Fly
Stylogaster neglecta
This odd-looking fly hovers around flowers and occasionally lands to feed on nectar. It has long, bent mouthparts that easily reach nectar in blue vervain flowers and other flowers with tubular corollas.

Its slender abdomen and lengthy legs hang downward while it hover. Females use this pointed abdomen to lay eggs into their hosts (crickets). Eggs are oblong in shape and barbed to help secure them into the hosts' abdomens. When the eggs hatch, larvae burrow into the host and feed on non-essential parts of the host's internal tissues. Just before pupation they finish feeding on essential organs in the abdomen and kill the host. Thick-headed flies pupate safely in the shelter of the host's exoskeleton.

There are neotropical *Stylogaster* species that prey on grasshoppers and cockroaches associated with army raid ants. These flies hover around an army raid ant swarm, waiting to target grasshoppers or cockroaches that are flushed out by the swarm.

BLUE (SWAMP) VERVAIN ~ *Verbena hastata*

POLLINATOR PROFILE

Sweat Bees, *Halictus* spp.
Visiting a variety of flower types, sweat bees are common throughout the growing season. Bees in the *Halictus* genus can have a range of nesting types from solitary to eusocial. *See p. 14 for more information.*

Most sweat bees nest in the ground, preferring flat ground over slopes. They typically choose sites with loose, sandy-loam soils or soils easy to excavate. Individual brood cells are constructed branching off from the main tunnel. Females line these cells with a wax-like substance to provide water proofing. This substance is secreted from their Dufour's gland located at the end of their abdomen.

Their common name is derived from the fact that they land on humans to feed on sweat for the salt (above).

PLANT - INSECT INTERACTIONS

Green Sweat Bees, *Agapostemon* spp. *left*
Small Carpenter Bees, *Ceratina* spp. *right*

Bumble Bees, *Bombus* spp. *left*
Long-Horned Bees, *Melissodes* spp. *right*

Leafcutter Bees, *Megachile* spp. *left, right*

Mining Bee, *Calliopsis andreniformis*
male left, female right

Pollinators of Native Plants

PLANT - INSECT INTERACTIONS

FLOWER MORPHOLOGY, DEVELOPMENT & RESOURCE ACCESS

Blue vervain flowers develop from the bottom of the spike upward. Similar to hoary vervain flowers (*Verbena stricta*, p. 128), the flowers are curved and become horizontal near the corolla opening. This horizontal opening helps protect the floral resources from rain entering the corolla.

Each individual flower lasts about six days. With the long floral spikes and densely packed flowers on each spike, the blooming period of blue vervain is often over two months. This is an excellent plant to cover the succession of flowers needed to support a diversity of pollinator species.

The corolla opening is ringed with stiff hairs that help keep out small insects such as ants that pilfer nectar. In the center of the hairs is a small opening that provides a portal for insects to probe the flowers for nectar. Each flower has four filaments fused to the corolla tube and arranged in two pairs. One pair is near the corolla opening so that pollen is deposited onto the pollinator's proboscis as it is withdrawn from the flower corolla.

The style is short, about half the length of the corolla, and located close to the pair of lower anthers. If no cross-pollination occurs, the flowers are self-compatible and likely self-pollinate from the lower anthers' pollen contacting the receptive stigma. The flowers are protandrous (anthers dehiscing first followed by stigma receptivity). Most floral visits by pollinators are for nectar secreted from a disc at the base of the ovary.

Silver Spotted Skipper
Epargyreus clarus
The silver spotted skipper is a regular visitor of blue vervain for nectar. One of the largest skippers, its size and markings make it easier to identify compared to other skipper species. In the northern part of their range (Minnesota, southern Ontario and the New England states), there is one generation, in the South, two generations per year. In the North, adults are active in early summer feeding on nectar from a number of flowers.

Caterpillar host plants include various legumes such as false indigo, *Amorpha* sp.

COMMON IRONWEED ~ *Vernonia fasciculata*

FLOWERING PERIOD

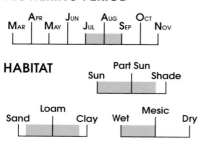

HABITAT

RANGE

HEIGHT 36 - 72" tall

FLOWER
Deep Pink - Purple
15 - 30 Disc Florets
5 Lobes
Flat-Topped Cluster

LEAF
Lanceolate
Alternate
Finely Toothed
Central Light Vein

FRUIT
Achene, Scales

ROOT
Fibrous

PLANT NOTES
Common ironweed is a very suitable plant for a pond, creek or lake edge. Use as backdrop in a low-lying moist location such as a rain garden. The unique, rich purple flowers make it an excellent candidate to combine with any other flower color especially yellow or orange.

COMPLEMENTARY PLANTS
Spotted Joe Pye Weed   Common Boneset
Culver's Root   Swamp Milkweed

INSECT NOTES
Both pollen and nectar rewards are offered to visiting insects. The most common insect visitors are bees, butterflies and skippers. Long-horned bees, *Melissodes* spp., in particular are frequent visitors: two species are pollen-collecting specialists.

PLANT - INSECT INTERACTIONS

HONEY BEES

LARVAL HOST PLANT

Parthenice Tiger Moth, *Grammia parthenice*

Green Sweat Bees, *Agapostemon* spp. *left*
Bumble Bees, *Bombus* spp. *right*

Leafcutter Bees, *Megachile* spp. *left*
Long-Horned Bees, *Melissodes* spp. *right*

Syrphid Flies, *Eristalis* spp. *left*
These syrphid flies are excellent bumble bee mimics and visit common ironweed to feed on nectar.
Soldier Beetles, *Chauliognathus* spp. *right*

SPECIALIST BEES

Long-Horned Bees
Melissodes vernoniae
Melissodes denticulata

Peck's Skipper
Polites peckius
The Peck's skipper is a frequent visitor of common ironweed. Silver spotted skippers and tawny edge skippers are regular visitors as well.

Eastern Tiger Swallowtail
Papilio glaucus
The eastern tiger swallowtail butterfly visits the flowers for nectar. Other butterfly visitors include the monarch, great spangled fritillary, gray hairstreak, sulphurs and other swallowtail species.

CULVER'S ROOT ~ *Veronicastrum virginicum*

FLOWERING PERIOD

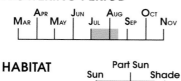

HABITAT

RANGE

HEIGHT 36 - 72" tall

FLOWER	LEAF
White, Tubular	Lanceolate
4-Parted	Whorled with
Terminal Cluster	3 - 6 Stalked Leaves
Several Spikes	Toothed

FRUIT	ROOT
Tiny Seed	Fibrous, Rhizome

PLANT NOTES

The tall, white candelabra-like flower spikes provide a nice vertical element in the landscape. It is one of a few perennials with whorled leaves; these dark green whorls create tiers that set off the narrow, white flower heads. The roots are rhizomatous and plants can spread quickly in humus-rich soils. Culver's root typically flowers for over a month.

COMPLEMENTARY PLANTS

Common Ironweed	Blue Vervain
Swamp Milkweed	Spotted Joe Pye Weed

INSECT NOTES

Bees, flies and butterflies are the most frequent visitors. Flowers develop from the bottom of the spike upward. Anthers elongate first past the corolla opening, dehiscing and offering pollen. The small style elongates afterward. Anthers spread away from the stigma to prevent self-pollination.

Pollinators of Native Plants

PLANT - INSECT INTERACTIONS

 HONEY BEES

LARVAL HOST PLANT

Culver's Root Borer Moth
Papaipema sciata

Leafcutter Bees, *Megachile* spp. *left*

Leafcutter bees feed on the nectar. The anthers extend past the tubular flower and pollen is deposited on the long hairs of leafcutter abdomens.

Rusty Patched Bumble Bee *right*
Bombus affinis See profile p. 201.

Long-Horned Bee
Melissodes bimaculata

This long-horned bee is all black except for two white spots near the base of the abdomen. Similar to other long-horned bees, the female has long pollen-collecting hairs on their lower hind legs. When full of pollen, it resembles bright yellow bicycle saddle bags. Its range includes most of the eastern United States although a few observations have been recorded in the Rocky Mountain states.

Sweat Bees, *Lasioglossum* spp. *left*

From anthers that extend past the tubular flowers, sweat bees collect and feed on pollen. These bees, although short-tongued, are capable of reaching nectar in the small flowers.

Yellow-Faced Bees, *Hylaeus* spp. *right*

Most yellow-faced bees are tiny enough to crawl into the flower corolla to feed on nectar. They have not been observed feeding on or collecting pollen.

Green Sweat Bees *left*
Agapostemon spp.
Sweat Bees, *Halictus* spp. *right*

Sweat bees are regular visitors, effectively transporting culver's root pollen and are considered effective pollinators.

Pollinators of Native Plants

CULVER'S ROOT ~ *Veronicastrum virginicum*

PREDATOR PROFILE

PLANT - INSECT INTERACTIONS

Thread-Waisted Wasps, *Ammophila* spp.

Females excavate nests in sandy or loose soil before hunting for prey. The burrow is typically dug perpendicular to the soil surface with one cell at the bottom. The female scrapes at the soil with her mandibles or forelegs. Collecting soil between her head and forelegs as she digs, she backs out of the nest and dumps the soil away from the nest entrance. The nest entrance is often concealed with sand or an appropriate-sized pebble to keep out unwanted fly cleptoparasites. Paralyzed prey (sawfly larvae or hairless caterpillars) are flown or dragged back to the nest and the nest entrance is reopened.

PREDATOR PROFILE

Great Golden Digger Wasp
Sphex ichneumoneus

The great golden digger wasp is solitary and nests in the ground. This large, brightly colored wasp preys on crickets and katydids. Females can be observed excavating nests in mid-summer in sandy soil. As soil is excavated from the burrow, females hold the clumps of soil between their mandibles and forelegs, back out of the nest and deposit the clumps away from the nest entrance.

Females sting and paralyze prey, then fly back to the nest using their legs to clutch the prey beneath them. Prey is placed on the ground near the nest entrance; the nest is checked before dragging the prey inside. Females often drag the prey backward into the burrow grasping it with their mandibles. Once the prey is cached, a single egg is laid on each cricket or katydid. When the larva hatches, it feeds on the prey provided then prepares to pupate.

Great Black Wasp *left*
Sphex pensylvanicus

The great black wasp is a regular visitor of flowers in summer and feeds on nectar.

Thread-Waisted Wasp *right*
Eremnophila aureonotata

PLANT - INSECT INTERACTIONS

HONEY BEES

Syrphid Flies, *Eristalis* spp. *left*
These large syrphid flies are very convincing mimics of bumble bees. They feed on both pollen and nectar of culver's root.

Tachinid Flies, *Archytas* spp. *right*
Tachinid flies are common in the summer visiting flowers to feed on nectar. *See profile p. 125.*

Red Admiral Butterfly, *Vanessa atalanta*
Azure Butterflies, *Celastrina* spp. *right*
Butterflies probe for nectar at the top of the flower spike where flowers are barely open but offering nectar. Flower visits can last for several minutes as they investigate each small tubular flower.

Eastern Tailed Blue Butterfly *left*
Everes comyntas
Soldier Beetles, *Chauliognathus* spp. *right*

PARASITOID PROFILE

Thick-Headed Flies
***Physocephala* spp.**
Female thick-headed flies are aerial acrobats, some with the ability to parasitize their host (bees and wasps) as they fly through the air or when they visit plants such as culver's root.

Eggs are laid on the host. The larva hatches and burrows into the host and feeds as an internal parasite in the host's abdomen. The larva orients itself with its hind end near the base of the abdomen. It begins by consuming less vital parts, then the vital organs above and eventually kills the host.

The host dies sometime before the larva is ready to pupate and the larva uses the host's exoskeleton as a shelter as it finishes pupation. Thick-headed flies are wasp mimics with a slender, wasp-like waist, enlarged abdomen and black coloring. They visit flowers including culver's root to feed on nectar.

REFERENCES

Alemán, M., Figueroa-Fleming, T., Etcheverry, Á., Sühring, S., & Ortega-Baes, P. The explosive pollination mechanism in Papilionoideae (Leguminosae): an analysis with three Desmodium species. *Plant Systematics and Evolution*, 1-10.

Arnett, R. H., Jr., & Thomas, M. C. (Eds.). (2001). *American beetles: Archostemata, myxophaga, adephaga, polyphaga: Staphyliniformia.* (Vol. 1). Boca Raton, FL: CRC Press LLC.

Arnett, R. H., Thomas, M. C., Skelley, P. E., & Frank, J. H. (Eds.). (2002). *American Beetles, Volume II: Polyphaga: Scarabaeoidea through Curculionoidea* (Vol. 2). Boca Raton, FL: CRC Press LLC.

Arnett, R. H., Jr. (1993). *American insects: a handbook of the insects of America north of Mexico.* Gainesville, FL: Sandhill Crane Press.

Barth, F. G. (1991). *Insects and flowers: the biology of a partnership.* NJ: Princeton University Press.

Beattie, A. J. (1969). Studies in the pollination ecology of Viola. 1. The pollen-content of stigmatic cavities. *Watsonia, 7*(3), 142-156. Retrieved from http://archive.bsbi.org.uk/Wats7p142.pdf

Beattie, A. J. (1971). Pollination mechanisms in Viola. *New Phytologist, 70*(2), 343-360. Retrieved from http://www.jstor.org/stable/2430674

Beattie, A. J. (1972). The pollination ecology of Viola. 2. Pollen loads of insect-visitors. *Watsonia, 9,* 13-25. Retrieved from http://archive.bsbi.org.uk/Wats9p13.pdf

Beattie, A. J. (1974). Floral evolution in Viola. *Annals of the Missouri Botanical Garden*, 781-793. Retrieved from http://www.jstor.org/stable/2395029

Bertin, R. I., & Sholes, O. D. (1993). Weather, pollination and the phenology of Geranium maculatum. *American Midland Naturalist*, 52-66. Retrieved from http://www.jstor.org/stable/2426435

Black, M. R., & Judziewicz, E. J. (2009). *Wildflowers of Wisconsin and the Great Lakes region* (2nd. ed.). Madison, WI: University of Wisconsin Press.

Black, S. H., Shepherd, M., & Vaughan, M. (2011). Rangeland management for pollinators. *Rangelands, 33*(3), 9-13. Retrieved from http://www.xerces.org/wp-content/uploads/2008/06/Rangeland-Management-for-Pollinators_SHB-MDS-MV.pdf

Blanchan, N. (1900). *Nature's garden.* Garden City, NY: Garden City.

Blatchley, W. S., & Leng, C. W. (1916). *Rhynchophora or weevils of north eastern America.* The Nature Publishing Company. Retrieved from books.google.com/books?id=j-IkAAAAYAAJ

Bock, J. H., & Peterson, S. J. (1975). Reproductive biology of Pulsatilla patens (Ranunculaceae). *American Midland Naturalist*, 476-478. Retrieved from http://www.jstor.org/stable/2424441

Brett, J. F., & Posluszny, U. (1982). Floral development in Caulophyllum thalictroides (Berberidaceae). *Canadian Journal of Botany, 60*(10), 2133-2141. doi:10.1139/b82-262

Britton, N. L., & Brown, A. (1970). *An illustrated flora of the Northern United States and Canada* (2nd. ed., Vol. 1-3). New York, NY: Dover.

Campbell, J. W., Hanula, J. L., & Waldrop, T. A. (2007). Effects of prescribed fire and fire surrogates on floral visiting insects of the blue ridge province in North Carolina. *Biological conservation, 134*(3), 393-404. Retrieved from ftp://192.139.6.163/pub/fire/Alexander/USFS_RD_WildlandFireReview/references/campbell_hanula_waldrop_2007.pdf

Cane, J. H. (1991). Soils of ground-nesting bees (Hymenoptera: Apoidea): texture, moisture, cell depth and climate. Journal of the Kansas Entomological Society, 406-413. Retrieved from http://xa.yimg.com/kq/groups/17598545/201795555/name/CaneNestingSoilsBeesJKES1991.pdf

Cane, J. H. (2006). An evaluation of pollination mechanisms for purple prairie-clover, Dalea purpurea (Fabaceae: Amorpheae). *The American Midland Naturalist, 156*(1), 193-197. Retrieved from http://www.jstor.org/stable/4094681

Clinebell, R. R., & Bernhardt, P. (1998). The pollination ecology of five species of Penstemon (Scrophulariaceae) in the tallgrass prairie. *Annals of the Missouri Botanical Garden*, 126-136. Retrieved from http://www.jstor.org/stable/2992002

Clinebell, R. R. (2002). Foraging ecology in selected prairie wildflowers (Echinacea, Liatris, Monarda, and Veronicastrum) in Missouri prairie remnants and restorations. In *Proceedings of the 18th north America Prairie Conference. Truman State University, Kirksville, Missouri* (pp.194-212). Retrieved from http://www.litzsinger.org/research/clinebell.pdf

Pollinators of Native Plants

Corbet, S. A., Chapman, H., & Saville, N. (1988). Vibratory pollen collection and flower form: bumble-bees on Actinidia, Symphytum, Borago and Polygonatum. *Functional Ecology*, 147-155. Retrieved from http://www.jstor.org/stable/2389689

Costelloe, B. H. (1988). Pollination ecology of Gentiana andrewsii. *The Ohio Journal of Science, 88*(4), 132-138. Retrieved from https://kb.osu.edu/dspace/bitstream/handle/1811/23269/v088n4_132.pdf?sequence=1

Cowan, D. P., & Waldbauer, G. P. (1984). Seasonal occurrence and mating at flowers by Ancistrocerus antilope (Hymenoptera: Eumenidae). Proceedings of the *Entomological Society of Washington, 86*(4), 930-934.

Crosswhite, F. S., & Crosswhite, C. D. (1966). Insect pollinators of Penstemon series Graciles (Scrophulariaceae) with notes on Osmia and other Megachilidae. *American Midland Naturalist*, 450-467. Retrieved from http://www.jstor.org/stable/2423097

Cruden, R. W., Hermanutz, L., & Shuttleworth, J. (1984). The pollination biology and breeding system of Monarda fistulosa (Labiatae). *Oecologia, 64*(1), 104-110. Retrieved from http://www.jstor.org/stable/4217429

Culley, T. M. (2002). Reproductive biology and delayed selfing in Viola pubescens (Violaceae), an understory herb with chasmogamous and cleistogamous flowers. *International Journal of Plant Sciences, 163*(1), 113-122. Retrieved from http://www.jstor.org/stable/10.1086/324180

Danderson, C. A., & Molano-Flores, B. (2010). Effects of herbivory and inflorescence size on insect visitation to Eryngium yuccifolium (Apiaceae) a prairie plant. *The American Midland Naturalist, 163*(1), 234-246. Retrieved from http://www.jstor.org/stable/25602357

Dickinson, J. A., & McKONE, M. J. (1992). Insect floral visitors to four species of tall-grass prairie composite (Asteraceae: Heliantheae). *Prairie Naturalist, 24*, 159-159. Retrieved from http://apps.carleton.edu/campus/arb/assets/Dickinson___McKone__92__Insect_Floral_Visitors_Prairie_Naturalist.pdf

Dieringer, G., & Cabrera, L. (2002). The interaction between pollinator size and the bristle staminode of Penstemon digitalis (Scrophulariaceae). *American Journal of Botany, 89*(6), 991-997. Retrieved from http://www.jstor.org/stable/4131391

Dietz, R. A. (1952). Variation in the perfoliate Uvularias. *Annals of the Missouri Botanical Garden, 39*(3), 219-247. Retrieved from http://www.jstor.org/stable/2394524

Dobson, H. E. M. (1987). Role of flower and pollen aromas in host-plant recognition by solitary bees. *Oecologia, 72*(4), 618-623. Retrieved from http://www.jstor.org/stable/4218316

Douglas, K. L., & Cruden, R. W. (1994). The reproductive biology of Anemone canadensis (Ranunculaceae): breeding system and facilitation of sexual selection. *American Journal of Botany*, 314-321. Retrieved from http://www.jstor.org/stable/2445458

Eckert, C., & Schaefer, A. (1998). Does self-pollination provide reproductive assurance in Aquilegia canadensis (Ranunculaceae)? *American Journal of Botany, 85*(7), 919-919. Retrieved from http://www.jstor.org/stable/2446357

Estes, J. R., & Thorp, R. W. (1975). Pollination ecology of Pyrrhopappus carolinianus (Compositae). *American Journal of Botany*, 148-159. Retrieved from: http://www.jstor.org/stable/2441589

Evans, E. W., Smith, C. C., & Gendron, R. P. (1989). Timing of reproduction in a prairie legume: seasonal impacts of insects consuming flowers and seeds. *Oecologia, 78*(2), 220-230. Retrieved from http://www.jstor.org/stable/4218854

Evans, E. W. (1990). Dynamics of an Aggregation of Blister Beetles (Coleoptera: Meloidae) Attacking a Prairie Legume. *Journal of the Kansas Entomological Society*, 616-625. Retrieved from http://www.jstor.org/stable/25085226

Evans, F. C. (1984). Bee-flower interactions on an old field in southeastern Michigan. In *North American Prairie Conference*. Retrieved from: http://images.library.wisc.edu/EcoNatRes/EFacs/NAPC/NAPC09/reference/econatres.napc09.fevans.pdf

Fenster, C. B., Armbruster, W. S., Wilson, P., Dudash, M. R., & Thomson, J. D. (2004). Pollination syndromes and floral specialization. *Annual Review of Ecology, Evolution, and Systematics*, 375-403. Retrieved from http://web.pdx.edu/~cruzan/Fenster et al 2004.pdf

Pollinators of Native Plants

REFERENCES

Fiedler, A., Tuell, J., Isaacs, R., & Landis, D. (2007). *Attracting beneficial insects with native flowering plants*. Michigan State University, Extension Service.

Fishbein, M., & Venable, D. L. (1996). Diversity and temporal change in the effective pollinators of Asclepias tuberosa. *Ecology*, 1061-1073. Retrieved from: http://www.jstor.org/stable/2265576

Frankie, G. W., Thorp, R. W., Schindler, M., Hernandez, J., Ertter, B., & Rizzardi, M. (2005). Ecological patterns of bees and their host ornamental flowers in two northern California cities. *Journal of the Kansas Entomological Society*, 227-246. Retrieved from http://www.jstor.org/stable/25086268

Frelich, L. E., Hale, C. M., Scheu, S., Holdsworth, A. R., Heneghan, L., Bohlen, P. J., & Reich, P. B. (2006). Earthworm invasion into previously earthworm-free temperate and boreal forests. *Biological invasions, 8*(6), 1235-1245. Retrieved from http://mx1.boulderlake.org/worms/downloads/publications/Frelich et al 2006.pdf

Galen, C., & Kevan, P. G. (1980). Scent and color, floral polymorphisms and pollination biology in Polemonium viscosum Nutt. *American Midland Naturalist*, 281-289. Retrieved from http://www.jstor.org/stable/2424867

Garibaldi, L. A., Steffan-Dewenter, I., Winfree, R., Aizen, M. A., Bommarco, R., Cunningham, S. A., ... & Klein, A. M. (2013). Wild pollinators enhance fruit set of crops regardless of honey bee abundance. *Science, 339*(6127), 1608-1611. Retrieved from http://www.iee.unibe.ch/unibe/philnat/biology/zoologie/ecol/content/e7049/e267480/e267538/e271515/e293460/Garibaldi_2013_Science.pdf

Gibbs, J., & Sheffield, C. S. (2009). Rapid Range Expansion of the Wool-Carder Bee, Anthidium manicatum (Linnaeus)(Hymenoptera: Megachilidae), in North America. *Journal of the Kansas Entomological Society, 82*(1), 21-29. Retrieved from http://www.jstor.org/stable/25568936

Glassberg, J. (2001). *Butterflies through Binoculars: The East*. New York, NY: Oxford University Press.

Graenicher, S. (1900) The fertilization and insect visitors of our earliest entomophilous flowers. *Bulletin of the Wisconsin Natural History Society*, 1, 73-84. Retrieved from books.google.com/books?id=N_XOAAAAMAAJ

Graenicher, S. (1900). The Syrphidae of Milwaukee County. *Bulletin of the Wisconsin Natural History Society*, 1, 167-177.

Graenicher, S. (1902). Flowers adapted to flesh-flies. *Bulletin of the Wisconsin Natural History Society, 1*(1), 33.

Graenicher, S. (1906). Some notes on the pollination of flowers. *Bulletin of the Wisconsin Natural History Society, 4*, 12-21.

Graenicher, S. (1909). Wisconsin flowers and their pollination. *Bulletin of the Wisconsin Natural History Society, 7*, 19.

Graenicher, S. (1910). The bee-flies (Bombyliidae) in their relations to flowers. *Bulletin of the Wisconsin Natural History Society, 8*, 91-101.

Graham, E. E., Tooker, J. F., & Hanks, L. M. (2012). Floral Host Plants of Adult Beetles in Central Illinois: An Historical Perspective. *Annals of the Entomological Society of America, 105*(2), 287-297. Retrieved from http://www.life.illinois.edu/hanks/pdfs/Graham et al 2012 floral hosts of beetles AESA 105.pdf

Grissell, E., & Crissell, E. (2006). *Insects and gardens: in pursuit of a garden ecology*. Portland, Oregon: Timber Press.

Grissell, E. (2010). *Bees, Wasps, and Ants: The Indispensable Role of Hymenoptera in Gardens*. Portland, Oregon: Timber Press.

Haddock, R. C., & Chaplin, S. J. (1982). Pollination and seed production in two phenologically divergent prairie legumes (Baptisia leucophaea and B. leucantha). *American Midland Naturalist*, 175-186. Retrieved from http://www.jstor.org/stable/2425307

Hahn, J. (2006, May 1). Be on the watch for columbine sawfly. *Yard & Garden Line News 8*(6). Retrieved from http://www.extension.umn.edu/yardandgarden/YGLNews/YGLNews-May0106.html#csf

Hahn, J. (2009). *Insects of the North Woods*. Duluth, MN: Kollath + Stensaas.

Hannan, G. L., & Prucher, H. A. (1996). Reproductive biology of Caulophyllum thalictroides (Berberidaceae), an early flowering perennial of eastern North America. *American Midland Naturalist*, 267-277. Retrieved from http://www.jstor.org/stable/2426731

Heinrich, B. (1975). Energetics of Pollination. *Annual Review of Ecology and Systematics*, *6*, 139-170. Retrieved from http://www.jstor.org/stable/2096828

Heinrich, B. (1976). Bumblebee Foraging and the Economics of Sociality: How have bumblebees evolved to use a large variety of flowers efficiently? Individual bees have specialized behavioral repertories, and the colony, collectively, can harvest food from many different resources. *American Scientist, 64*(4), 384-395. Retrieved from http://www.jstor.org/stable/27847342

Heinrich, B. (1976). The foraging specializations of individual bumblebees. *Ecological Monographs*, 105-128. Retrieved from http://www.pollinators.info/wp-content/uploads/2012/02/1942246.pdf

Hendrix, S. D. (2001). Population size and reproduction in Phlox pilosa. *Conservation Biology, 14*(1), 304-313. Retrieved from http://www.jstor.org/stable/2641929

Herlihy, C. R., & Eckert, C. G. (2007). Evolutionary analysis of a key floral trait in Aquilegia canadensis (Ranunculaceae): genetic variation in herkogamy and its effect on the mating system. *Evolution, 61*(7), 1661-1674. Retrieved from http://www.jstor.org/stable/4621407

Horn, S., & Hanula, J. L. (2004). Impact of seed predators on the herb Baptisia lanceolata (Fabales: Fabaceae). *Florida Entomologist, 87*(3), 398-400. Retrieved from http://www.fcla.edu/FlaEnt/fe87p398.pdf

Ivey, C. T., Martinez, P., & Wyatt, R. (2003). Variation in pollinator effectiveness in swamp milkweed, Asclepias incarnata (Apocynaceae). *American Journal of Botany, 90*(2), 214-225. Retrieved from http://www.jstor.org/stable/4124176

Johnson, S. D., Horn, K. C., Savage, A. M., Windhager, S., Simmons, M. T., & Rudgers, J. A. (2008). Timing of prescribed burns affects abundance and composition of arthropods in the Texas hill country. *The Southwestern Naturalist, 53*(2), 137-145. Retrieved from http://ecologyofmutualism.com/ecologyofmutualism.com_files/JohnsonetalSwestNat08.pdf

Johnston, M. O. (1991). Natural selection on floral traits in two species of Lobelia with different pollinators. *Evolution*, 1468-1479. Retrieved from http://www.jstor.org/stable/2409893

Johnston, M. O. (1992). Effects of cross and self-fertilization on progeny fitness in Lobelia cardinalis and L. siphilitica. *Evolution*, 688-702. Retrieved from http://www.jstor.org/stable/2409638

Jürgens, A., & Dötterl, S. (2004). Chemical composition of anther volatiles in Ranunculaceae: genera-specific profiles in Anemone, Aquilegia, Caltha, Pulsatilla, Ranunculus, and Trollius species. *American Journal of Botany, 91*(12), 1969-1980. Retrieved from http://www.amjbot.org/content/91/12/1969.full

Kampny, C. M., Dickinson, T. A., & Dengler, N. G. (1993). Quantitative comparison of floral development in Veronica chamaedrys and Veronicastrum virginicum (Scrophulariaceae). *American Journal of Botany*, 449-460. Retrieved from http://www.jstor.org/stable/2445391

Kaplan, S. M., & Mulcahy, D. L. (1971). Mode of pollination and floral sexuality in Thalictrum. *Evolution*, 659-668. Retrieved from http://www.jstor.org/stable/2406946

Kearns, C. A. & D. W. Inouye, D. W. (1993). *Techniques for pollination biologists*. Niwot, Colorado: University Press of Colorado.

Kephart, S. R. (1983). The partitioning of pollinators among three species of Asclepias. *Ecology*, 120-133. Retrieved from http://www.jstor.org/stable/1937335

Krall, B. S., Bartelt, R. J., Lewis, C. J., & Whitman, D. W. (1999). Chemical defense in the stink bug Cosmopepla bimaculata. *Journal of Chemical Ecology, 25*(11), 2477-2494.

Kremen, C., Williams, N. M., & Thorp, R. W. (2002). Crop pollination from native bees at risk from agricultural intensification. *Proceedings of the National Academy of Sciences, 99*(26), 16812-16816. Retrieved from http://www.pnas.org/content/99/26/16812.full

Krombein, K. V., Hard, P. D., Jr., Smith, D. R., & Burks, B. D. (1979). *Catalog of Hymenoptera in America north of Mexico: Symphyta and apocrita (parasitica)* (Vol. 1). Washington, DC: Smithsonian Institution Press.

Krombein, K. V., Hard, P. D., Jr., Smith, D. R., & Burks, B. D. (1979). *Catalog of Hymenoptera in America north of Mexico: Apocrita (aculeata)* (Vol. 2). Washington, DC: Smithsonian Institution Press.

Krombein, K. V., Hard, P. D., Jr., & Smith, D. R.(1979). *Catalog of Hymenoptera in America north of Mexico: Indexes* (Vol. 3). Washington, DC: Smithsonian Institution Press.

LaBerge, W. E. (1956). *A Revision of the Bees of the Genus Melissodes in North and Central America: Part I (Hymenoptera, Apidae)*. University of Kansas.

Larson, D. L., Royer, R. A., & Royer, M. R. (2006). Insect visitation and pollen deposition in an invaded prairie plant community. *Biological Conservation, 130*(1), 148-159. Retrieved from http://digitalcommons.unl.edu/cgi/viewcontent.cgi?article=1068&context=usgsnpwrc

Levin, D. A. (1968). The structure of a polyspecies hybrid swarm in Liatris. *Evolution*, 352-372. Retrieved from http://www.jstor.org/stable/2406534

Levin, D. A., & Kerster, H. (1969). Density-dependent gene dispersal in Liatris. *American Naturalist*, 61-74. Retrieved from http://www.jstor.org/stable/2459468

Levin, D. A., & Berube, D. E. (1972). Phlox and Colias: the efficiency of a pollination system. *Evolution*, 242-250. Retrieved from http://www.jstor.org/stable/2407034

Lindsey, A. H. (1984). Reproductive biology of Apiacea. I. Floral vistors to Thaspium and Zizia and their importance in pollination. *American Journal of Botany*, 375-387. Retrieved from http://www.jstor.org/stable/2443496

Lowry, P. P., & Jones, A. G. (1984). Systematics of Osmorhiza Raf.(Apiaceae: Apioideae). *Annals of the Missouri Botanical Garden*, 1128-1171. Retrieved from http://www.jstor.org/stable/2399249

Lyon, D. L. (1992). Bee pollination of facultatively xenogamous Sanguinaria canadensis L. *Bulletin of the Torrey Botanical Club*, 368-375. Retrieved from http://www.jstor.org/stable/2996724

Macior, L. W. (1966). Foraging behavior of Bombus (Hymenoptera: Apidae) in relation to Aquilegia pollination. *American Journal of Botany*, 302-309. Retrieved from http://www.jstor.org/stable/2439803

Macior, L. W. (1970). The pollination ecology of Dicentra cucullaria. *American Journal of Botany*, 6-11. Retrieved from http://www.jstor.org/stable/2440374

Macior, L. W. (1978). Pollination interactions in sympatric Dicentra species. *American Journal of Botany*, 57-62. Retrieved from http://www.jstor.org/stable/2442554

MacRae, T. C. (1991). The Buprestidae (Coleoptera) of Missouri. *Insecta Mundi*, 411.

Mader, E., Spivak, M., & Evans, E. (2010). *Managing alternative pollinators: A handbook for beekeepeers, growers, and conservationists*. Ithaca, NY: NRAES (Natural Resource, Agriculture, and Engineering Service).

Mader, E., Shepherd, M., Vaughn, M., & Black, S. H. (2011). *Attracting Native Pollinators: The Xerces Society Guide Protecting North America's Bees and Butterflies*. North Adams, MA: Storey.

Mader, E., Spivak, M., Evans, E., & Vaughan, M. *Alternative Pollinators*. Retrieved from: http://files.meetup.com/3992742/native%20bees.pdf

Marschalek, D. A. (2013). *Blister beetles (Coleoptera: Meloidae) of Wisconsin: Distribution and ecology.* (Doctoral dissertation, University of Wisconsin-Madison). Retrieved from http://depot.library.wisc.edu/repository/fedora/1711.dl:CG32FRISRZ5KL87/datastreams/REF/content

Marshall, S. A. (2006). *Insects: their natural history and diversity: with a photographic guide to insects of eastern North America*. Richmond Hill, Canada: Firefly Books.

Marshall, S. A. (2012). *Flies: the natural history and diversity of Diptera*. Buffalo, New York: Firefly Books.

Mawdsley, J. R. (2002). Ecological notes on species of Cleridae (Insecta: Coleoptera) associated with the prairie flora of central North America. *Great Lakes Entomologist, 35*(1), 15-22.

McAlpine, J. F., Peterson, B. V., Shewell, G. E., Teskey, H. J., Vockeroth, J. R., & Wood, D. M. (Eds.). (1987). *Manual of nearctic diptera* (Monograph No. 28, Vol. 2). Ottawa, Canada: Agriculture Canada.

McCrea, K. D., & Levy, M. (1983). Photographic visualization of floral colors as perceived by honeybee pollinators. *American Journal of Botany*, 369-375. Retrieved from: http://www.jstor.org/stable/2443245

McKinney, A. M., & Goodell, K. (2011). Plant–pollinator interactions between an invasive and native plant vary between sites with different flowering phenology. *Plant Ecology, 212*(6), 1025-1035.

Miller, S. R., Gaebel, R., Mitchell, R. J., & Arduser, M. (2002). Occurrence of two species of old world bees, Anthidium manicatum and A. oblongatum (Apoidea: Megachilidae), in northern Ohio and southern Michigan. *Great Lakes Entomologist, 35*(1), 65-70. Retrieved from http://www3.uakron.edu/biology/mitchell/pdfs/Miller et al 2002.pdf

---

Pollinators of Native Plants

Mitchell, T. B. (1960). *Bees of the eastern United States (Vol. 1)*. North Carolina Agricultural Experiment Station. Retrieved from http://insectmuseum.org/easternBees.php

Michener, C. D., Brothers, D. J., & Kamm, D. R. (1971). Interactions in colonies of primitively social bees: Artificial colonies of Lasioglossum zephyrum. *Proceedings of the National Academy of Sciences*, 68(6), 1241-1245. Retrieved from http://www.pnas.org/content/68/6/1241.full.pdf

Michener, C. D. (1974). *The social behavior of the bees: a comparative study* (Vol. 73, No. 87379). Belknap Press.

Michener, C. D. (2000). *The bees of the world*. Baltimore, MD: Johns Hopkins University Press.

Moisset, B. (2012, December 7). Monarchs and their enemies [Blog post]. Retrieved from http://pollinators.blogspot.com/2012/11/monarchs-and-their-enemies.html

Molano-Flores, B., & Hendrix, S. D. (1999). The effects of population size and density on the reproductive output of Anemone canadensis L.(Ranunculaceae). *International Journal of Plant Sciences, 160*(4), 759-766. Retrieved from http://www.jstor.org/stable/10.1086/314161

Molano-Flores, B. (2001). Reproductive biology of Eryngium yuccifolium (Apiaceae), a prairie species. *Journal of the Torrey Botanical Society*, 1-6. Retrieved from http://www.jstor.org/stable/3088654

Motten, A. F. (1986). Pollination ecology of the spring wildflower community of a temperate deciduous forest. *Ecological Monographs*, 21-42. Retrieved from http://www.jstor.org/stable/2937269

Moure, J. S., & Hurd, P. D., Jr. (1987). *An annotated catalog of the halictid bees of the Western Hemisphere (hymenoptera: halictidae)*. Washington, DC: Smithsonian Institution Press.

New Hampshire Wildlife Action Plan. (n.d.). *Species profile: Frosted elfin*. Retrieved from http://www.wildlife.state.nh.us/Wildlife/Wildlife_Plan/WAP_species_PDFs/Invertibrates/Frosted Elfin.pdf

Newmaster, S. G., Harris, A. G., & Kershaw, L. J. (1997). *Wetland plants of Ontario*. Edmonton, Canada: Lone Pine.

Nyman, Y. (1993). The pollen-collecting hairs of Campanula (Campanulaceae). II. Function and adaptive significance in relation to pollination. *American Journal of Botany*, 1437-1443. Retrieved from http://www.jstor.org/stable/2445673

O'Neill, K. M. (2001). *Solitary wasps: behavior and natural history*. Ithaca, NY: Cornell University Press.

Pammel, L. H. (1898). *Flower ecology*. Press of JB Hungerford.

Panzer, R. (2002). Compatibility of prescribed burning with the conservation of insects in small, isolated prairie reserves. *Conservation Biology, 16*(5), 1296-1307. Retrieved from ftp://ftp.dnr.state.mn.us/pub/eco/NHNRP/SWAP/Daren's prairie insect publications/panzer_2002_consbio_presescribed burning insects.pdf

Paulissen, M. A. (1987). Exploitation by, and the effects of, caterpillar grazers on the annual, Rudbeckia hirta (Compositae). *American Midland Naturalist*, 439-441. Retrieved from http://www.jstor.org/stable/2425987

Pellmyr, O. (1985). The pollination biology of Actaea pachypoda and A. rubra (including A. erythrocarpa) in northern Michigan and Finland. *Bulletin of the Torrey Botanical Club*, 265-273. Retrieved from http://www.jstor.org/stable/2996542

Perkins, W. E., Estes, J. R., & Thorp, R. W. (1975). Pollination ecology of interspecific hybridization in Verbena. *Bulletin of the Torrey Botanical Club*, 194-198. Retrieved from http://www.jstor.org/stable/2484941

Petersen, C. E., & Sleboda, J. A. (1994). Selective pod abortion by Baptisia leucantha (Fabaceae) as affected by a curculionid seed predator, Apion rostrum (Coleoptera). *Great Lakes Entomologist, 27*, 143-143. Retrieved from http://insects.ummz.lsa.umich.edu/mes/gle-pdfs/vol27no3.pdf#page=18

Petersen, C. E. (1997). Bee visitors of four reconstructed tallgrass prairies in northeastern Illinois. In *Proceedings of the Fifteenth North American Prairie Conference. Bend, Oregon: Natural Areas Association* (pp. 200-206). Retrieved from http://images.library.wisc.edu/EcoNatRes/EFacs/NAPC/NAPC15/reference/econatres.napc15.cpetersen.pdf

Petersen, C. E., Petersen, R. E., & Meek, R. (2006). Comparison of common factors affecting seed yield in the congeners, Baptisia alba and Baptisia bracteata. *Transactions of the Illinois Academy of Science, 99*, 31-36. Retrieved from http://ilacadofsci.com/wp-content/uploads/2013/03/099-03MS2509-print.pdf

REFERENCES

Peterson, R. L., Scott, M. G., & Miller, S. L. (1979). Some aspects of carpel structure in Caltha palustris L. (Ranunculaceae). *American Journal of Botany*, 334-342. Retrieved from http://www.jstor.org/stable/2442611

Platt, W. J., Hill, G. R., & Clark, S. (1974). Seed production in a prairie legume (Astragalus canadensis L.). *Oecologia, 17*(1), 55-63. Retrieved from http://www.jstor.org/stable/4215023

Praz, C. J., Müller, A., & Dorn, S. (2008). Host recognition in a pollen-specialist bee: evidence for a genetic basis. *Apidologie, 39*(5), 547-557. Retrieved from http://www.jstor.org/stable/4218316

Predny, M. L., & Chamberlain, J. L. (2005). *Bloodroot (Sanguinaria canadensis): an annotated bibliography*. US Department of Agriculture, Forest Service, Southern Research Station. Retrieved from http://www.sfp. forprod.vt.edu/pubs/sfpdoc8.pdf

Rafferty, N. E., & Ives, A. R. (2011). Effects of experimental shifts in flowering phenology on plant–pollinator interactions. *Ecology Letters, 14*(1), 69-74. Retrieved from http://faculty.bennington.edu/~kwoods/classes/Ecology/readings/rafferty - 2011 - effects of experimental shifts.pdf

Reed, C. (1993). Reconstruction of Pollinator Communities on Restored Prairies in Eastern Minnesota: final Report to the Minnesota Department of Natural Resources, Nongame Wildlife Program. *Minnesota Department of Natural Resources, Minnesota*. Retrieved from http://www.catherinecreed.com/assets/writings/1993_reed.pdf

Reed, C. C. (1995). Species richness of insects on prairie flowers in southeastern Minnesota. In *Proceedings of the 14th Annual North American Prairie Conference*. Kansas State University Press, Manhattan, Kansas, USA (pp. 103-115). Retrieved from http://cedarcreek.umn.edu/biblio/fulltext/t1600.pdf

Robertson, C. (1889). Flowers and insects. I. *Botanical Gazette*, 14(5), 120-126.

Robertson, C. (1892). Flowers and insects. VIII. *Botanical Gazette, 17*(6), 173-179. Retrieved from http://www.jstor.org/stable/2994167

Roulston, T. A. H., Cane, J. H., & Buchmann, S. L. (2000). What governs protein content of pollen: pollinator preferences, pollen-pistil interactions, or phylogeny?. *Ecological Monographs, 70*(4), 617-643.

Rudall, P. J., Bateman, R. M., Fay, M. F., & Eastman, A. (2002). Floral anatomy and systematics of Alliaceae with particular reference to Gilliesia, a presumed insect mimic with strongly zygomorphic flowers. *American Journal of Botany, 89*(12), 1867-1883. Retrieved from http://www.jstor.org/stable/4122742

Russo, L., DeBarros, N., Yang, S., Shea, K., & Mortensen, D. (2013). Supporting crop pollinators with floral resources: network-based phenological matching. *Ecology and Evolution*. doi: 10.1002/ece3.703

Sauer, S. B. (2005). Prairie Apioninae (Coleoptera: Brentidae) of Wisconsin: Collections and distributions. *Insecta Mundi*, 90. Retrieved from http://digitalcommons.unl.edu/cgi/viewcontent.cgi?article=1089&context=insectamundi

Savile, D. B. O. (1953). Splash-cup dispersal mechanism in Chrysosplenium and Mitella. *Science, 117*(3036), 250-251.

Schaal, B. A. (1978). Density dependent foraging on Liatris pycnostachya. *Evolution, 32*(2), 452-454. Retrieved from http://www.jstor.org/stable/2407611

Schemske, D. W., Willson, M. F., Melampy, M. N., Miller, L. J., Verner, L., Schemske, K. M., & Best, L. B. (1978). Flowering ecology of some spring woodland herbs. *Ecology*, 351-366. Retrieved from http://www.jstor.org/stable/1936379

Shenk, G. K. (2005). Developmentally plastic responses to pollinators by Lupinus perennis flowers and what they tell us about the pollination mechanism in the general Lupine flower. Retrieved from http://proquest.umi.com/pqdlink?did=990279341&Fmt=7&clientId=79356&RQT=309&VName=PQD

Sinclair, C. B. (1968). Pollination, hybridization, and isolation factors in the erect Tradescantias. *Bulletin of the Torrey Botanical Club*, 232-240. Retrieved from http://www.jstor.org/stable/2483670

Sogaard, J. (2009). *Moths & Caterpillars of the North Woods*. Duluth, MN: Kollath + Stensaas.

Spencer, K. A., & Steyskal, G. C. (1986). *Manual of the Agromyzidae (Diptera) of the United States* (U.S. Department of Agriculture, Agriculture Handbook No. 638). Washington, DC: Government Printing Office.

Springer, C. A., & Goodrich, M. A. (1983). A revision of the family Byturidae (Coleoptera) for North America. *The Coleopterists' Bulletin*, 183-192. Retrieved from http://www.jstor.org/stable/4008013

Pollinators of Native Plants

Strange, J. P., Koch, J. B., Gonzalez, V. H., Nemelka, L., & Griswold, T. (2011). Global invasion by Anthidium manicatum (Linnaeus)(Hymenoptera: Megachilidae): assessing potential distribution in North America and beyond. *Biological Invasions, 13*(9), 2115-2133. Retrieved from http://apoidea.lifedesks.org/files/apoidea/strange_2011_anthidium_manicatum.pdf

Struven, R. D., Wall, J. E., & Heitler, F. B. (1994). Insect pollinators of 12 milkweed (Asclepias) species. In *Proceedings of the Thirteenth North American Prairie Conference. RG Wickett, PD Lewis, A. Woodliffe & P. Pratt (editors), Department of Parks & Recreation, Windsor, Ontario, Canada* (pp. 45-60).

Tripp, E. A., & Manos, P. S. (2008). Is floral specialization an evolutionary dead-end? pollination system transitions in Ruellia (Acanthaceae). *Evolution, 62*(7), 1712-1737. doi: 10.111 l/j. 1558-5646.2008. 00398.X

Tuell, J. K., Fiedler, A. K., Landis, D., & Isaacs, R. (2008). Visitation by wild and managed bees (Hymenoptera: Apoidea) to eastern US native plants for use in conservation programs. *Environmental Entomology, 37*(3), 707-718. Retrieved from http://www.landislab.ent.msu.edu/pdf/Landis%20PDF%20Collection/5.Tuell. Fiedler.Landis.Isaacs.2008.Visitation%20by%20Wild.pdf

Wagner, D. L. (2005). *Caterpillars of eastern North America: A guide to identification and natural history.* Princeton, NJ: Princeton University Press.

Waser, N. M., & Ollerton, J. (Eds.). (2006). *Plant-pollinator interactions: From specialization to generalization.* Chicago, IL: University of Chicago Press.

Weber, L. (2002). *Spiders of the North Woods.* Duluth, MN: Kollath + Stensaas.

Wells, E. F. (1984). A revision of the genus Heuchera (Saxifragaceae) in eastern North America. *Systematic Botany Monographs*, 45-121. Retrieved from http://www.jstor.org/stable/25027594

Whatley, J. M. (1984). The ultrastructure of plastids in the petals of Caltha palustris L. *New Phytologist, 97*(2), 227-231. Retrieved from http://www.jstor.org/stable/2432302

Whigham, D. (1974). An ecological life history study of Uvularia perfoliata L. *American Midland Naturalist*, 343-359. Retrieved from http://www.jstor.org/stable/2424326

White, R. E. (1983). *A field guide to the beetles of North America.* Boston: MA: Houghton Mifflin.

Williams, C. F., & Guries, R. P. (1994). Genetic consequences of seed dispersal in three sympatric forest herbs. Hierarchical population-genetic structure. *Evolution*, 791-805. Retrieved from http://www.jstor.org/stable/2410487

Willmer, P., Stanley, D. A., Steijven, K., Matthews, I. M., & Nuttman, C. V. (2009). Bidirectional flower color and shape changes allow a second opportunity for pollination. *Current Biology, 19*(11), 919-923. Retrieved from http://www.sciencedirect.com/science/article/pii/S0960982209009798

Willmer, P. (2011). *Pollination and floral ecology.* Princeton University Press.

Willson, M. F., Miller, L. J., & Rathcke, B. J. (1979). Floral display in Phlox and Geranium: adaptive aspects. *Evolution*, 52-63. Retrieved from http://www.jstor.org/stable/2407365

Wist, T. J., & Davis, A. R. (2006). Floral nectar production and nectary anatomy and ultrastructure of Echinacea purpurea (Asteraceae). *Annals of Botany, 97*(2), 177-193. doi:10.1093/aob/mcj027

Wojcik, V. A., Frankie, G. W., Thorp, R. W., & Hernandez, J. L. (2008). Seasonality in bees and their floral resource plants at a constructed urban bee habitat in Berkeley, California. *Journal of the Kansas Entomological Society, 81*(1), 15-28. Retrieved from http://www.jstor.org/stable/25086414

Wratten, S. D., Gillespie, M., Decourtye, A., Mader, E., & Desneux, N. (2012). Pollinator habitat enhancement: Benefits to other ecosystem services. *Agriculture, Ecosystems & Environment, 159*, 112-122. Retrieved from http://www.researchgate.net/publication/230807681_Pollinator_ habitat_enhancement_Benefits_to_other_ecosystem_services/file/79e41504a16d65a445.pdf

Yanega, D. (1996). *Field guide to northeastern longhorned beetles (Coleoptera: Cerambycidae).* Champaign, IL: Illinois Natural History Survey.

Yeo, P. F., & Corbet, S. A. (1983). *Solitary wasps.* Cambridge, UK: Cambridge University Press.

Zomlefer, W. B. (1994). *Guide to flowering plant families.* Chapel Hill, NC: University of North Carolina Press.

WEBSITES CONSULTED

The Biota of North America Program
http://www.bonap.org

BugGuide
http://bugguide.net

Butterflies and Moths of North America
http://www.butterfliesandmoths.org

Canadian National Collection of Insects, Arachnids and Nematodes
http://canacoll.org

Discover Life
http://www.discoverlife.org

Heteropteran Systematics Lab @ UCR (University of California Riverside)
http://www.heteroptera.ucr.edu

Illinois Wildflowers
http://www.illinoiswildflowers.info

Lady Bird Johnson Wildflower Center Native Plant Database
http://www.wildflower.org/plants

Michigan State University, Native Plants and Ecosystem Services
http://nativeplants.msu.edu

Microleps.org
http://www.microleps.org/Guide/Heliodinidae/index.html

Minnesota Wildflowers
http://www.minnesotawildflowers.info

Natural History Museum Database of the World's Lepidopteran Hostplants
http://www.nhm.ac.uk/research-curation/research/projects/hostplants/search/index.dsml

The New York Botanical Garden
http://www.nybg.org

Pollinator Conservation Digital Library
http://libraryportals.org/PCDL

USDA Plants Database
http://plants.usda.gov

Working with Cerceris fumipennis
http://www.cerceris.info

The Xerces Society for Invertebrate Conservation
http://www.xerces.org

Pollinators of Native Plants

ILLUSTRATION & PHOTOGRAPHY CREDITS

All illustrations were drawn by the author, Heather Holm.

All photographs in the book were taken by the author, © Heather Holm, with the exception of the following:

Katy Chayka
© 2011, Bottle Gentian, series of five photos of bumble bee entering and exiting flower, p. 203.

Peter Dzuik
© 2001, Milbert's Tortoiseshell Butterflies, *Nymphalis urticae*, p. 201.
© 2008, Prairie Blazingstar, *Liatris pycnostachya*, bottom image, p. 206.
© 2008, Tiger Moth, *Grammia arge*, p. 207.

Michelle Kalantari
© 2011, Peck's Skipper Butterfly, *Polites peckius,* p. 51.
© 2010, Paper Wasps, *Polistes* spp., p. 61.
© 2010, Moth, *Anagrapha* spp., p. 96.
© 2012, Eastern Tiger Swallowtail, *Papilio glaucus*, p. 127.
© 2010, Sweat Bee, *Lasioglossum* spp., p. 187.
© 2010, Azure Butterflies, *Celastrina* spp., p. 201.
© 2005, White Admiral Butterflies, *Limenitis arthemis arthemis,* p. 201.
© 2009, Peck's Skipper Butterfly, *Polites peckius,* p. 229.
© 2008, Eastern Tiger Swallowtail, *Papilio glaucus*, p. 229.

Michael Lynch
© 2012, Syrphid Flies, *Brachypalpus* spp., p. 55.

Kim Phillips
© 2013, Large Carpenter Bee, *Xylocopa virginica,* female, p. 267.
© 2013, Large Carpenter Bee, *Xylocopa virginica,* male, p. 267.

BEE - NATIVE PLANT INTERACTIONS

Species	Common Name	Andrena	Anthophora	Agapostemon	Augochlora	Bombus	Ceratina	Coelioxys	Colletes	Halictus	Hylaeus	Heriades	Lasioglossum	Megachile	Melissodes	Osmia	Nomada	Sphecodes	Triepeolus
Actaea pachypoda	White Baneberry												■						
Agastache foeniculum	Fragrant Hyssop					■	■	■		■	■	■	■	■					
Allium cernuum	Nodding Onion			■		■				■			■	■	■				
Anemone acutiloba	Sharp-Lobed Hepatica	■					■						■						
Anemone canadensis	Canada Anemone	■		■			■			■	■		■						
Anemone patens	American Pasqueflower	■		■						■			■						
Aquilegia canadensis	Wild Columbine					■							■						
Arnoglossum atriplicifolium	Pale Indian Plantain					■				■			■						
Aruncus dioicus	Goat's Beard	■				■	■			■			■				■		
Asclepias incarnata	Swamp Milkweed					■			■	■	■	■	■	■	■				
Asclepias tuberosa	Butterfly Milkweed					■	■	■	■	■	■	■	■	■	■	■			
Baptisia lactea	Wild White Indigo					■							■						
Caltha palustris	Marsh Marigold	■															■		
Campanula rotundifolia	Harebell		■	■	■		■						■	■	■	■			
Chelone glabra	White Turtlehead					■								■					
Coreopsis palmata	Prairie Coreopsis	■		■		■	■	■		■			■	■	■	■			
Dalea purpurea	Purple Prairie Clover	■	■	■		■	■	■	■	■	■	■	■	■	■				■
Desmodium canadense	Showy Tick Trefoil					■				■			■	■	■				
Dicentra cucullaria	Dutchman's Breeches	■	■											■		■			
Echinacea pallida	Pale Purple Coneflower	■		■		■	■	■		■			■	■	■	■			
Echinacea purpurea	Purple Coneflower			■		■	■			■			■	■	■	■			■
Eryngium yuccifolium	Rattlesnake Master			■		■	■	■		■	■		■	■	■		■	■	
Eupatorium perfoliatum	Common Boneset	■				■			■	■	■		■	■	■			■	
Eurybia macrophylla	Large-Leaved Aster	■				■	■	■		■			■	■		■			
Eutrochium maculatum	Spotted Joe Pye Weed					■		■					■	■					
Gentiana andrewsii	Bottle Gentian					■													
Geranium maculatum	Wild Geranium	■	■	■		■	■			■			■				■	■	
Geum triflorum	Prairie Smoke					■							■						
Helianthus maximiliani	Maximilian Sunflower					■				■				■					
Heliopsis helianthoides	False Sunflower	■		■		■	■	■		■			■	■	■	■			■
Heuchera richardsonii	Prairie Alumroot								■				■						
Hydrophyllum virginianum	Virginia Waterleaf	■	■			■	■	■					■			■	■		
Hypericum pyramidatum	Great St. John's Wort			■		■							■	■					

Note: Incomplete list, compiled from research and observations at time of book printing.

BEE - NATIVE PLANT INTERACTIONS

		Andrena	Anthophora	Agapostemon	Augochlora	Bombus	Ceratina	Coelioxys	Colletes	Halictus	Heriades	Hylaeus	Lasioglossum	Megachile	Melissodes	Osmia	Nomada	Sphecodes	Triepeolus
Liatris ligulistylis	Meadow Blazingstar		■	■		■	■						■	■					
Liatris pycnostachya	Prairie Blazingstar					■	■			■			■	■	■				■
Lobelia siphilitica	Great Blue Lobelia		■			■	■					■	■		■				
Lupinus perennis	Wild Lupine	■				■	■					■	■	■		■			
Maianthemum racemosum	False Solomon's Seal				■					■			■					■	
Mitella diphylla	Bishop's Cap						■			■	■								
Monarda fistulosa	Wild Bergamot	■	■	■	■	■	■	■	■	■	■	■	■	■	■				■
Monarda punctata	Spotted Bee Balm					■			■				■		■				
Osmorhiza longistylis	Sweet Cicely	■		■	■					■	■		■	■		■	■	■	
Parthenium integrifolium	Wild Quinine	■		■			■			■	■	■	■	■			■		
Penstemon digitalis	Smooth Beard Tongue	■	■	■		■	■			■	■		■	■		■			
Phlox pilosa	Prairie Phlox		■		■	■	■					■		■					
Physostegia virginiana	Obedient Plant			■		■				■		■	■	■	■				
Polemonium reptans	Jacob's Ladder	■	■	■		■	■			■			■				■	■	
Polygonatum biflorum	Solomon's Seal		■			■	■						■						
Potentilla arguta	Prairie Cinquefoil	■					■			■	■	■	■						
Pycnanthemum virginianum	Virg. Mountain Mint	■		■		■	■	■		■	■	■	■	■				■	■
Ratibida pinnata	Yellow Coneflower	■		■	■	■		■		■			■	■	■				■
Rudbeckia hirta	Black-Eyed Susan	■		■	■	■	■			■			■	■		■			■
Ruellia humilis	Wild Petunia			■	■	■	■						■	■					
Sanguinaria canadensis	Bloodroot	■				■	■			■			■			■	■		
Silphium perfoliatum	Cup Plant	■		■		■	■	■		■			■	■	■				■
Solidago flexicaulis	Zigzag Goldenrod	■		■		■		■					■	■					
Solidago rigida	Stiff Goldenrod	■				■	■		■	■			■	■	■		■		
Symphyotrichum novae-angliae	New England Aster	■		■		■	■			■	■		■	■	■				■
Thalictrum thalictroides	Rue Anemone	■				■	■			■			■			■	■		
Tradescantia ohiensis	Ohio Spiderwort	■		■		■	■			■			■	■		■			
Uvularia grandiflora	Large-Fl. Bellwort	■				■				■			■			■			
Verbena hastata	Blue Vervain			■		■	■	■		■		■	■		■	■	■		■
Verbena stricta	Hoary Vervain	■				■	■	■		■			■	■		■		■	■
Vernonia fasciculata	Common Ironweed			■		■	■			■	■		■	■					■
Veronicastrum virginicum	Culver's Root		■	■		■				■	■	■	■	■					
Viola pubescens	Downy Yellow Violet	■	■			■	■			■			■			■	■		
Zizia aurea	Golden Alexanders	■		■	■	■	■			■		■	■			■	■	■	

PREDATORY WASP - NATIVE PLANT INTERACTIONS

Scientific Name	Common Name	Ammophila	Ancistrocerus	Bicyrtes	Cerceris	Dolichovespula	Eremnophila	Eumenes	Euodynerus	Isodontia	Myzinum	Parancistrocerus	Parazumia	Polistes	Prionyx	Sphex ichneum.	Sphex pensylvan.	Tachytes	Vespula
Arnoglossum atriplicifolium	Pale Indian Plantain	■		■				■		■						■	■		
Asclepias incarnata	Swamp Milkweed				■	■		■	■	■	■			■		■	■	■	■
Asclepias tuberosa	Butterfly Milkweed	■													■	■			
Coreopsis palmata	Prairie Coreopsis	■		■	■				■						■				
Dalea purpurea	Purple Prairie Clover	■			■			■	■		■				■				
Echinacea pallida	Pale Purple Coneflower	■																	
Echinacea purpurea	Purple Coneflower	■																■	
Eryngium yuccifolium	Rattlesnake Master	■	■	■	■			■	■	■	■	■			■	■	■	■	■
Eupatorium perfoliatum	Common Boneset	■	■	■	■	■	■	■	■	■	■	■		■			■		
Eurybia macrophylla	Large-Leaved Aster	■	■					■	■			■		■					
Heliopsis helianthoides	False Sunflower	■																	
Hydrophyllum virginianum	Virginia Waterleaf		■					■											
Lupinus perennis	Wild Lupine													■					
Monarda fistulosa	Wild Bergamot				■				■			■	■				■		
Monarda punctata	Spotted Bee Balm												■			■	■		
Osmorhiza longistylis	Sweet Cicely		■					■											
Parthenium integrifolium	Wild Quinine	■			■			■		■	■			■					
Penstemon digitalis	Smooth Penstemon								■										
Pycnanthemum virginianum	Virg. Mountain Mint	■	■		■	■	■	■	■	■	■	■		■		■	■	■	
Ratibida pinnata	Yellow Coneflower	■		■	■				■						■	■			
Rudbeckia hirta	Black-Eyed Susan	■	■	■					■							■			
Ruellia humilis	Wild Petunia													■					
Silphium perfoliatum	Cup Plant	■												■					
Solidago flexicaulis	Zigzag Goldenrod		■				■							■					■
Solidago rigida	Stiff Goldenrod	■	■		■			■	■	■	■			■		■	■		■
Verbena hastata	Blue Vervain	■			■			■								■	■		
Verbena stricta	Hoary Vervain	■									■								
Veronicastrum virginicum	Culver's Root	■														■	■		
Zizia aurea	Golden Alexanders		■					■	■		■			■					

BEE TONGUE LENGTHS

CHARTS

SHORT TONGUE → LONG TONGUE

FAMILY	GENUS		BODY LENGTH (mm)	TONGUE LENGTH (mm)
Colletidae	Hylaeus	Yellow-Faced Bees	5 - 7	1 - 2
	Colletes	Cellophane Bees	6 - 12	2 - 4
Andrenidae	Andrena	Mining Bees	7 - 15	2 - 4
Halictidae	Sphecodes	Cuckoo Bees	6 - 8	2 - 3
	Halictus	Sweat Bees	5 - 12	2 - 6
	Lasioglossum	Small Sweat Bees	5 - 12	2 - 6
Megachilidae	Coelioxys	Cuckoo Bees	12	4
	Osmia	Mason Bees	6 - 11	7 - 9
	Megachile	Leafcutter Bees	6 - 9	9 - 12
Apidae	Nomada	Cuckoo Bees	9 - 12	4 - 5
	Apis mellifera	Honey Bees (Worker)	10 - 14	5 - 8
	Anthophora	Digger Bees	9 - 15	8 - 21
	Bombus	Bumble Bees	9 - 22	5 - 11
		Short-Tongued	Worker	5 - 6
			Queen	8 - 9
		Medium-Tongued	Worker	7 - 8
			Queen	8 - 9
		Long-Tongued	Worker	9 - 10
			Queen	10 - 11
		Very Long-Tongued	Worker	12 - 13
			Queen	14 - 16

Bee Tongue Lengths *(Modified from Willmer, 2011.)*

FLOWERING TIMELINE - PRAIRIE

SCIENTIFIC NAME	COMMON NAME	MAR	APR	MAY	JUN	JUL	AUG	SEP	OCT
Agastache foeniculum	Fragrant Hyssop				■	■	■		
Allium cernuum	Nodding Onion								
Anemone patens	American Pasqueflower	■	■	■					
Arnoglossum atriplicifolium	Pale Indian Plantain					■			
Asclepias tuberosa	Butterfly Milkweed				■				
Baptisia lactea	Wild White Indigo			■					
Campanula rotundifolia	Harebell							■	
Coreopsis palmata	Prairie Coreopsis								
Dalea purpurea	Purple Prairie Clover				■				
Echinacea pallida	Pale Purple Coneflower					■			
Echinacea purpurea	Purple Coneflower					■			
Eryngium yuccifolium	Rattlesnake Master						■		
Geum triflorum	Prairie Smoke			■	■				
Helianthus maximilianii	Maximilian Sunflower							■	■
Heliopsis helianthoides	False Sunflower					■	■		

FLOWERING TIMELINE - PRAIRIE

SCIENTIFIC NAME	COMMON NAME	MAR	APR	MAY	JUN	JUL	AUG	SEP	OCT
Heuchera richardsonii	Prairie Alumroot						X		
Liatris ligulistylis	Meadow Blazingstar							X	
Lupinus perennis	Wild Lupine			X	X				
Monarda fistulosa	Wild Bergamot					X			
Monarda punctata	Spotted Bee Balm					X	X	X	
Parthenium integrifolium	Wild Quinine								
Penstemon digitalis	Smooth Penstemon				X	X			
Phlox pilosa	Prairie (Downy) Phlox								
Potentilla arguta	Prairie Cinquefoil								
Ratibida pinnata	Yellow Coneflower								
Rudbeckia hirta	Black-Eyed Susan					X	X	X	X
Ruellia humilis	Wild Petunia						X		
Solidago rigida	Stiff Goldenrod						X	X	X
Tradescantia ohiensis	Ohio Spiderwort								
Verbena stricta	Hoary Vervain					X	X	X	
Zizia aurea	Golden Alexanders								

FLOWERING TIMELINE - WOODLAND EDGE

SCIENTIFIC NAME	COMMON NAME	MAR	APR	MAY	JUN	JUL	AUG	SEP	OCT
Actaea pachypoda	White Baneberry			■					
Anemone acutiloba	Sharp-Lobed Hepatica		■						
Aquilegia canadensis	Wild Columbine			■	■				
Aruncus dioicus	Goat's Beard								
Dicentra cucullaria	Dutchman's Breeches		■						
Eurybia macrophylla	Large-Leaved Aster						■		
Geranium maculatum	Wild Geranium			■					
Hydrophyllum virginianum	Virginia Waterleaf			■					
Maianthemum racemosum	False Solomon's Seal			■					
Mitella diphylla	Bishop's Cap								
Osmorhiza longistylis	Long-Styled Sweet Cicely			■					
Polemonium reptans	Jacob's Ladder			■					
Polygonatum biflorum	Solomon's Seal			■	■				
Sanguinaria canadensis	Bloodroot								
Solidago flexicaulis	Zigzag Goldenrod							■	
Thalictrum thalictroides	Rue Anemone								
Uvularia grandiflora	Large-Flowered Bellwort		■						
Viola pubescens	Downy Yellow Violet								

Pollinators of Native Plants

FLOWERING TIMELINE - WETLAND EDGE

SCIENTIFIC NAME	COMMON NAME	MAR	APR	MAY	JUN	JUL	AUG	SEP	OCT
Anemone canadensis	Canada Anemone			■	■				
Asclepias incarnata	Swamp Milkweed					■	■		
Caltha palustris	Marsh Marigold		■	■					
Chelone glabra	White Turtlehead						■	■	
Desmodium canadense	Canada Tick Trefoil					■			
Eupatorium perfoliatum	Common Boneset						■	■	
Eutrochium maculatum	Spotted Joe Pye Weed					■	■		
Gentiana andrewsii	Bottle Gentian						■	■	
Hypericum pyramidatum	Great St. John's Wort					■			
Liatris pycnostachya	Prairie Blazingstar					■	■		
Lobelia siphilitica	Great Blue Lobelia						■		
Physostegia virginiana	Obedient Plant					■	■		
Pycnanthemum virginianum	Virginia Mountain Mint					■	■		
Silphium perfoliatum	Cup Plant					■	■		
Symphyotrichum novae-angliae	New Enlgand Aster						■	■	■
Verbena hastata	Blue Vervain					■	■		
Vernonia fasciculata	Common Ironweed					■	■		
Veronicastrum virginicum	Culver's Root					■			

Abdomen
Insect: third part of the tripartite body (head, thorax, abdomen).

Antenna (Antennae - plural)
One of a pair of appendages borne on the head of an insect, often segmented, bearing sensilla (olfactory, tactile).

Aposematism
Combination of a warning signal with unprofitability or toxicity of a potential food item, most commonly through the form of warning coloration.

Bee Bread
A mixture of pollen and nectar prepared by a female bee used to feed bee larvae.

Biennial
A plant that takes two years to complete its life cycle and produces flowers in the second year.

Brood Cell
An egg-laying site in a bee nest where a larva develops.

Buzz Pollination (Sonication)
A technique used to dislodge pollen from anthers with small pores or longitudinal slits. Grasping the flower's anthers, bees rapidly move their flight muscles to vibrate the anthers and dislodge pollen. Commonly used by bumble bees and some solitary bee species.

Cleptoparasite
An insect that does not construct or provision its own nest but instead lays its eggs in the nest of another insect species. Cleptoparasitic bee larva hatch and often kill the host larva and consume the provisions provided by the host.

Corbicula (Corbiculae - plural)
A pollen basket on the hind tibia of female *Apis*, *Bombus*, stingless bees and euglossine bees.

Corolla
Collective term for the flower petals.

Crop
Insects: Enlarged area of the foregut used for storing food provisions.

Dehiscence
Opening of the anthers to release pollen.

Diapause
A period of suspended development in an insect, typically during unfavorable environmental conditions.

Dichogamy
The sequential development of male and female floral reproductive parts in plants.

Dioecious
A plant having male and female reproductive organs in separate plants.

Dufour's Gland
A gland near the ovipositor in bees, wasps and ants. The gland secretes pheromones as well as secretions. The secretions are mixed with provisions and/ or used to waterproof brood cells.

Elytra
The hard forewings of beetles that provide protection.

Floral Constancy
The tendency of a pollinator to move reliably between flowers of the same plant species.

Genotype
The genetic makeup of an organism with reference to a single, set, or complex of traits.

Glossa
The terminal portion of a bee's tongue.

Herkogamy
The spatial separation of male and female floral reproductive parts.

Host Plant (Larval)
A specific plant species or genus that a butterfly or moth larva (caterpillar) feeds upon.

Hyperparasitoid
A parasitic insect that develops upon another parasitic insect larva.

Instar
A phase between two periods of molting in the development of an insect larva.

Larva (Larvae - plural)
The active immature form of an insect developing between egg and pupa with complete metamorphosis.

Mimicry
A plant or animal that resembles another plant or animal by evolving to have similar traits that provide a benefit.

Monoecious
A plant having both male and female reproductive organs in the same plant.

Nymph
A newly hatched insect undergoing molts with incomplete metamorphosis. Young resemble adults.

Ovipositor
An appendage used for egg-laying, near the base of an insect's abdomen.

Perennial
A plant that persists for a few to many years and typically flowers yearly.

Phenotype
The expression of a specific trait based on genetic and environmental influences.

Pistillate Flowers
A flower in the female reproductive phase: style elongation and stigma receptivity.

Protandry
Plant: The development of male reproductive parts of a flower before the development of female reproductive parts.
Insect: The adult emergence of male insects before the emergence of female insects from a nest.

Protogyny
Plant: The development of female reproductive parts of a flower before the development of male reproductive parts.
Insect: The adult emergence of female insects before the emergence of male insects from a nest.

Pupa (Pupae - plural)
The developmental stage for insects with complete metamorphosis between the larval and adult stage.

Scopa (Scopae - plural)
A concentration of hairs on a bee's leg or abdomen that is used for pollen storage.

Sonication - *See* Buzz Pollination

Staminate Flowers
A flower that is in the male reproductive phase: anther development and dehiscence.

Staminode (Staminodia - plural)
A sterile stamen on a flower that does not produce reproductive pollen.

Stylopodium (Stylopodia - plural)
An enlargement at the base of the style.

Thorax
Insect: second part of the tripartite body (head, thorax, abdomen).

Trichome
A hair-like growth, often glandular and oil-producing, on a plant's surface.

LEAF SHAPE

LEAF EDGE

LEAF ARRANGEMENT

LEAF DIVISIONS

ROOTS

FRUIT

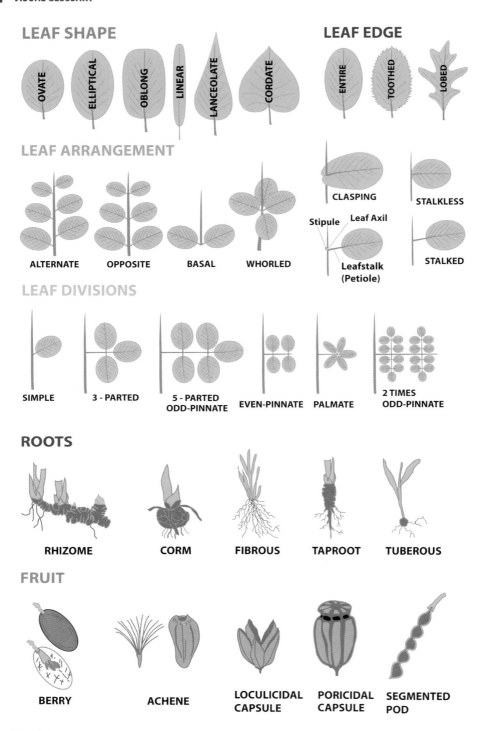

TYPES OF INFLORESCENCES

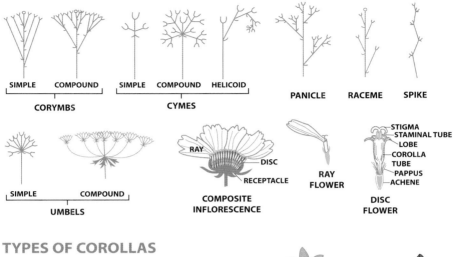

| SIMPLE | COMPOUND | SIMPLE | COMPOUND | HELICOID | PANICLE | RACEME | SPIKE |

CORYMBS

CYMES

| SIMPLE | COMPOUND |

UMBELS

STIGMA
STAMINAL TUBE
LOBE
COROLLA
TUBE
PAPPUS
ACHENE

RAY

DISC

RECEPTACLE

RAY FLOWER

COMPOSITE INFLORESCENCE

DISC FLOWER

TYPES OF COROLLAS

STANDARD

WING
KEEL

| BILABIATE | CAMPANULATE (BELL-SHAPED) | HOOD & HORN | TUBULAR | CARINATE |

NECTARIES

FLOWER COMPONENTS

STIGMA

PISTIL { STYLE

OVARY

OVULE

ANTHER
FILAMENT } STAMEN

PETAL

SEPAL NECTARIES   STAMINAL NECTARIES

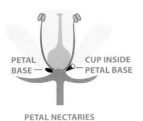

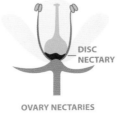

PETAL BASE — CUP INSIDE PETAL BASE

DISC NECTARY

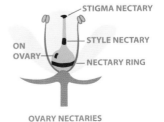

STIGMA NECTARY

STYLE NECTARY

ON OVARY

NECTARY RING

PETAL NECTARIES   OVARY NECTARIES

OVARY NECTARIES

BEE ILLUSTRATIONS - ANATOMY, LIFE CYCLE, NESTS, POLLINATION

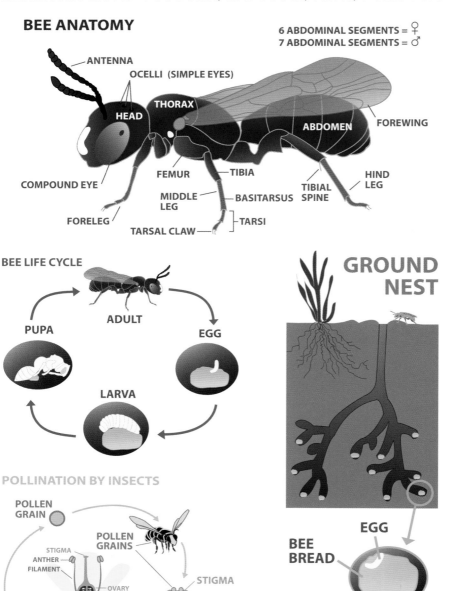

BEE ANATOMY

6 ABDOMINAL SEGMENTS = ♀
7 ABDOMINAL SEGMENTS = ♂

ANTENNA
OCELLI (SIMPLE EYES)
THORAX
HEAD
ABDOMEN
FOREWING
COMPOUND EYE
FEMUR
TIBIA
HIND LEG
MIDDLE LEG
BASITARSUS
TIBIAL SPINE
FORELEG
TARSAL CLAW
TARSI

BEE LIFE CYCLE

ADULT
PUPA
EGG
LARVA

POLLINATION BY INSECTS

POLLEN GRAIN
POLLEN GRAINS
STIGMA
ANTHER
FILAMENT
OVARY
STIGMA
STYLE
POLLEN TUBE
ANTHER
POLLEN GRAINS
SPERM
FILAMENT
OVARY
OVULE

GROUND NEST

EGG
BEE BREAD

CAVITY NEST

FAMILY COLLETIDAE

FAMILY COLLETIDAE Profile p. 53
Cellophane (Polyester) Bees, *Colletes* spp.

Nest
Ground, often near water or on slopes or
  embankments, dense aggregations

Nest Soil Type
Sand, loamy sand, loam, clay loam

Nest Lining Mixture of Dufour's gland and salivary
  gland secretions; product is a cellophane-like
  material; brushed on with short, bilobed glossa

Active Late spring - summer

Size Small - medium, 7 - 15 mm (0.3 - 0.6 in)

Tongue Length
Short, 1 - 3 mm (0.04 - 0.12 in), two-lobed

Color Black and white banding on abdomen

Appearance
Hairy head and thorax
Heart-shaped face (strongly converging eyes)

Pollen Collection
Scopae, upper hind legs and thorax

Flight Distance ∼ 500 ft, 150 m

MALE

FAMILY COLLETIDAE
Yellow-Faced Bees, *Hylaeus* spp.

Nest
Preexisting cavities: wood, stems or twigs

Nest Lining
Silk-like salivary gland secretions, brushed on
  with glossa

Active
Late spring - late summer

Size
Small, 5 - 7 mm (0.2 - 0.3 in)

Tongue Length
Short, 1 - 2 mm (0.04 - 0.07 in)

Color Black with yellow markings

Appearance
Hairless, bilobed tongue
No pollen-collecting scopae

Pollen Collection
Pollen stored internally in crop

Profile p. 179

MALE

FAMILY ANDRENIDAE

FAMILY ANDRENIDAE
Mining Bees, *Andrena* spp.

MALE

Nest
Ground (sometimes lawns)
Nest soil type
Sand, sandy loam, silt loam
Active Spring - early summer, fall
Size
Small - medium
7 - 15 mm (0.3 - 0.6 in)
Tongue length
Short, 2 - 4 mm (0.07 - 0.15 in)
Color Black
Appearance
Moderately hairy, white to orange hairs,
  often with bands of hair on abdomen
Facial depressions (foveae) between
  the compound eyes
Pollen collection
Scopae upper hind legs
Flight distance ~ 500 yards, 450 m
Profile pp. 123 & 134

- -

FAMILY ANDRENIDAE
Mining Bees, *Calliopsis* spp.

Calliopsis andreniformis, male (left), female (right)

Nest Ground
Nest Lining
Wax-like secretion from
  Dufour's gland used to
  waterproof the brood cell
  and cover the bee bread
Active
Late Spring - Early Fall
Size
Small - medium,
7 - 9 mm (0.3 - 0.35 in)
Color Black
Males often with yellow or
  cream markings on the
  face, legs and thorax
Appearance
Moderately hairy
Pollen collection
Scopae hind legs

Pollinators of Native Plants

FAMILY HALICTIDAE

FAMILY HALICTIDAE   **Profile p. 226**
Sweat Bees, *Halictus* spp.

Nest Ground
Nest Soil Type
Loamy sand, sandy loam
Nest Lining Wax-like substance
Active Summer
Size Small - medium, 5 - 15 mm (0.2 - 0.6 in)
Tongue Length
Short - medium, 2 - 6 mm (0.08 - 0.2 in)
Color Dark gray, black
Appearance Pale bands of hair on outer edge
  of abdominal segments
Pollen Collection Scopae hind legs
Other Feeds on human sweat for salts
Flight Distance ~ 200 yd, 180 m

MALE

- -

FAMILY HALICTIDAE
Sweat Bees, *Lasioglossum* spp.

Nest Ground
Nest Soil Type Silt Loam
Nest Lining Wax-like substance
Active Early spring - summer
Size Small - medium, 3 - 10 mm (0.1 - 0.4 in)
Tongue Length
Short - medium, 2 - 6 mm (0.08 - 0.2 in)
Color Dull gray, black, metallic
Appearance Often with pale bands of hair along
  the base of abdominal segments or uniformly
  fuzzy (subgenus *Dialictus*)
Pollen Collection Scopae hind legs
Flight Distance ~ 200 yd, 180 m

MALE

FAMILY HALICTIDAE

FAMILY HALICTIDAE
Green Sweat Bees, *Agapostemon* spp.

Nest Ground
Nest Soil Type
Sandy loam
Active Late spring - fall
Size Small - medium, 7 - 15 mm (0.3 - 0.6 in)
Tongue Length Short, 2 - 6 mm (0.08 - 0.2 in)
Color
Bright green head and thorax, some species with
green abdomen, other species with black and
white (females), or black and yellow (males)
striped abdomen
Pollen Collection Scopae hind legs
Profile p. 218

MALE

FAMILY HALICTIDAE
Cuckoo Bees, *Sphecodes* spp.

Nest No nest
Cleptoparasite of sweat bees
Active Late spring - summer
Size Medium
5 - 15 mm (0.2 - 0.6 in)
Tongue Length
Short, 2 - 3 mm (0.08 - 0.1 in)
Color Black, dark red abdomen (female)
Appearance Sparsely haired, coarsely pitted
Pollen Collection None

260

FAMILY HALICTIDAE and MEGACHILIDAE

FAMILY HALICTIDAE
Augochlorini Tribe
Sweat Bees, *Augochlora pura*

Nest Solitary
Nest Location Rotting wood,
  preexisting cavities in logs on ground
Active Summer
Size Small, 5 - 10 mm (0.2 - 0.4 in)
Tongue Length
Short, 2 - 3 mm (0.08 - 0.1 in)
Color Bright green or blue-green,
  metallic or brassy
Appearance Very sparsely haired
Pollen Collection Scopae hind legs
Flight Distance ∼ 490 ft, 150 m

FAMILY HALICTIDAE
Augochlorini Tribe
Sweat Bees, *Augochlorella* spp.

Nest Ground
Active Summer
Size Medium, 4.5 - 8 mm (0.18 - 0.3 in)
Tongue Length
Short, 2 - 3 mm (0.08 - 0.1 in)
Color Golden-green with coppery
  or red sheen
Appearance Sparsely haired
Pollen Collection Scopae hind legs

FAMILY MEGACHILIDAE
Mason Bees, *Osmia* spp.

Nest
Preexisting cavities: wood, stems, rock
  crevices, snail shells, old wasp nests
Nest Divisions
Mud, leaves, sand, gravel, wood chips
Active Spring - early summer
Size
Small - medium, 6 - 11 mm (0.2 - 0.4 in)
Tongue Length
Medium - long, 7 - 9 mm (0.3 - 0.4 in)
Color
Blue, green, metallic, dull appearing black
Appearance
Moderately hairy, bulky, large
  head and mandibles
Pollen Collection Abdominal scopae
Flight Distance ∼ 300 ft, 91 m
Profile p. 93

FAMILY MEGACHILIDAE

FAMILY MEGACHILIDAE
Leafcutter Bees, *Megachile* spp.

Nest
Preexisting cavities: wood, stems, rocks
Ground
Nest Divisions
Leaves, petals, resin, mud
Active Early - late summer
Size
Medium - large, 7 - 10 mm (0.2 - 0.4 in)
Tongue Length
Medium - long, 9 - 12 mm (0.35 - 0.5 in)
Color Dark gray, black
Appearance
Female: Pale hair bands (often), large
  mandibles, broad head, flattened or
  upturned abdomen, tapered
Male: Long hairs on forelegs
Pollen Collection
Abdominal scopae
Flight Distance ~ 500 yards, 450 m
Profile pp. 86 & 121

- -

FAMILY MEGACHILIDAE
Small Resin Bees, *Heriades* spp.

Nest
Preexisting cavities: wood, stems
Nest Divisions
Resin, sealed with sand,
  wood fibers, plant fragments
Active
Late spring - summer
Size
Small, 4 - 7 mm (0.15 - 0.28 in)
Tongue Length Short
Color Black, pale abdominal bands
Appearance
Concave abdomen, pitted surface,
  short hair
Pollen Collection
Abdominal scopae

Pollinators of Native Plants

FAMILY MEGACHILIDAE

FAMILY MEGACHILIDAE
Mason Bees, *Hoplitis* spp.

Nest Preexisting cavities: pithy stems, wood, old nests in soil or old mud nests
Nest Divisions Chewed leaves, pebbles, sand, clay, wood fiber
Active Spring - summer
Size Small to medium
  5 - 15 mm (0.2 - 0.6 in)
Color Black or metallic (western species)
Appearance Slender, robust, hairy face
Pollen Collection Abdominal scopae

FAMILY MEGACHILIDAE
Cuckoo Bees, *Coelioxys* spp.

Nest
No nest, cleptoparasite of leafcutter bees
Active Early summer - late fall
Size Medium, 12 mm (0.5 in)
Tongue Length
Short, 4 mm (0.15 in)
Color Dark gray, black
Appearance
Hair on eyes
Female: narrow, tapered abdomen
Male: short spines, last abdominal segment
Pollen Collection None, no nest provisioned
Profile p. 61

MALE

FAMILY MEGACHILIDAE
Carder Bees, *Anthidium* spp.

Nest Preexisting cavities: soil, wood, stems
Nest Divisions Plant hairs and trichomes, resin
Nest Closure Wood fibers
Active Late spring - summer
Size Small - medium, 7 - 15 mm (0.3 - 0.8 in)
Tongue Length Short, 4 mm (0.15 in)
Color Dark gray, black with yellow/white bands
Appearance Robust, sparsely haired
Pollen Collection Abdominal scopae
Profile p. 127

Pollinators of Native Plants

FAMILY APIDAE

FAMILY APIDAE   Profile p. 21

Bumble Bees, *Bombus* spp.

Nest Colony (eusocial)
Nest Location Rodent holes, leaf piles, ground
Nest Materials
Wax (nectar pots), leaves (insulation)
Active Spring - late fall
Size Medium - large, 10 - 23 mm (0.4 - 0.9 in)
Tongue Length
Medium - long, 4 - 16 mm (0.15 - 0.6 in)
Color
Black, yellow, white or orange hair, black body
Appearance Stout, furry, robust, completely hairy
Pollen Collection
Pollen baskets on hind legs (corbiculae)
Flight Distance ∼ 1 mile, 1.6 km

FAMILY APIDAE
Digger Bees, *Anthophora* spp.

Nest Ground, *A. terminalis* (shown) nests in rotting wood
Nest Soil Type
Loam, sandy clay loam
Nest Lining Oil
Active Spring - late summer
Size Medium - large, 9 - 15 mm (0.35 - 0.6 in)
Tongue Length
Medium - long, 8 - 21 mm (0.3 - 0.8 in)
Color Black, pale bands, often yellow markings on face, especially males
Appearance Hairy, robust
Pollen Collection Long scopae hind legs
Profile p. 105

MALE

FAMILY APIDAE

FAMILY APIDAE
Cuckoo Bees, *Nomada* spp.

Nest No Nest
Cleptoparasite of ground-nesting bees
Active Early spring - early fall
Size Small - medium, 3 - 15 mm (0.1 - 0.6 in)
Tongue Length
Medium, 4 - 5 mm (0.15 - 0.2 in)
Color
Black, rusty red, yellow (white) markings
Appearance
Sparsely hairy, thick antennae, wasp-like
Pollen Collection None
Profile p. 151

FAMILY APIDAE
Cuckoo Bees, *Triepeolus* spp.

Nest No Nest
Cleptoparasite of long-horned bees (*Melissodes*)
Active Summer - fall
Size Medium, 3 - 15 mm (0.1 - 0.6 in)
Tongue Length
Medium, 4 - 5 mm (0.15 - 0.2 in)
Color Black with yellow or white markings
Appearance
Very short hair, appearing hairless
Pollen Collection None
Note: Similar in appearance to *Epeolus* spp.
Profile pp. 113 & 217

FAMILY APIDAE
Small Carpenter Bees, *Ceratina* spp.

Nest Pithy stems, wood
Vertical or angled nest orientation
Nest Divisions Pith and saliva
Active Early spring - summer
Size Small - medium, 3 - 15 mm (0.1 - 0.6 in)
Tongue Length
Medium, 5 - 9 mm (0.2 - 0.35 in)
Color Blue, black, green, metallic
Appearance
Cylindrical abdomen, sparsely haired, shiny,
often white (or yellow) patch on face
Pollen Collection Scopae hind legs
Flight Distance ~ 200 yd, 180 m
Profile p. 111

FAMILY APIDAE
Long-Horned Bees, *Melissodes* spp.

Nest Ground
Nest Lining Wax-like substance
Active Mid-summer - fall
Size Small - medium, 7 - 18 mm (0.3 - 0.7 in)
Tongue Length
Medium - long
Appearance
Robust and hairy, often with pale bands on
abdomen in the middle of the abdominal segments
Males: long antennae
Pollen Collection Long scopae on hind legs
Profile p. 69

MALE

FAMILY APIDAE

FAMILY APIDAE
Large Carpenter Bees
Xylocopa spp.

Nest
Excavated with mandibles
 in wood, plant stems
Nest Lining Sawdust (plant stems)
Active
Mid-summer - fall
Size
Large, 13 - 30 mm (0.5 - 1.25 in)
Tongue Length
Medium - long
Color
Black with yellow hairs, bumble bee-like
Appearance
Robust, hairy thorax, shiny black abdomen
Pollen Collection
Scopae hind legs
Flight Distance ~ 1 mile, 1.6 km

MALE

FAMILY APIDAE
Honey Bees, *Apis mellifera*

Nest Social, colony
Nest Location (Besides man-made hives)
Tree cavities, tree limbs or branches
Nest Materials
Wax: hexagonal cells
Active Early spring - late fall
Size Medium, 10 - 15 mm (0.4 - 0.6 in)
Tongue Length (Worker)
5 - 8 mm (0.2 - 0.3 in)
Color Black with golden hairs
Appearance
Moderately hairy, long abdomen
 with black or gold stripes, hairy eyes
Pollen Collection
Pollen baskets hind legs (corbiculae)
Flight Distance ~ 2 miles, 3.2 km

BOULEVARD POLLINATOR GARDEN - SUN, DRY

BOULEVARD POLLINATOR GARDEN - SAND TO SANDY LOAM SOILS, PLANT HEIGHTS UNDER 20 INCHES

PLANT LIST

A (7) Little Bluestem
Schizachyrium scoparium

B (19) Nodding Onion
Allium cernuum

C (9) Am. Pasqueflower
Anemone patens

D (15) Butterfly Milkweed
Asclepias tuberosa

E (14) June Grass
Koeleria macrantha

F (11) Harebell
Campanula rotundifolia

G (16) Purple Prairie Clover
Dalea purpurea

H (13) Prairie Alumroot
Heuchera richardsonii

I (14) Prairie Smoke
Geum triflorum

J (8) Spotted Bee Balm
Monarda punctata

K (6) Wild Petunia
Ruellia humilis

L (5) Prairie Phlox
Phlox pilosa

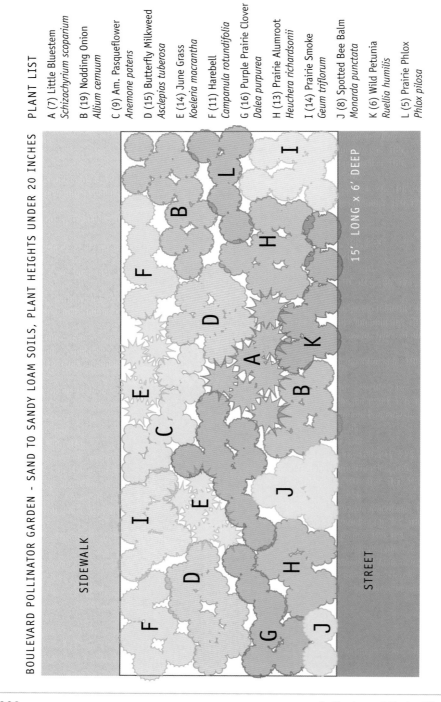

SIDEWALK

STREET

15' LONG x 6' DEEP

Pollinators of Native Plants

BOULEVARD POLLINATOR GARDEN - SHADE, MESIC

PLANT LIST

A (6) Wild Geranium
Geranium maculatum

B (19) Bishop's Cap
Mitella diphylla

C (9) Virginia Waterleaf
Hydrophyllum virginianum

D (15) Large-Leaved Aster
Eurybia macrophylla

E (14) Pennsylvania Sedge
Carex pensylvanica

F (17) Jacob's Ladder
Polemonium reptans

G (23) Zigzag Goldenrod
Solidago flexicaulis

H (15) False Solomon's Seal
Maianthemum racemosum

I (14) Downy Yellow Violet
Viola pubescens

BOULEVARD POLLINATOR GARDEN - SHADE, LOAM SOILS, PLANT HEIGHTS UNDER 20 INCHES

SIDEWALK

STREET

15' LONG x 6' DEEP

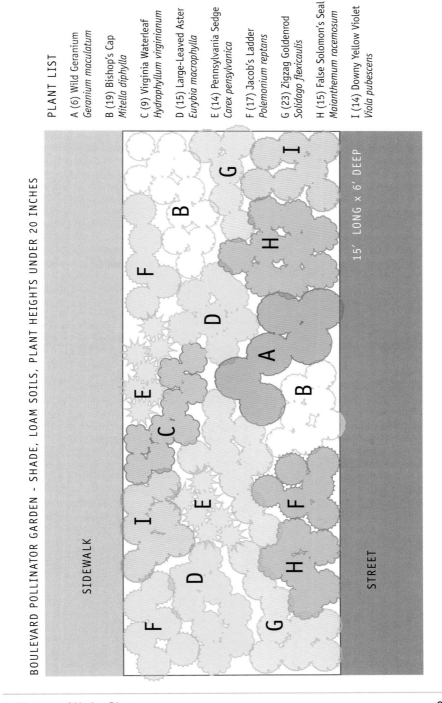

BIOSWALE / DITCH POLLINATOR GARDEN

PLANT LIST

A (11) Prairie Blazingstar
Liatris pycnostachya
B (8) Indian Grass
Sorghastrum nutans
C (6) Swamp Milkweed
Asclepias incarnata
D (5) Common Boneset
Eupatorium perfoliatum
E (3) Cup Plant
Silphium perfoliatum
F (10) Canada Anemone
Anemone canadensis
G (17) Great Blue Lobelia
Lobelia siphilitica
H (5) New England Aster
Symphyotrichum novae-angliae
I (4) Spotted Joe Pye Weed
Eutrochium maculatum
J (4) Great St. John's Wort
Hypericum pyramidatum
K (4) Mountain Mint
Pycnanthemum virginianum
L (7) White Turtlehead
Chelone glabra
M (4) Blue Vervain
Verbena hastata
N (8) Side Oats Gramma
Bouteloua curtipendula

BIOSWALE/DITCH/RAINGARDEN POLLINATOR GARDEN - SUN, LOAM TO CLAY-LOAM SOILS

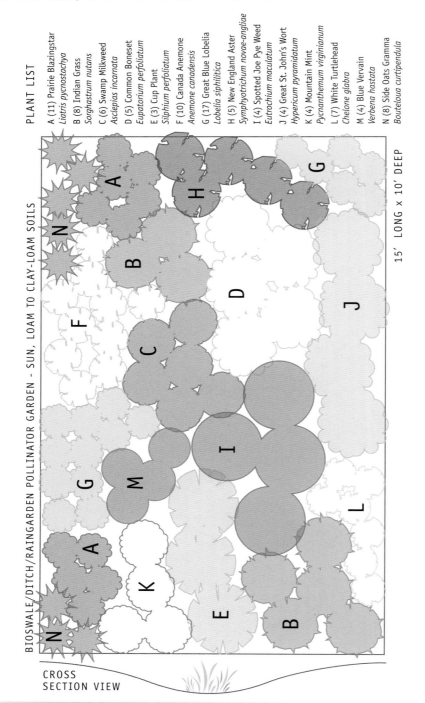

15' LONG x 10' DEEP

CROSS
SECTION VIEW

WOODLAND EDGE POLLINATOR GARDEN

PLANT LIST

A (5) White Baneberry
Actaea pachypoda

B (12) Wild Columbine
Aquilegia canadensis

C (13) Golden Alexanders
Zizia aurea

D (12) Wild Geranium
Geranium maculatum

E (13) Large-Leaved Aster
Eurybia macrophylla

F (14) Zigzag Goldenrod
Solidago flexicaulis

G (9) Long-Styled Sweet Cicely
Osmorhiza longistylis

H (7) Large-Flowered Bellwort
Uvularia grandiflora

I (5) Jacob's Ladder
Polemonium reptans

J (8) Rough Blazingstar
Liatris aspera

K (5) Ohio Spiderwort
Tradescantia ohiensis

L (5) Wild Quinine
Parthenium integrifolium

M (7) Black-Eyed Susan
Rudbeckia hirta

N (6) Wild Bergamot
Monarda fistulosa

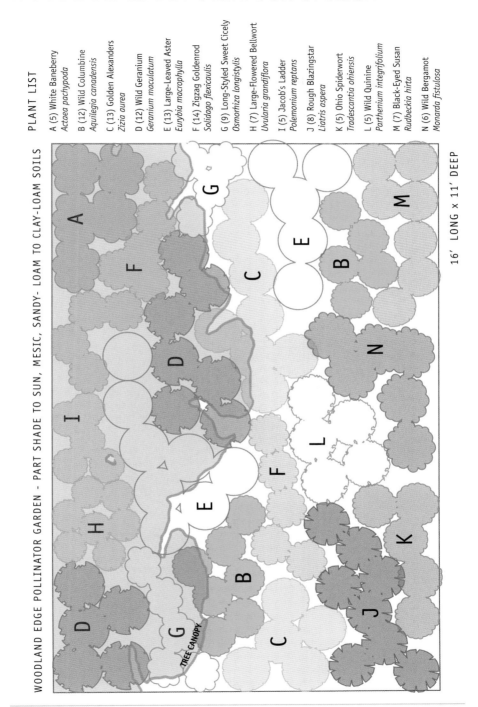

WOODLAND EDGE POLLINATOR GARDEN - PART SHADE TO SUN, MESIC, SANDY- LOAM TO CLAY-LOAM SOILS

TREE CANOPY

16' LONG x 11' DEEP

BUMBLE BEE (*Bombus*) GARDEN

PLANT LIST

A (15) Purple Prairie Clover
Dalea purpurea

B (5) Hoary Vervain
Verbena stricta

C (11) Golden Alexanders
Zizia aurea

D (6) Culver's Root
Veronicastrum virginicum

E (5) Pale Indian Plantain
Arnoglossum atriplicifolium

F (11) Stiff Goldenrod
Solidago rigida

G (4) Spotted Joe Pye Weed
Eutrochium maculatum

H (7) Meadow Blazingstar
Liatris ligulistylis

I (7) Smooth Beard Tongue
Penstemon digitalis

J (5) Yellow Coneflower
Ratibida pinnata

K (8) Fragrant Hyssop
Agastache foeniculum

L (6) Ohio Spiderwort
Tradescantia ohiensis

M (8) Black-Eyed Susan
Rudbeckia hirta

N (10) Wild Bergamot
Monarda fistulosa

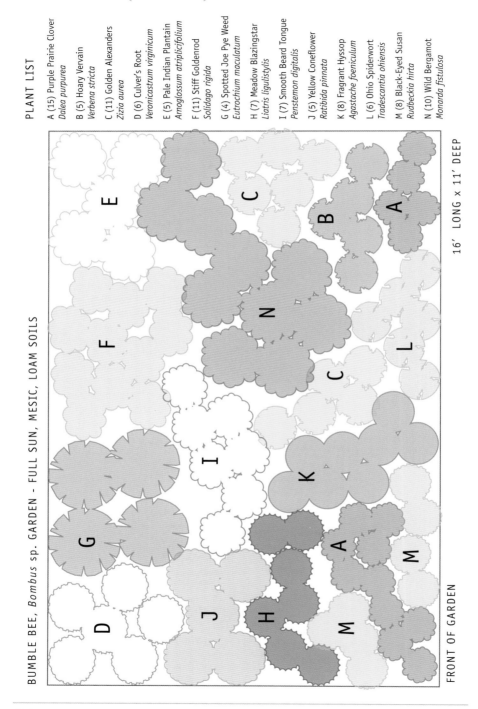

BUMBLE BEE, *Bombus* sp. GARDEN - FULL SUN, MESIC, LOAM SOILS

16' LONG x 11' DEEP

FRONT OF GARDEN

LEAFCUTTER BEE (*Megachile*) GARDEN

PLANT LIST

A (15) Purple Prairie Clover
Dalea purpurea

B (5) Hoary Vervain
Verbena stricta

C (11) Butterfly Milkweed
Asclepias tuberosa

D (6) Culver's Root
Veronicastrum virginicum

E (5) New England Aster
Symphyotrichum novae-angliae

F (11) Stiff Goldenrod
Solidago rigida

G (4) Spotted Joe Pye Weed
Eutrochium maculatum

H (7) Meadow Blazingstar
Liatris ligulistylis

I (7) Pale Purple Coneflower
Echinacea pallida

J (5) Yellow Coneflower
Ratibida pinnata

K (8) Fragrant Hyssop
Agastache foeniculum

L (6) Nodding Onion
Allium cernuum

M (8) Black-Eyed Susan
Rudbeckia hirta

N (10) Showy Tick Trefoil
Desmodium canadense

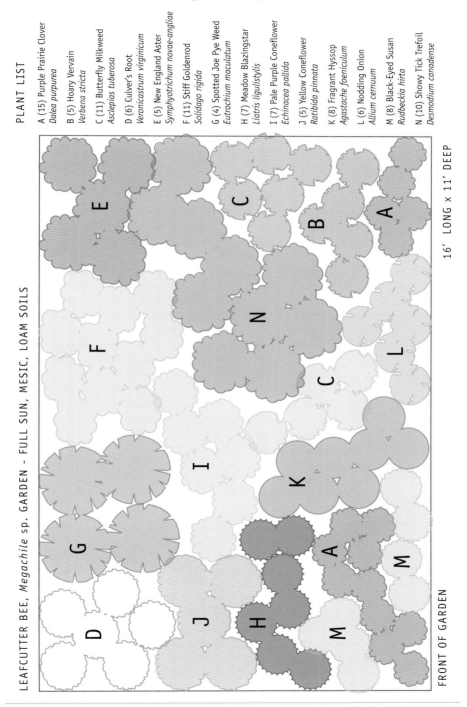

16' LONG x 11' DEEP

LEAFCUTTER BEE, *Megachile* sp. GARDEN - FULL SUN, MESIC, LOAM SOILS

FRONT OF GARDEN

MASON BEE (*Osmia*) GARDEN

PLANT LIST

A (15) Virginia Waterleaf
Hydrophyllum virginianum

B (12) Butterfly Milkweed
Asclepias tuberosa

C (13) Golden Alexanders
Zizia aurea

D (12) Wild Geranium
Geranium maculatum

E (13) Smooth Beard Tongue
Penstemon digitalis

F (14) Zigzag Goldenrod
Solidago flexicaulis

G (9) Long-Styled Sweet Cicely
Osmorhiza longistylis

H (7) Large-Flowered Bellwort
Uvularia grandiflora

I (10) Jacob's Ladder
Polemonium reptans

J (1) Wild Plum
Prunus americana

K (5) Ohio Spiderwort
Tradescantia ohiensis

L (11) Downy Yellow Violet
Viola pubescens

M (10) Harebell
Campanula rotundifolia

MASON BEE, *Osmia* sp. GARDEN - PART SHADE TO SUN, MESIC, SANDY- LOAM TO LOAM SOILS

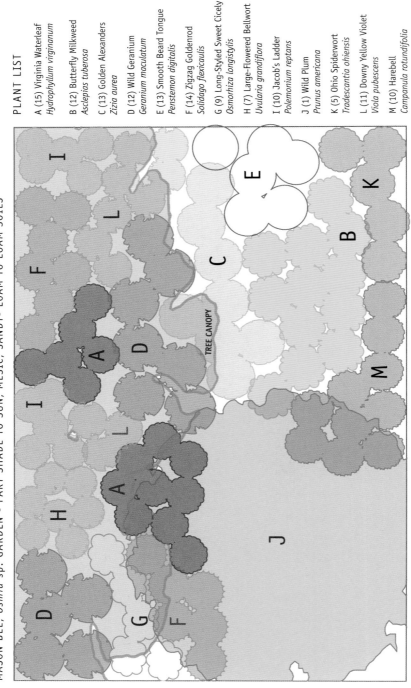

TREE CANOPY

16' LONG x 11' DEEP

Pollinators of Native Plants

BENEFICIAL INSECT GARDEN - FULL SUN, MESIC

PLANT LIST

A (15) Purple Prairie Clover
Dalea purpurea

B (5) Butterfly Milkweed
Asclepias tuberosa

C (11) Golden Alexanders
Zizia aurea

D (6) Virginia Mountain Mint
Pycnanthemum virginianum

E (5) Pale Indian Plantain
Arnoglossum atriplicifolium

F (11) Stiff Goldenrod
Solidago rigida

G (4) Common Boneset
Eupatorium perfoliatum

H (7) Wild Quinine
Parthenium integrifolium

I (7) Rattlesnake Master
Eryngium yuccifolium

J (5) Yellow Coneflower
Ratibida pinnata

K (8) Purple Coneflower
Echinacea purpurea

L (6) Hoary Vervain
Verbena stricta

M (8) Black-Eyed Susan
Rudbeckia hirta

N (10) Wild Bergamot
Monarda fistulosa

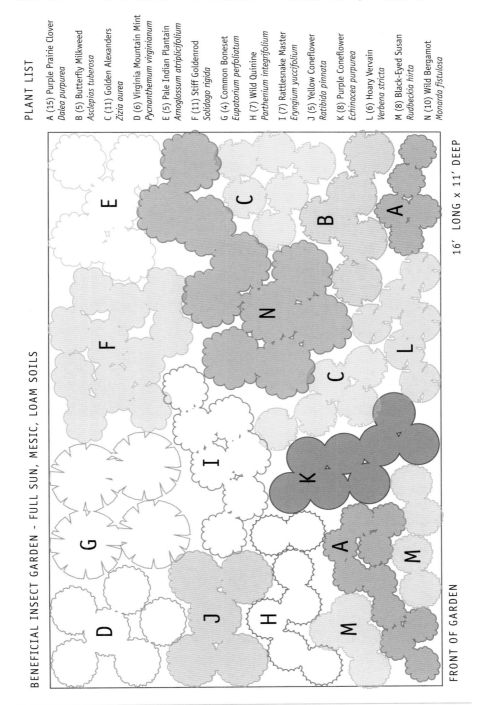

BENEFICIAL INSECT GARDEN - FULL SUN, MESIC, LOAM SOILS

16' LONG x 11' DEEP

FRONT OF GARDEN

Pollinators of Native Plants

BEES

Boldface page numbers indicate species profile.
Boldface Italic page numbers indicate genera information.

Bumble Bee, *Bombus* sp.
Pages: **16**, **64**, **97**, **107**, **129**, **143**, **163**, **201**, **213**, ***264***

Small Carpenter Bee,
Ceratina sp.
Pages: **111**, ***266***

Carder Bee, *Anthidium* sp.
Pages: **127**, ***263***

Long-Horned Bee,
Melissodes sp.
Pages: 19, 51, **69**, 231, ***266***

Digger Bee, *Anthophora* sp.
Pages: **105**, 209, ***264***

Mining Bee, *Andrena* sp.
Pages: **123**, **134**, 165, 173, ***258***

Leafcutter Bee, *Megachile* sp.
Pages: 20, **86**, **121**, ***262***

Small Resin Bee, *Heriades* sp.
Pages: **5**, 51, 53, 60, 69, 97, 187, 213, ***262***

Mason Bee, *Osmia* sp.
Pages: 34, 67, **93**, 134, 151, 153, ***261***

BEES

Yellow-Faced Bee,
Hylaeus sp.
Pages: 4, 17, 19, **179, 257**

Cellophane Bee, *Colletes* sp.
Pages: **53,** 159, **257**

Sweat Bee, *Lasioglossum
subgenus dialictus*
Pages: 9, 16, 67, 139, 165,
175, **259**

Green Sweat Bee,
Agapostemon sp.
Pages: 5, 21, **218, 260**

Sweat Bee, *Halictus* sp.
Pages: **226, 259**

Augochlorini Tribe
Pages: 86, 117,
149, 187, **261**

Cuckoo Bee, *Sphecodes* sp.
Pages: 101, **260**

Cuckoo Bee, *Nomada* sp.
Pages: **151, 265**

Cuckoo Bee, *Coelioxys* sp.
Pages: **61, 263**

Cuckoo Bee, *Triepeolus* sp.
Pages: **113, 217, 265**

WASPS

Great Black Wasp
Sphex pensylvanicus
Pages: 95, **184**

Great Golden Digger Wasp
Sphex ichneumoneus
Pages: 10, 185, **232**

Thread-Waisted Wasp
Prionyx sp.
Pages: 61, 79, 124

Thread-Waisted Wasp
Ammophila sp.
Pages: 57, 101, **232**

Bald-Faced Hornet
Dolichovespula maculata
Pages: 22, 196

Grass-Carrying Wasp
Isodontia sp.
Pages: 10, **197**

Paper Wasp, *Polistes* sp.
Pages: 22, **196**

Potter Wasp, *Eumenes* sp.
Pages: 124, 197

Yellowjacket Wasp,
Vespula sp.
Pages: 22, **124**, 185

Cuckoo Wasp, *Hedychrum* sp.
Pages: **198**, 214

Pollinators of Native Plants

WASPS

Boldface page numbers indicate species profile

Thynnid Wasp
Myzinum quinquecinctum
Pages: 41, 78, **198**, 214

Beetle Wasp
Cerceris sp.
Pages: 11, **79**, 197

Sand Wasp
Bicyrtes quadrifasciatus
Pages: 22, 57, **196**

Mason Wasp
Parazumia symmorpha
Pages: **95**

Beewolf
Philanthus gibbosus
Pages: 111, **118**, **197**, 214

Mason Wasp
Ancistrocerus sp.
Pages: 79, 124, **168**

Square-Headed Wasp
Tachytes sp.
Pages: **185**

Wood-boring Mason Wasp
Euodynerus foraminatus
Pages: **135**

Thread-Waisted Wasp
Eremnophila aureonotata
Pages: 168, 198, 232

Square-Headed Wasp
Ectemnius sp.
Pages: 124

BUTTERFLIES

Boldface page numbers indicate species profile

Great Spangled Fritillary
Speyeria cybele
Pages: 24, **59**, 74

Clouded Sulphur Butterfly
Colias philodice
Page: 63

Red Admiral Butterfly
Vanessa atalanta
Pages: 74, 183, 233

American Lady Butterfly
Vanessa virginiensis
Page: **74**

Common Ringlet Butterfly
Coenonympha tullia
Page: 85

Crescent Butterfly
Phyciodes sp.
Pages: 59, 85, 125, 222

Common Wood Nymph
Butterfly, *Cercyonis pegala*
Pages: 91, 103, 130

Painted Lady Butterfly
Vanessa cardui
Page: 91

Eastern Tiger Swallowtail
Papilio glaucus
Pages: 75, 96, 127,
201, 229

BUTTERFLIES

Boldface page numbers indicate species profile

Silver Spotted Skipper Butterfly
Epargyreus clarus
Pages: 51, 96, 130, 201, **227**

Monarch Butterfly
Danaus plexippus
Pages: **59**, 83, **91**, 96, 125, **183**, 199, 201

Cabbage White Butterfly
Pieris rapae
121, 130

Peck's Skipper
Polites peckius
Pages: 51, 91, 109, 229

Common Buckeye Butterfly
Junonia coenia
Pages: 121, **222**

Azure Butterflies,
Celastrina sp.
Pages: 114, 133, 155, 201, 233

Fiery Skipper
Hylephila phyleus
Pages: 130, 217

Milbert's Tortoiseshell Butterfly
Nymphalis urticae
Page: 201

Banded Hairstreak Butterfly
Satyrium calanus
Page: 215

White Admiral Butterfly
Limenitis arthemis arthemis
Page: 201

Eastern Tailed Blue Butterfly
Everes comyntas
Pages: 130, 233

Pollinators of Native Plants

Boldface page numbers indicate species profile

Virginia Creeper Clearwing
Moth, *Albuna fraxini*
Page: **199**

Tiger Moth, *Grammia arge*
Page: 207

Arcigera Flower Moth
Schinina arcigera
Page: **222**

Clearwing Moth
Synanthedon sp.
Page: 87

Grapeleaf Skeletonizer Moth
Harrisina americana
Page: **103**

Hummingbird Clearwing Moth
Hemaris sp.
Pages: 24, 96, 109, 183

Wavy-Lined Emerald Moth
Synchlora aerata
Pages: 87, **114**

Moth, *Anagrapha* sp.
Page: 96

Snout Moth
Pyrausta sp.
Pages: 67, 96, 103, 114

Garden Webworm Moth
Achyra rantalis
Page: 83

Clematis Clearwing Moth,
Alcathoe caudata
Page: 57

Moth, *Neoheliodines cliffordi*
Page: 155

Pollinators of Native Plants

FLIES

Syrphid Fly, *Allograpta* sp.
Pages: 53, 83, 157

Syrphid Fly, *Toxomerus* sp.
Pages: 27, 107, **115**

Syrphid Fly, *Pipiza* sp.
Pages: 109, 151

Syrphid Fly, *Spilomyia* sp.
Pages: 125, **169**

Syrphid Fly, *Helophilus* sp.
Pages: 91, 207

Syrphid Fly, *Eristalis* sp.
Pages: 26, 119, 131,
223, 225

Syrphid Fly, *Brachypalpus* sp.
Page: 55

Syrphid Fly, *Sphegina* sp.
Pages: 157, **159**

Syrphid Fly, *Ocyptamus* sp.
Page: **169**

FLIES

Boldface page numbers indicate species profile

Syrphid Fly, *Chrysotoxum* sp.
Page: 71

Syrphid Fly, *Merodon* sp.
Page: 127

Syrphid Fly,
Melanostoma sp.
Page: 171

Syrphid Fly, *Chrysogaster* sp.
Page: 181

Syrphid Fly, *Neoascia* sp.
Page: 189

Syrphid Fly, *Xylota* sp.
Page: 189

Syrphid Fly, *Tropidia* sp.
Pages: 107, 169, **181,** 184

Syrphid Fly, *Syritta* sp.
Page: 215

Syrphid Fly, *Lejops* sp.
Page: 189

Soldier Fly, *Odontomyia* sp.
Pages: 77, **102,** 215

Soldier Fly, *Stratiomys* sp.
Page: **102**

Frit Fly, *Malloewia* sp.
Page: 102

FLIES

Boldface page numbers indicate species profile

Tachinid Fly, *Gymnoclytia* sp.
Page: 199

Tachinid Fly, *Archytas* sp.
Pages: 27, 41, **125,** 184, 233

Tachinid Fly, *Siphona* sp.
Pages: 135, 157, 159

Thick-Headed Fly,
Stylogaster sp.
Page: **225**

Thick-Headed Fly, *Myopa* sp.
Pages: 27, 151

Thick-Headed Fly
Physocephala sp.
Pages: 27, 199, **233**

Green Bottle Fly, *Lucilia* sp.
Pages: 145, 184

Bee Fly, *Exoprosopa* sp.
Pages: **119,** 207

Sinuous Bee Fly
Hemipenthes sp.
Pages: 11, **85,** 127

Bee Fly, *Villa* sp.
Pages: 91, **119,** 184, 199

Bee Fly, *Bombylius* sp.
Pages: 26, 51, 55, **95,** 131,
223, 225

Pollinators of Native Plants

BEETLES

Boldface page numbers indicate species profile

Soldier Beetle,
Chauliognathus sp.
Pages: 23, 51, **96**, 118,
186, 223

Soldier Beetle,
Rhagonycha sp.
Page: 133

Milkweed Leaf Beetle,
Labidomera clivicollis
Pages: **61, 186**

Blister Beetle
Lytta sayi
Page: **63**

Blister Beetle
Nemognatha sp.
Pages: 11, 23, **118**

Red Milkweed Beetle
Tetraopes sp.
Page: 186

Ground Beetle, *Calleida* sp.
Page: 85

Wedge-Shaped Beetle
Macrosiagon sp.
Pages: 11, 23, **99**, 215

Ladybird Beetle
Cycloneda sp.
Pages: 41, **133, 219**

BEETLES

Boldface page numbers indicate species profile

Locust Borer Beetle
Megacyllene robiniae
Page: 125

Red-Shouldered Pine Beetle
Stictoleptura canadensis
Page: 77

Banded Long-Horn Beetle
Typocerus sp.
Pages: 75, 96, 186

Long-Horned Beetle
Strangalepta sp.
Page: 145

Long-Horned Beetle
Strangalia sp.
Page: 145

Long-Horned Beetle
Leptura sp.
Page: 145

Long-Horned Beetle
Anoplodera sp.
Page: 180

Long-Horned Beetle
Analeptura sp.
Page: 180

Long-Horned Beetle
Trigonarthris sp.
Page: 186

Pollinators of Native Plants

Boldface page numbers indicate species profile

Spotted Cucumber Beetle
Diabrotica undecimpunctata
Page: 83

Fruitworm Beetle
Byturus unicolor
Pages: 151, **180**

Tumbling Flower Beetle
Mordella sp.
Pages: 53, 180

Weevil, *Trichapion rostrum*
Page: **65**

Weevil
Cleopomiarus hispidulus
Page: 209

Lily of the Valley Weevil,
Hormorus sp.
Page: 155

Weevil
Idiostethus tubulatus
Page: 153

Fire-Colored Beetle,
Pedilus sp.
Pages: 145, **155**, 161

Long-Horned Beetle,
Euderces sp.
Pages: 155, 180, 186

BUGS, LACEWINGS, SPIDERS & ANTS

Boldface page numbers
indicate species profile

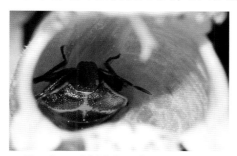

Two-Spotted Stink Bug, *Cosmopepla* sp.
Page: 211

Assasin Bug, *Zelus* sp.
Page: **195**

Jagged Ambush Bug, *Phymata* sp.
Pages: 10, **119**

Ebony Bug, *Corimelaena* sp.
Pages: 103, 133

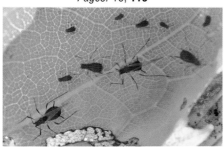

Brown Ambrosia Aphid, *Uroleucon* sp.
Page: **219**

Crab Spiders, Family Thomisidae
Pages: 10, 102, 135, **171,** 181

Brown Lacewing Larvae, Family Hemerobiidae
Pages: 41, **219**

Ants, Family Formicidae
Pages: 61, 115, 153, 189, 215

Pollinators of Native Plants

Boldface page numbers indicate species profile or definition.
Boldface Italic page numbers indicate genera information.

Pollinators of Native Plants

Pollinators of Native Plants

Pollinators of Native Plants

Pollinators of Native Plants

Pollinators of Native Plants

Pollinators of Native Plants

POLLINATOR	PLANT	DATE	NOTES

POLLINATOR	PLANT	DATE	NOTES

POLLINATOR	PLANT	DATE	NOTES

POLLINATOR	PLANT	DATE	NOTES

Heather Holm had an avid interest in natural history and botany at a young age, and spent much of her childhood exploring the woodlands and prairie on the family property in Canada, established by her great-great-grandfather in the 1850s. She studied horticulture and biology at the University of Guelph and later web programming and digital design at Seneca college, Canada.

Heather is a biologist, pollinator conservationist, and award-winning author. In addition to assisting with native bee research projects, she informs and educates audiences nation-wide, through her writing and many presentations, about the fascinating world of native pollinators and beneficial insects, and the native plant communities that support them.

Her second book, *Bees*, published in 2017, has won six book awards including the 2018 American Horticultural Society Book Award. Her latest book, *Wasps: Their Biology, Diversity, and Role as Beneficial Insects and Pollinators of Native Plants*, was published in 2021. Heather's expertise includes the interactions between native pollinators and native plants, and the natural history and biology of native bees and predatory wasps occurring in the Upper Midwest and Northeast.

In her spare time, Heather is an active community supporter, writing grants and coordinating neighborhood volunteer landscape restoration projects. Currently, she is working on three projects with volunteers, restoring approximately ten acres of city-owned park land in her neighborhood for pollinators and people. She lives in Minnesota with her husband. Follow Heather online:

Author Website
www.PollinatorsNativePlants.com

Facebook
PollinatorsNativePlants
RestoringTheLandscape

iNaturalist
www.inaturalist.org/people/heatherholm

Instagram
beesnativeplants

Twitter
beesnativeplant

Join her Facebook group to **share your observations and pollinator photos**:
www.facebook.com/groups/PollinatorsNativePlants